RUSSIAN RESEARCH CENTER STUDIES 31

Stalin's Failure in China

1924–1927

The Russian Research Center of Harvard University is supported by a grant from the Carnegie Corporation. The Center carries out interdisciplinary study of Russian institutions and behavior and related subjects.

RUSSIAN RESEARCH CENTER STUDIES

1. *Public Opinion in Soviet Russia: A Study in Mass Persuasion,* by Alex Inkeles
2. *Soviet Politics — The Dilemma of Power: The Role of Ideas in Social Change,* by Barrington Moore, Jr.
3. *Justice in Russia: An Interpretation of Soviet Law,* by Harold J. Berman
4. *Chinese Communism and the Rise of Mao,* by Benjamin I. Schwartz
5. *Titoism and the Cominform,* by Adam B. Ulam
6. *A Documentary History of Chinese Communism,* by Conrad Brandt, Benjamin Schwartz, and John K. Fairbank
7. *The New Man in Soviet Psychology,* by Raymond A. Bauer
8. *Soviet Opposition to Stalin: A Case Study in World War II,* by George Fischer
9. *Minerals: A Key to Soviet Power,* by Demitri B. Shimkin
10. *Soviet Law in Action: The Recollected Cases of a Soviet Lawyer,* by Harold J. Berman and Boris A. Konstantinovsky
11. *How Russia Is Ruled,* by Merle Fainsod
12. *Terror and Progress USSR: Some Sources of Change and Stability in the Soviet Dictatorship,* by Barrington Moore, Jr.
13. *The Formation of the Soviet Union: Communism and Nationalism, 1917–1923,* by Richard Pipes
14. *Marxism: The Unity of Theory and Practice,* by Alfred G. Meyer
15. *Soviet Industrial Production, 1928–1951,* by Donald R. Hodgman
16. *Soviet Taxation: The Fiscal and Monetary Problems of a Planned Economy,* by Franklyn D. Holzman
17. *Soviet Military Law and Administration,* by Harold J. Berman and Miroslav Kerner
18. *Documents on Soviet Military Law and Administration,* edited and translated by Harold J. Berman and Miroslav Kerner
19. *The Russian Marxists and the Origins of Bolshevism,* by Leopold H. Haimson
20. *The Permanent Purge: Politics in Soviet Totalitarianism,* by Zbigniew K. Brzezinski
21. *Belorussia: The Making of a Nation,* by Nicholas P. Vakar
22. *A Bibliographical Guide to Belorussia,* by Nicholas P. Vakar
23. *The Balkans in Our Time,* by Robert Lee Wolff
24. *How the Soviet System Works: Cultural, Psychological, and Social Themes,* by Raymond A. Bauer, Alex Inkeles, and Clyde Kluckhohn*
25. *The Economics of Soviet Steel,* by M. Gardner Clark
26. *Leninism,* by Alfred G. Meyer
27. *Factory and Manager in the USSR,* by Joseph S. Berliner*
28. *Soviet Transportation Policy,* by Holland Hunter
29. *Doctor and Patient in Soviet Russia,* by Mark G. Field*
30. *Russian Liberalism,* by George Fischer
31. *Stalin's Failure in China, 1924–1927,* by Conrad Brandt

* Publications of the Harvard Project on the Soviet Social System.

Stalin's Failure in China

1924–1927

Conrad Brandt

HARVARD UNIVERSITY PRESS
Cambridge, Massachusetts
1958

This volume was prepared under a grant from the Carnegie Corporation of New York. That Corporation is not, however, the author, owner, publisher, or proprietor of this publication and is not to be understood as approving by virtue of its grant any of the statements made or views expressed therein.

Library of Congress Catalog Card Number 58-12963
Printed in the United States of America

The strength of Marxism lies in its ability to foretell.
Trotsky

You are too shallow, Hastings, much too shallow,
To sound the bottom of the after-times.
King Henry IV, Part II

PREFACE

About the first mass upheaval in China's struggle toward modern nationhood — her "Great Revolution" of the 1920's — much more has been written than is known. There is no obscurer period in the recent past of any large country, and no new society that has emerged out of profounder chaos. A nationalist upsurge, a strong labor movement, an agrarian explosion: for all these China was ripe; but ripeness in history often stops short of ultimate fruition. That it did not in this case was made sure by deliberate planning, by the planning and prodding, the aid and advice, of the Soviets.

Without Soviet munitions and Soviet advice on party organization, China's "Great Revolution" would certainly have been delayed; and without inspiration from Soviet dogma it would certainly have been less forceful. The arms and advisers provided by Moscow did much to unify China, but the doctrine of imperialism which it proclaimed did more to unite the Chinese. It sank into minds that struggled to explain, and to cure, the ills of the country; and it sank into hearts that rejected the West and yet desired its methods. Above all, it became a creed with the pacemakers of revolution, a premise that they shared often unawares, beneath differences more patent. Sun Yat-sen was a convert, as was his successor, Chiang Kai-shek, who outdid him in fervor just as he was outdone by his own successor, Mao Tse-tung. The progressive vehemence with which these three have embraced the foreign dogma is paralleled by the progressive success with which they rallied their country.

The doctrine of imperialism as it reached China had been formulated by Lenin as part of his effort to make common cause with the subject peoples of Asia. The Chinese revolution by rewarding this effort bears witness to Lenin's foresight; yet it did not take the course he marked out, nor that which his heirs thought proper. How it persistently jumped the tracks of "inevitable" development is the principal theme which runs through this book — a rather wearisome *leitmotif*. We pursue it through 1927, when the Chinese Communist Party, taking Stalin's advice on how to gain power, very nearly destroyed itself. The substance of our tale ends there; but enough will be told of the sequel to show that our monotonous theme can be traced through at least two more decades. When the Chinese Communists did at long last edge forward toward seizing power, Stalin attempted to hold them back: he feared one more '27.*

He feared another debacle in China even though, unlike twenty years earlier, he did not have to cope with obstreperous comrades waiting to pounce on his blunders. The criticism which he had incurred on that previous occasion would not, while he lived, repeat itself: he had disposed of his critics. In 1927, they had still been able to make his failure in China the subject of an open debate: the last such debate in the party. They had maintained that the Chinese Communists might have won except for his bungling; he had maintained that, if properly followed, his policy would have been perfect. The debate aroused mighty passions because actually under attack was Stalin's entire leadership and not merely his China policy. Thus the China problem assumed for the Soviets a purely Russian dimension, reaching deep down into their affairs as a major domestic issue.

Most responsible for this development was the brilliant Leon Trotsky, at one time the strongest of Stalin's rivals and then his most bitter critic. Trotsky pounced on the bad news from

* By his own admission, he advised them in '46 or '47 to make peace with Chiang Kai-shek. Vladimir Dedijer, *Tito Speaks*, p. 331.

China and warned of worse news to come, and soon his prophecy was fulfilled — in fact, sooner than he had expected. Proven right in this case, he claimed later, in exile, that he had been right all along; and it seemed (were there not quotations to prove it?) that his argument was irrefutable. The record seemed to speak for itself — at least as he chose to cite it, and as it has been reviewed in a book by an author under his influence.*

Trotsky's claims as a prophet cannot be examined in the short space of a preface; but what follows will show (or so I hope) that they have been grossly inflated. He almost ignored the revolution in China till it was about to founder, till even with less than prophetic vision one could see disaster approaching. To be sure, he did see the danger then, whereas Stalin went on playing ostrich; but by that time the end was already at hand, the ultimate massacre certain. Losses might possibly have been cut if Stalin had listened to Trotsky; but how could he listen to his opponent at the height of his struggle against him? The struggle blocked off his alternatives, left him no choice in China but to pursue the dangerous course which past choices had somehow set for him. Whether these past choices had been his or (as he asserted) Lenin's became a hotly debated issue in the Bolshevik party. We shall have to discuss it ourselves; but here it need only be mentioned that these choices had been active and passive, that some of them had been omissions.

In fact, these omissions had left such gaps in the Soviet plan for China that they affected its operation deeply if not decisively. Some of Lenin's and Stalin's silences therefore deserve to be noted almost as carefully as their dicta, solemn but vague, on the subject. It has been the fashion to quote these dicta as proof of the simple thesis that what happened

* Harold Isaacs, *The Tragedy of the Chinese Revolution.*

in China was according to plan: a Muscovite manipulation. The Communists and their loudest opponents could agree on this thesis; for it was simple, and all zealots meet on the common ground of simplicity.

Almost as simple and over-schematic is another thesis which, instead of exaggerating, belittles the Soviet impact on China. Now we hear barely any echo of Soviet events in China, so loud is the rumble of Chinese history describing another cycle. We see one more dynastic succession after others before it and like it, installing a new ruler on an old throne without breaking a deep continuity. We think of some ancient emperors rather than Lenin and Stalin, who (if indeed they matter at all) perform the function of catalysts.*

Thus the revolutionary decades preceding Mao Tse-tung's rise to power emerge from this thesis not like a beginning but like a mere interregnum. The ancient pattern of dynastic succession can indeed be traced through these decades: the old rule dissolves into civil war; out of chaos congeals the new rule. The literate class, either holding office or aspiring to do so, throws its support to the usurper: he becomes, without fuss, legitimate. This being the pattern, what more need be said? Is our present purpose merely to dwell on the latest variation of a theme already familiar? Not quite: this book would not have been written unless I believed, perhaps wrongly, that even Stalin's failure in China affected her history deeply. It would not have been written unless I believed that Mao Tse-tung's final triumph was the ultimate outcome — unforeseen and unplanned — of the first Soviet stab into China.

To explain the antecedents of Mao's rise to power is only a first step, of course, toward explaining that rise itself. I shall

* For the most erudite version of this thesis, see C. P. Fitzgerald's *Revolution in China*.

content myself with that first step; for to advance beyond this would take us away from solid ground into rarefied speculation. To the extent that such speculation can be well-informed and intelligent, it has already been undertaken by two competent scholars.* Let us therefore leave the subject alone until we have new materials with which to fill or narrow the gaps in our present knowledge. If we attempt to cover these gaps by the sweep of some easy formula, we only succeed in building traps — and may be the first to fall into them.

Not that the pitfalls of simplification can be wholly avoided: there are many of them along our way as we study the mid-1920's. This was the period when the French foreign minister had reason to ask: *Qu'est-ce que c'est que la Chine?* — what was this China in which civil war had become the sport of generals? To answer, we should have to piece together the generals' private kingdoms and deal at length with cliques and cabals and regional bonds and alignments. We should have to draw on a fund of knowledge such as I, for one, have not acquired; the answer will therefore not be forthcoming from the study before us. In fact, it looks as if far from resolving the complexities of the period, I may succeed in adding to them, in confounding confusion still further. The reader will gain a foretaste of this as I trace out the contours of the fragmented world, the laboring chaos, which he is about to enter.

He will find a China with two governments pretending to speak for the nation and yet with no government at all having more than local authority. In the north was Peking, the legal capital recognized by the powers, a coveted prize in the civil war, forever changing possession. To the south

* Robert C. North, *Moscow and Chinese Communists*, chapter XI; Benjamin I. Schwartz, *Chinese Communism and the Rise of Mao*, chapter XII.

was the rival capital, Canton, headquarters of revolution, of the Nationalist Party or Kuomintang which would one day rule all of the country. Affiliated with the Kuomintang was the Chinese Communist Party, its helpful ally and deadly rival, supporting and undermining it. The two parties exercised joint control over Canton and areas around it; but elsewhere they were strictly outlawed, though not quite suppressed, by the warlords. Having to operate secretly throughout a divided country, both parties lost the cohesiveness that they possessed on paper. The Kuomintang leaders lost touch with their followers as these fell in with the Communists; the Communist leaders lost touch with each other as their party sank into regionalism. Its Canton branch became nearly the equal of the Central Committee in Shanghai; in fact, it is known (though details are obscure) that the two were often at loggerheads.

Hence we cannot speak collectively of either one of these parties without lumping together, in each case, a number of separate bodies. Such lumping cannot be wholly avoided in a coherent narrative; and surely there has been some of it in our present study. But I hope not too much, having done my best to avoid an effect of unity where the real diversities are known and where I thought them important. That this volume is nevertheless so small is due to the exclusiveness with which I have chosen what to discuss and what to pass over in silence. If my choice seems arbitrary at times, my scope excessively limited, the fault is only partly my own, and partly that of my sources.

Many of these are Communist; they yield only such information as we can extract from between the refrains of latter-day Marxist "analysis." Others, of the opposite bias, are equally problematic: even a bias shared by oneself is capable of distorting. Not one of the books that deal at some length with the 1920's in China gives a straightforward, comprehensive account of the history of the period. What accuracy can we therefore expect from a study like this one, for which the materials have come almost wholly from inaccurate sources?

Not as much, surely, as one would like, yet more than seems at first possible: sources that are contradictory often correct each other. Different versions of one event tell more than a single official one; and polemics invariably bring out truth, if only by puncturing falsehoods. Thus we would certainly know much less of Stalin's failure in China if we did not have the literature of his polemic with Trotsky. We would not know the magnitude of his failure, nor that of his efforts to hide it, had it not been for Trotsky and the Opposition exposing his tricks and evasions. Are we, conversely, indebted to Stalin and to publicists in his service for having exposed the dishonesties in the Trotskyite argument? Not very much: the chief concern of those who replied to Trotsky was not to disprove his argument but to defame his person. The most damaging evidence against Trotsky comes therefore not from his enemies but, strange to say, from Trotsky himself: from his letters and memoranda.*

We have no comparable source in Chinese; but the best information we do have comes also from former Communist leaders who went into opposition. Ch'en Tu-hsiu, who led the Communist Party during the "Great Revolution," made important disclosures when removed from his post to expiate for Stalin's failure.† No less important are the recollections (due to be published in English) of another former Communist leader, now an exile in Hongkong. Chang Kuo-t'ao will become a familiar name to the readers of this study; for

* In the Trotsky Archives, Houghton Library, Harvard University.
† Ch'en Tu-hsiu, *Kao ch'üan tang t'ung-chih shu.*

in the period with which it deals, he ranked very high in the party. He ranked higher than most of its present chiefs, including Mao Tse-tung, its chairman, with whom he collided in the mid-1930's and who subsequently expelled him.

"Information obtained from Chang Kuo-t'ao," a recurrent phrase in my footnotes, denotes information obtained through interviews during a stay in Hongkong. Some scholars may bridle: interviews? gossip as source material? one more intrusion of journalism into historical method? They may bridle still more upon finding out that even the *printed* sources which students of modern China must use are permeated with gossip. Yet it is precisely for checking such sources that interviews can be useful—*are* useful if based on specific questions about specific topics. The scope of my interviews with Mr. Chang was therefore kept purposely narrow: we would discuss only one event, one episode, at a sitting.

All told, I feel that Mr. Chang's comments have added more to this study than any other single source, except for the Trotsky papers. I wish to record my thanks to him as well as to the foundation which made our interviews possible: the Social Science Research Council. I am indebted to the Council not only for its generosity but for helping in many personal ways, whenever help was required.

In the course of my research, when feeling adrift on a meaningless ocean of data, I would often consult a colleague or friend to regain my sense of direction. To mention only a few of these would be an injustice to many; I therefore thank them without listing names, at the risk of seeming ungracious. Those directly concerned will know, I believe, that my thanks, although briefly stated, are not on that account a mere phrase but express a genuine feeling.

This book has been written under the joint sponsorship of the Russian Research Center and the Research Program in Chinese Economic and Political Studies, Harvard University. The help and encouragement I received from both enabled me to entertain such thought as the following pages may contain.

C. B.

CONTENTS

Stalin's Failure in China

1924–1927

CHAPTER I

LENIN AND ASIAN NATIONALISM: SOURCES OF AN ALLIANCE

Comintern strategy in China grew out of Lenin's awareness of Asian nationalism as an indispensable ally of the Western proletariat in its struggle for power. Never before had a socialist leader given more than a passing nod to the half-articulate aspirations of the "backward" East. From Marx to Kautsky, social democracy treated the Orient as only a passive victim of imperialism, to be freed automatically by the victory of the Western workers. Asian freedom became in fact a part of the white man's burden; and the "sleeping giant" Napoleon had feared was left to stir in his sleep. It remained for Lenin to arouse the giant in order to harness him to the cause of world revolution. This alone goes to show how very keen was Lenin's political instinct.

Lenin's discovery of the East as a potential ally is the more remarkable because it did not come to him as a by-product of discouragement with the West.[1] On the contrary, his courtship of Asian nationalism began while he still held high hopes for a quick victory in Europe. In March 1919 the Russian Communist Party adopted a program which officially linked its cause to that of all oppressed nations.[2] In November of the same year, Lenin explained what was involved in this program.

Addressing the Second All-Russian Congress of the Communist Organizations of the Peoples of the East, Lenin enjoined his Asian disciples to "adapt communist theory and practice to conditions where the bulk of the people are peasants." They were to fight "not against capital but against medieval remnants," not against bourgeois but against feudal exploiters. In fact, they were to join hands with the bourgeoisie; for it too stood opposed to feudalism, and it too aimed at putting an end to Western imperialist dominance. To overthrow native feudalism and foreign imperialism were the twin tasks confronting revolutionary Asia; and the accomplishment of these tasks would be a bourgeois revolution. Charged with leading the bourgeoisie into its own revolution, the Asian Communists bore a heavy responsibility; for upon their success depended not merely the liberation of Asia but that of Europe as well. Lenin believed—at least at this point—that without a bourgeois revolution in the East the Western proletariat could not come to power.[3]

Thus the future of Europe could not unfold unless Asia caught up with the European past. How it would catch up was a central theme in Lenin's doctrine of imperialism. The Asian bourgeoisie would play a historically progressive part like that which the French bourgeoisie had played in eighteenth century Europe. The Western proletariat and the Asian bourgeoisie had a common interest in colonial revolution, because the existing order in Asia hindered the progress of both. Imperialism weakened the Western proletariat in that it won surplus profits for monopoly capital: profits drawn from overseas markets and foreign investments and shared with a part of the working class to turn it into a labor aristocracy forgetful of its class interests. On the other hand, imperialism weakened the Asian bourgeoisie by stifling native industry and fostering native feudalism as its mercenary and proconsul. Hence colonial revolution would clear the way of the Asian bourgeoisie to capitalism and that of the Western proletariat to socialism. A harmony of interests thus prevailed not only among the workers of the whole world (the original Marxian vision) but also between the workers and the bourgeois nationalists of the subject East.[4]

This wider harmony, it seemed to Lenin, was one of the major achievements of the Russian October Revolution.[5] Since then, all movements for national liberation had been gathered into the world revolution of the proletariat. The Communist slogan had become: Workers and oppressed peoples of the world, unite! [6] But the October Revolution had not only allied communism to Asian nationalism: it had also made possible the replacement of this alliance by the ultimate Marxian harmony of world socialism. The victory of socialism in Russia had saved all backward countries from the historical necessity of passing through a capitalist stage; they could now, with the aid of established soviet governments, take a short-cut to communism.[7] Of course, this required guidance by native Communist parties, which would draw a mass following — mostly of peasants — into toilers' councils or soviets.[8]

At least this was the rosy perspective which Lenin held up to the Second Congress of the Comintern in the summer of 1920. At this congress "all Eastern delegates felt that the line in the East was directed toward immediate revolutionary upheavals on a large scale." [9] Such was the mood of the congress which translated Lenin's theory of colonial revolution into a set of practical directives.

The resultant *Theses on the National and Colonial Question*, drafted by Lenin, stipulated that the Communists should form "temporary agreements or even alliances" with national liberation movements in dependent countries. Lenin did not say what form such temporary agreements or alliances were to take, nor how long they were to last. He merely laid down the rule that the Communists should not merge with their nationalist allies but should always preserve "the independent character of the proletarian movement — even in its germinal form." [10] This meant — as he himself explained elsewhere —

that they were not to sacrifice their freedom to "educate" and organize the masses.[11]

The practical difficulties this involved did not become fully apparent until after Lenin had passed from the scene and Stalin had become his successor. The zigzags of Stalin's course in China, his attempts to reconcile opposites, derived from the ambiguities in Lenin's original master plan. Yet in the consequent fiasco Stalin's critics in the Bolshevik party accused him of having perverted this plan and thus brought about its miscarriage. Actually, Lenin had been so vague that *both* Stalin and his critics could pose as defenders of the faith and cite him as their authority.

Some of this vagueness was natural in a set of directives intended to guide revolutionaries in many different countries. But some of it was due to the fact that two conflicting opinions, only partially reconciled, had found their way into the Theses. The committee which had prepared the Theses for submission to the Second Congress had been the scene of a tug-of-war between Lenin and a young Indian Communist. The Indian, Roy, had declared with fervor that the workers in his own country were strong enough to stand up for their rights without leaning on bourgeois allies. Accordingly, he had objected to that part of Lenin's theses which bound all Communists in the East to give support to the nationalists. He had also prepared his own theses, which the weary committee, anxious to cut the discussion short, simply appended to Lenin's.[12]

The congress approved the double theses without any opposition, even though one delegate pointed out that they contradicted each other.[13] So they did indeed, and quite unavoidably, considering that Roy and Lenin held different views of Asia's place in the coming world revolution. Lenin, though firmly determined to draw Asia into the struggle, retained nonetheless the old Marxist belief that the West would be its chief battleground. But Roy, an Asian, believed that Asia would be far more important, since the workers of Europe had in effect become shareholders of imperialism.[14] Their Asian brethren would therefore provide the chief force in the world revolution, but only if — contrary to Lenin's advice — they stayed out of bourgeois alliances.[15]

These differences between Lenin and Roy were later exploited by Stalin to prove the legitimate descent of his policy in China. Refusing to accede to Trotsky's demand that he call for soviets in China, Stalin maintained that by doing so he would follow Roy, not Lenin. Only Roy, he claimed, had regarded countries such as China and India — countries that were *relatively* advanced — as fit for sovietization. Lenin, by contrast, had referred only to the most backward areas (as, for instance, to Turkestan) when he called for soviets in Asia.[16]

Thus Stalin demonstrated that a lack of theoretical brilliance may well be accompanied by finesse in scholastic argumentation. It is true that that clause in Lenin's theses which dealt with the question of soviets had been inserted by the committee of which Roy was also a member.[17] But Lenin had not opposed this insertion; elsewhere at the Second Congress he said that "wherever conditions permit," soviets should be set up in Asia.[18] Nor did he distinguish in this context between more and less backward countries; in fact, his theses came under attack for lumping them all together.[19] He did single out Russian Turkestan as a totally backward area; but this was to show the party's success in sovietizing Central Asia.[20] If he meant to imply that in China and India such success was out of the question, he failed to convey this inner meaning to his closest associates.[21]

Thus Stalin went back to the records of the Second Comintern Congress to make up a spurious precedent that would vindicate his China policy. From the same records he also extracted an equally spurious precedent for that part of his China policy which made it in fact unprecedented. Nowhere in the world but in China did Communist Party members belong to another party as well, as they belonged to the Kuomintang. However, Stalin could point to the fact that Lenin, at the Second Congress, had ordered the British Communists to enter the Labour Party.

As we saw, Lenin never specified the form which "temporary agreements or even alliances" with Asian nationalism were to take. Hence Stalin had to seek doctrinal sanction for Communist membership in the Kuomintang by falling back on a European precedent. Whether Lenin would have thought this precedent applicable is, of course, somewhat doubtful. But Stalin allowed no such doubts.

Stalin could interpret Lenin as he wished, but there remained within him a hard core of the disciple's faith, of unquestioning attachment. To find precedents for his own acts among those of his predecessor was only a formula, of course, to legitimize his succession. But precedents carry their own weight; and thus, at a crucial juncture, Stalin saw the Kuomintang in the same light in which Lenin had looked at Labour.

Why had Lenin set this precedent, so dangerous to the proletarian "independence" which he preached at all other times? The answer is that he regarded the Labour Party as a promising medium through which to reach — and convert — the British workers. He believed that Labour was not a "party in the ordinary sense of the word" but a composite body leaving "sufficient liberty to all political parties within it." It was a workers' party only in so far as it consisted of workers; politically, it was a "bourgeois party through and through," led by petty-bourgeois reformers. Fortunately, its discipline was weak; thus the Communists in it would be able to discredit its leadership in the eyes of its rank-and-file members.[22]

What made Lenin so hopeful in this respect was Labour's federate structure, which he thought would permit the free growth and free functioning of a Communist faction inside it. His hope was not blind: he realized that those at the top of this structure might save themselves — as they actually did — by refusing to let in the Communists.[23] Yet he framed his policy assuming the opposite and also assuming, mistakenly, that the freedom of criticism in Labour's ranks meant an absence of all party discipline.

This mistake sprang from his inability (inherent in communist thinking) to understand a workers' party not dedicated to communism. A party, in the system of Marx, represents one single class interest; and communism, it is simply assumed, is the class interest of the workers. What then if a workers' party is "bourgeois"? How can one cross the chasm between the fact of its class composition and the fiction of its "true" interest? Two bridges have served men of many faiths to connect a fact with a fiction: either they transform the fact till it fits or else they condemn it morally. Lenin did both in order to prove that the Labour Party was bourgeois: he transformed it into a party of parties and he branded its leaders as "traitors." His lieutenant Zinoviev, the Comintern chairman, went even one step further: he denied the Labour Party the right to be called as much as a party. The Labour Party, he pointed out to the Second Comintern Congress, was merely a "blurred and solely parliamentary political association." [24]

The British Communists at the Congress balked at this definition; their principal spokesmen voiced dissent from the Lenin-Zinoviev policy. Their future leader, William Gallagher, complained that he and his comrades were being asked to give up ground that years of struggle had gained for them.[25] Lenin replied as follows:

> The method of the old International was to leave such questions to the individual parties in the countries concerned. That is basically wrong. It is quite possible that we do not know conditions in this or that party quite exactly; but our business here is to lay down the tactics of a Communist party in principle.[26]

Thus Lenin used the strong arm of Comintern discipline to push his scheme through the congress; yet behind the scenes he himself shrugged it off as an unpromising venture.[27] He shrugged off his statements in its defense as if they were inconsequential; but after his death they were to live on as part of Leninist doctrine. As such they were to have their effect on the policy of his successor not, as one might think, toward the Labour Party, but strangely enough, toward the Kuomintang.

This came about because Lenin had never informed his followers how they were to deal with nationalist parties as distinguished from nationalist movements. He had spoken of liberation movements, not of parties, at the Second Congress; hence those who came after him could only guess how he would have dealt with parties. Also, he had left it to his heirs to solve the insoluble problem of finding a Marxist definition for Asian nationalist parties. What class did such parties represent, considering that many classes responded to their patriotic appeal regardless of social distinctions? Were they multiclass parties? So it seemed; but then multiclass definitions, however accurate they might be in fact, could not possibly be strictly Marxist. Stalin's critics reminded him of this after he had "solved" the problem by applying varying multiclass terms to the undefinable Kuomintang. Now there was only one way out (and it was an escape with a precedent): to deprive the Kuomintang, by force of words, of its right to be called a party. This Stalin and his henchmen set out to do in the spring of 1927, with a zeal for verbalizing that seems strange in hard-headed Bolshevik realists. A "revolutionary parliament," a "peculiar semi-party," a " 'representative' organization of the soviet type": these were some of their names for the Kuomintang.[28]

Once it had been semantically established that the Kuomintang was not a party, it became possible to resolve another vexatious problem. It could be shown that this quasi-party offered its Communist members the same opportunities that Lenin had seen in the Labour Party in Britain. The Labour Party and the Kuomintang were, to be sure, quite dissimilar; but then there was nothing, in Stalin's view, to stop him from making them less so. In May 1927, he therefore issued instructions that the Kuomintang should forthwith be transformed into a federate body.

The boldness of this attempt to make facts accord with a fiction becomes clearer when we look at the facts — the stark facts — of Kuomintang power. The Kuomintang was very much of a party, patterned on the Bolshevik model; and then it was also a military force, ready to put down insurrection. In fact, the party had fallen so much under the sway of its army that generals, not apparatus-men, were wont to enforce its discipline. Stalin did not see that this party regime with an army standing behind it would resist and defeat his open attempt to disrupt its entire structure.

What accounts for such blindness? Ignorance of matters Chinese, no doubt, and the clever diplomacy of the Kuomintang generals. But this diplomacy could not have ensnared the far from gullible Soviets, if these had not felt compelled by their creed to invest their allies in class roles. As it was, they converted each Chinese general with whom they had struck a bargain into a "revolutionary bourgeois," though in fact he could not be called either. When such an ally showed his true face, he ceased to be "revolutionary"; but the role he had played would forthwith be assigned to another, like-minded actor. Thus a series of warlords played their parts as allies of world revolution, receiving Moscow's generous help and returning oaths of allegiance. When each finished his part by a sudden exit, Moscow would cry out "Treason!," shocked and surprised by the actor's refusal to go on with his acting. Only the moral fiction of a "betrayal" could now save its first assumption, unfounded but indispensable, of the general's class allegiance.

Stalin did, to be sure, go on record with the much quoted dictum that "in China armed revolution is fighting against armed counterrevolution." [29] But in practice he could not tell the two apart until after events had made the distinction for him. Those on the scene, whether Chinese Communists or Soviet advisers, were of course somewhat more discerning. Thus Stalin received repeated warnings of each successive "betrayal." But to be forewarned did not make him foresee.

The claim of Marxism to be a science rests on its claim to yield foresight. But it was precisely the Marxist-Leninist equipment of Stalin's mind which blurred his foresight in China. This equipment did not register a Chiang Kai-shek as a man of flesh, blood, and will, but merely as the organic particle of a class layer, to be shed in the next molting season of revolution. Stalin never suspected that this particle hid his own likeness.

Not that he let himself be enslaved by the tenets of his doctrine. He was always ready to twist them around until they suited his purpose. Yet ready as he was to adjust to reality, he usually saw reality in the Marxist-Leninist mirror.

This "reality" inside Stalin's mind was hardened by his conflict with Trotsky. The Trotskyites, in disputing his claim to the apostolic succession, accused him with fundamentalist zeal of having perverted the scripture. Thus they ascribed the successive defeats of the Chinese revolution to his unorthodox leadership, his betrayal of Lenin. In order to maintain his position, Stalin had to refute them, even to the point of denying facts that were actually quite undeniable. Because his opponents pointed out that the Kuomintang was turning against him, he had to pretend (and perhaps believed) that most of it would remain loyal. Even after the Kuomintang formally expelled the Communists, Stalin pretended that the two-party bloc remained as solid as ever. The bloc had become such a powerful symbol of his side in the factional struggle that he could not let go of it, even though it no longer existed.

What divided Stalin and Trotsky on the China issue was their obsession with different Leninist stereotypes. These stereotypes came from the same matrix: the National and Colonial Theses of the Second Comintern Congress. Stalin found in the Theses canonical justification of his decision to give support to the party of Chinese nationalism. But in order to carry out this decision, he had to ignore the Theses — or rather, distort their true intent — with respect to Chinese soviets. Soviets, he thought (and rightly so), would have provoked a showdown, earlier than was profitable, with the Kuomintang leaders. Trotsky shut his eyes to this dilemma when he demanded soviets in the belief that these might yet save the Chinese revolution. He took his stand on one part of the Theses while Stalin took his on another, so that the same scripture lent support to their mutual recriminations.

In the course of this argument, Stalin fell back on yet another slogan, one coined by Lenin in 1905 during Russia's first revolution. Lenin had hoped that this revolution would end in the establishment, by his own Social Democrats and their allies, of a republican government. He had termed this coalition of republican parties a democratic dictatorship — democratic within, dictatorial without — of the proletariat and peasantry. But the revolution went down in defeat; and Lenin's premature slogan had to be put away on a shelf for possible future usage. But in fact it was never used again; for in the next revolution — that which started in February 1917 — Lenin changed his mind about it. On Trotsky's advice, he now demanded that all power go to the soviets — not to the kind of coalition that he had envisaged previously.

When Stalin revived Lenin's ancient slogan in 1927, he did not say, of course, that Lenin himself had very soon discarded it. The coalition of which Lenin had spoken reminded him of the alliance between the two parties that now led the way in the Chinese revolution. Once this alliance had shaken off its traitorous bourgeois adherents, it would "inevitably" grow into a "democratic dictatorship." [30] Stalin felt confident of this outcome, although his original purpose in resorting to Lenin's formula may have been to lay down a smoke screen. But if he had intended to screen off the Kuomintang from the eyes of his and its critics, he had only succeeded in blinding himself as to its real nature. For Lenin's "democratic dictatorship" had denoted a coalition between entirely separate parties "never merging [their] organizations." [31] No such coalition existed in China; for here the Communist Party was organizationally intertwined with the party to which it was allied. Stalin hoped, to be sure, that precisely because of the tightness of this alliance, the Communists would find it easier to win the leading role in it. He persisted in mistaking the influence that they had won with the masses for power by which they could overcome the might of the Kuomintang armies.

Thus both he and Trotsky looked at China through the Leninist prism; yet neither (as subsequent chapters will show) distinguished himself by clear vision. Must we blame Lenin because his disciples found in his theses on Asia not so much a source of enlightenment as one of confusion and conflict? Hardly; for Lenin had only envisaged general prospects in Asia; he had never laid down a hard-and-fast rule for exploiting these prospects. Though his premises and objectives were fixed, being those of the Marxist system, he had, after all, progressed beyond Marx precisely by his empiricism. Thus he had marked out some courses of action that were mutually exclusive — and left the ultimate choice between them up to future experience.

But when he called for broad coalitions *and* for soviets in Asia, he probably thought of closely successive, not of alternative, measures. While he did ask that the formation of soviets should be given immediate attention, he did not, of course, ignore the prime need to train Asian cadres to run them. He stressed that the European proletariat, wherever it was in power, would have to think of this Asian need and undertake this training. Nowhere in this context did he make mention of the united-front tactic; but he probably intended it to be used during the training period. Alliances with Asian nationalism would allow the Comintern sufficient time in which to raise and train its Asian cadres. Lenin did not say how much time would be needed for this purpose; but he hoped that aid from the Soviet West would cut it down to a minimum.[32]

Thus Lenin's high hopes for the East rested on nothing firmer than his high hopes for the West, for victory in Europe. Hence it was not defeats in Asia but defeats in Europe which caused the first sharp revision of his Asian program. In 1922, at the Fourth Comintern Congress, the high hopes of two years before were formally abandoned. The Chinese Communists were told not to go on dreaming, idly and irresponsibly, of soviets and of socialism. Instead, they were to bend their efforts toward a steady widening, by means of a united front, of their party's influence. The Comintern had thus cast off its own youthful illusions and chosen to pursue the course that seemed to be the safest.

Had Lenin sounded the retreat? Had it been his idea to make the Chinese Communists auxiliaries of the Kuomintang? We cannot say: he never commented—not, at least, in public—on the unusual alliance taking shape in China. In 1922, he still paid some attention, though only intermittently, to policy decisions. But he was mortally ill—and steeped in Russian problems: hardly, it seems, in a position to give much thought to China. The question of how the master *would* have dealt with China therefore became, after his death, a much debated issue.

Such arguments are sheer speculation, except for those who subsume under Marxist principles what Lenin *did* do, and then deduce from these principles what he *would* do at any given juncture. Non-Marxists cannot be so certain: they can only venture a guess on the basis of precedent. But in the case of the Kuomintang alliance, exact precedent is lacking, so that the guesser must fall back on the best possible analogy. This he finds in Lenin's policy toward Turkey and other countries of the Near and Middle East.

The first ones to draw this analogy were the Bolshevik critics of Stalin's China policy. Stalin's chief agent in China, Borodin, had been Lenin's chief agent in Turkey; he had represented the Comintern at the headquarters of the Turkish General Kemal before he represented it at the headquarters of General Chiang Kai-shek. Kemal had hailed communism in Moscow the better to extirpate communism at home. Thus Stalin's critics had reason to warn of a "Kemalist" development in China. Stalin, of course, had to deny that there could be such a development.[33]

Briefly, Lenin's policy in Turkey, Afghanistan, and Persia was to ally himself with any nationalist leaders opposed to Britain, even though they might be opposed to communism as well. Or, as one of his Turkish allies (Enver Pasha) put it: anyone who was anti-British was also a Bolshevik.[34] When some purist German comrades objected to finding a man of Enver's caliber in their camp, they were told by the Comintern chairman that "one looks for help wherever one can find it."[35] Yet what had Lenin said on this subject only a few months before?

His *Theses on the National and Colonial Question* had demanded a "resolute struggle against pseudo-communist revolutionary liberation movements . . . which put on a communist coloring." They had explained that support of such movements served only to "rally elements of future proletarian parties together" and to "nurture their consciousness of . . . the [future] struggle with bourgeois-democratic movements in their nations."[36]

How did Lenin apply the *Theses* in his dealings with Kemal? He concluded an alliance with him in March 1921, only a few weeks after Kemal's police had waylaid and murdered a group of Turkish Communists on their return from Moscow. If Lenin knew of this incident, he ignored it, perhaps in view of the courtesy — not to say, deference — with which Kemal treated the Soviets. Kemal called his government (which included legitimist supporters of the ex-Sultan) a "council of people's commissars," and maintained liaison with the Comintern through Turkish Communist delegates. That these delegates represented a bogus communist party set up for Kemal's own purposes had escaped the Russians' attention. But eventually they had their eyes opened: in mid-1921, a genuine Turkish Communist delegate exposed his counterfeit comrades. But even this delegate had to pledge allegiance to Kemal, because the Comintern required such allegiance up to late 1922.[37]

This Turkish interlude illustrates a point which is neither new nor startling in itself. Just as Marx refused to be bound by "Marxism," Lenin was no slave to "Leninism." He was free to break his own precepts, to contradict himself "dialectically" in tune with the historical process for which he acted as oracle. But once he had died, his every word became law, his every move a model. His self-contradictions disappeared within the false consistency, the rigged-up whole, of an "ism."

Such posthumous systematizing involves a retroactive denial of choice, in that whatever the dead leader did becomes the *only* course that he could have wisely chosen. By extension, what the dead leader *would* do now becomes also a single certainty. But if his disciples disagree as to where this certainty lies, then the view of the strongest becomes *the* truth, a pure truth upheld by terror.

To distill an "ism" from the liquid uncertainties of a man's life requires that the ingredients of his decisions (periods, places, influences) should be sorted out according to the compound desired. The "Leninist" myths concocted by Stalin and Trotsky in their dispute about China offer a good example. Stalin brought forth a "Lenin" untouched by Trotsky's influence, a "Lenin" who, since 1905, had worked chiefly through coalitions. Trotsky brought forth a "Lenin" who looked almost like his disciple, a "Lenin" who, since 1917, had relied above all on soviets. Stalin's "Lenin" reflected the deft maneuverer; Trotsky's, the bold man of action; but neither reflected the real man: the living, developing paradox.

What, then, do ordinary men stand to gain from steeping themselves in the passionate pedantries of a Marxist-Leninist argument? Such debates appear arid at first sight and would indeed be irrelevant, if they did not leave so deep a mark upon so much human experience. As it is, men have died because of them, because of conflicting notions about questions of doctrine or of belief that seem very abstruse from a distance. Such questions do not move the unbeliever; for him, they lack all reality; and yet it may well be his blood that is shed in the course of their resolution. Thus the Chinese people found that debates of which most of them knew nothing — debates in the Russian capital — impinged deeply on their own destiny.

CHAPTER II

THE COMINTERN AND SUN YAT-SEN: PRELIMINARIES OF AN ALLIANCE

In historical perspective, the accomplished fact often passes for a conclusion long foregone. An event is ascribed to one origin sorted out from all causal clutter; and hindsight imputes foresight to the fumblings of the past. Such imputation is apt to occur in all efforts to reconstruct history; but it is most deeply imbedded in Western thought and most rigidly codified in Marxian determinism.

Foresight is, in fact, a misnomer for instinctive awareness of existing potentialities. Lenin "foresaw" the Asian revolution when he found Asia ready to respond to revolutionary action. But the action which evoked this response in China cannot be traced back to Lenin, and may well have been taken without his knowledge. In fact, this action was probably initiated for a purpose opposed to Lenin's own.

Lenin "foresaw" that the Communists in the East were too weak to stage a revolution without support from "bourgeois" nationalism. But in China the revolution was launched by a peculiar combination of Communists and nationalists in a single party. This combination was not of the Comintern's invention but was devised by the father of Chinese nationalism, Sun Yat-sen, for the double purpose of controlling and exploiting the Communists. The actual entry of the Chinese Communists into the Kuomintang was ordered by H. Maring, a minor Comintern functionary who claims to have acted on his own responsibility.

That the Communists chose Sun Yat-sen as their ally may also appear logical in hindsight. But such logic omits the hesitations and resistances which delayed, and might well have blocked, the alliance. Sun was by no means the only ally sought out by the Comintern: his favor was courted only after that of the northern warlord Wu P'ei-fu had already been secured. Conversely, the Comintern was not the only ally sought out by Sun; he allied himself with it only after his last overture to the West had been rebuffed. Furthermore, the alliance met resistance among the Chinese Communists, who never overcame their suspicion of Sun's motives.

There was therefore no historical necessity in Sun's Russian orientation. He was, to be sure, quite well known to the Kremlin; in fact, he had occupied Lenin's thoughts as early as 1912. At that time, Lenin had criticized him for believing, like the Russian Populists,* that "backward" countries would not have to go through a capitalist stage.[1] But this "reactionary" doctrine became Lenin's own after the success of the Russian revolution, which set a precedent for passing directly to socialism. Sun, for his part, had lost faith in parliamentary democracy when the first Chinese parliament succumbed to a military coup in November 1913. Under the impact of this defeat (the "18th Brumaire" of the Chinese revolution), Sun had rebuilt the Kuomintang into an autocratic body designed to wield one-party rule under himself.[2] Thus entirely independent forces had driven Lenin and Sun toward each other — yet forces so strong that it is a tribute to history's deviousness how slowly their alliance came about.

Sun had sent congratulations to Lenin on his accession to power in 1917 and had, in return, received written pledges of solidarity from Soviet Foreign Commissar Chicherin.[3] But this exchange only foreshadowed the pact which was blueprinted

* The Populists were agrarian socialists who exerted much influence on Russian thought and politics during the last quarter of the nineteenth century.

in 1922, sealed in 1923, and implemented in 1924. No collaboration with Chinese nationalism could take shape before a link had been formed through a native Communist party. Hence the Comintern had to think first of building a Chinese section, and then of inducing it to work side by side with its class enemy.

Communism, in the China of early 1920, was the newly found faith of groping intellectuals, not the platform of a political party. The fifty-odd students who composed Marxist study groups in Peking and Shanghai had no roots in social-democratic thought nor any experience in political work. Their leaders, Li Ta-chao and Ch'en Tu-hsiu, were university professors who had never passed through the school of revolutionary leadership which had already brought Sun to the threshold of Leninist party concepts. Both Li and Ch'en had played prominent parts in the May 4 Movement of 1919, the first outburst of Chinese nationalism; but both had only supported, not organized or led it — just as both had come to Marxism not by spontaneous search but under the impact of the Russian revolution.[4] Clearly, such men required firm guidance by experienced Comintern hands in order to convert a Marxist sect into a Communist party.

It is symptomatic of the mystery which still shrouds past Comintern moves that its first act of intervention in China cannot be clearly established. Standard sources identify this act with the mission of Grigorii Voitinsky in the spring of 1920.[5] But one Chinese Communist author gives the following account of an earlier, unsuccessful mission, not recorded elsewhere:

> At the beginning of 1920, the Comintern dispatched a Korean comrade named Kim Sen — who had attended its first congress — to China in order to lay the groundwork for the organization of a Communist

party. When he arrived in China, he contacted Huang Chieh-min, a member of the Ta-t'ung Party,* and twenty-one anarchists, and organized a Communist party which elected a Central Executive Committee of nineteen. Ch'en Tu-hsiu opposed this organization on the ground that a Communist party made up of such elements would certainly collapse. Before long, this small organization did fall apart. This was the failure of the first attempt to set up a Communist party.[6]

Whatever the accuracy of this story, it probably errs in crediting Ch'en with such a high standard of orthodoxy at so early a date. Actually Ch'en accepted, until well into 1921, the support of a motley crowd of malcontents, ranging from anarchists to anti-militarists and anti-Confucianists.[7] When he founded the Chinese Socialist Youth Corps in August 1920 (one month ahead of the Communist Party) he took in many such radicals. This laxity of admission standards reflects a looseness of principle but also, no doubt, a deliberate groping toward the broadest possible mass support. It is certain that by mid-1920 Ch'en Tu-hsiu was no longer ignorant of how a Bolshevik apparatus should be set up and operated. Lengthy consultations with the Comintern emissary, Voitinsky, had preceded the establishment of the Chinese Socialist Youth Corps. When the first party nucleus was formed in September 1920, Voitinsky appeared openly at Ch'en's side as his helper and adviser.[8]

As a newcomer to China, Voitinsky could not make out all the shades in the hazy spectrum of Chinese radicalism. Hence he did not curb the hospitality with which the Communists welcomed opponents—*any* opponents—of the existing order. Thus the Socialist Youth Corps grew less and less socialist, until, in May 1921, Ch'en Tu-hsiu dissolved and re-formed it.[9]

* This refers to adherents of the constitutional monarchist K'ang Yu-wei, who inspired the "Hundred Days of Reform" of the Manchu Emperor Kuang Hsü in 1898.

Subsequently the Youth Corps became a fortress of Jacobin intransigence.

Even the Communist Party itself was by no means entirely communist when it met for its First Congress in July 1921. Among its sixty to seventy members, it still harbored "democratic socialists" and anarchists. A "democratic" minority, led by Li Han-ch'ing* and Ch'en Kung-po, urged that the party program should be shelved pending an inquiry into the merits of Western social democracy as compared to those of Russian communism. The majority voted against this view, thus launching the party of Chinese Marxism into Russian waters.[10] But for some unknown reason the party did not yet affiliate with the Comintern.†

Because the First Congress issued no public statement whatever, our knowledge of its decisions comes wholly from second-hand sources. An official party history[11] tells us that the "congress decided to support Sun Yat-sen's progressive movement in the form of a two-party alliance." ‡ Actually, this decision seems to have originated with the Comintern delegate; for in a previous resolution passed by majority vote the congress had declared itself equally opposed to the Canton and Peking governments.[12] Moreover, even the minority which

* Though a person by that name appears in a Japanese biographical dictionary (*Gendai Chūgoku jimmei jiten*, p. 608), the "Li" in question is almost certainly Li Han-chün, a prominent "legal" Marxist known to have been at the congress (*Chung-kuo hsien-tai ko-ming yün-tung shih*, p. 89). This is the reason why "Han-ch'ing" has simply been rendered as "Han-chün" in the *Documents on Communism, Nationalism, and Soviet Advisers in China* (pp. 53–54).

† One source suggests that the Comintern delegate himself advised against affiliation, lest the party compromise its "Chineseness" in patriotic eyes (Robert Payne, *Mao Tse-tung*, p. 73). But no evidence to support this story is cited.

‡ "Two-party alliance" is a free translation of *tang-wai ho-tso*, "outside party collaboration." What is meant is a united front without interlocking memberships — a so-called "bloc without."

favored an alliance with Canton comprised an important faction which opposed an alliance with Sun. This group, led by Ch'en Kung-po and T'an P'ing-shan, proposed that the party should make common cause with a certain General Ch'en Chiung-ming, who, as military governor of Kwangtung Province, held the real power in the south.[13]

Sun Yat-sen owed his position in the Canton government entirely to General Ch'en, who had made himself master of Kwangtung Province late in 1920.* A warlord with a flair for reform, Ch'en had invited both Sun and Ch'en Tu-hsiu to enter his government.† This had won him such widespread support among Chinese liberals that when he finally broke with Sun two years later, the "most progressive elements" in the country were said to be backing him.[14] At least he had reformed a provincial government, while Sun had done very little beyond pushing quite impracticable schemes for the conquest of the whole country. The cause of reform thus seemed better served by the general turned reformer than by the reformer who fancied himself in the role of generalissimo.

Within the Communist Party, too, it was a group of reformers — the "democratic" minority — who took the side of Ch'en Chiung-ming. It is true that at the beginning of the First Party Congress even comrades of a deeper Bolshevik hue (such as T'an P'ing-shan) had backed him. But these retreated when the Comintern delegate turned out to champion Sun's cause, so that the "democrats" were left alone in the camp of the opposition. Their struggle did not last long, to be sure: soon after the congress ended, their leader, Ch'en Kung-po,

* General Ch'en had cast in his lot with the revolutionists during both the republican revolution of 1911 and the "second revolution" against Yüan Shih-k'ai two years later.

† Ch'en Tu-hsiu became chairman of the Board of Education, with the result that the Board became an important center of Communist power in Kwangtung.

conceded defeat by resigning his party membership.* Though this meant the end of all support for Ch'en Chiung-ming among the Communists, it did not mean that they had now come to feel more affectionate toward his rival. Their feelings toward Sun remained so cool that one may very well wonder how close they would ever have drawn to him if the Comintern had not pushed them.

The Comintern delegate at the First Party Congress was the Dutchman Maring,† who had taught the Communists in the Netherlands Indies how to use the united-front tactic.[15] Maring had doubtless heard of Sun during his stay in the Indies, for Sun derived much of his support from the Chinese in Southeast Asia. It must have been for some reason like this — not as a matter of principle — that Maring favored Sun over Ch'en Chiung-ming as an ally for the Chinese Communists. He certainly had no scruples about striking bargains with warlords: his first act after arriving in China was to negotiate with one of them. While stopping in Peking on his way to the First Party Congress in Shanghai he had conferred with Wu P'ei-fu, then the strongest warlord in North China.‡ In return for his promise to support Wu against any of his rivals,§ Wu had consented to give free rein to the Com-

* The party formalized Ch'en's withdrawal by expelling him in January 1923. As elastic in his principles as most Chinese politicians of the day, Ch'en wound up in the Kuomintang left wing, in which he became a leading figure ranking next to Wang Ching-wei and Liao Chung-k'ai. In 1939 he followed Wang into the Japanese camp and succeeded him, in March 1944, as head of the puppet government in Nanking.

† Maring's real name was Sneevliet. Many English-language sources give his name as "Malin," which is simply the way in which the Chinese pronounce Maring.

‡ Marshal Wu P'ei-fu was a leader of the Chihli clique, which dominated the Peking government from 1920 to 1924. He subsequently shifted his seat of power to Central China, whence he was dislodged by the Northern Expedition in 1926.

§ Communist commissars helped Wu to protect his rail lines when he defended his domain against the Manchurian warlord Chang Tso-lin in 1922.

munists in his area. Since the area he ruled was sparsely industrialized, it was mainly the railway workers whom the Communists were able to organize as a result of this bargain. The Ministry of Communications in Peking (like the Board of Education in Canton) became the center from which they spread the party's influence downward.[16] Moscow prided itself on Maring's coup: at last—said one of its spokesmen—it had become possible to gain a foothold among the workers of North China.[17] The Chinese Communists remained more skeptical: they had, to be sure, gained their foothold; but they knew, because they knew Wu P'ei-fu, that this foothold was very slippery.

"The tactic of a rapprochement with Wu P'ei-fu found its principal defendant in the Comintern representative," a Chinese Communist leader wrote later. "At the time there were, to be sure, one or two comrades who placed unfounded hopes on Wu; but this was not a general phenomenon."[18] The "phenomenon" caused the deepest split in the party branch at Peking, where "left" oppositionists rose up to protest when Li Ta-chao announced the new policy.[19] The leftists, grouped around Chang Kuo-t'ao, had no chance of winning the argument; but before long Wu himself furnished proof of how right they had been to distrust him.

On February 7, 1923, a meeting of railway workers at Chengchow, on the line between Peking and Hankow, was broken up by Wu's soldiery. Sixty workers were killed in a massacre which left its imprint on history in that it profoundly affected the outlook of the Chinese Communist leaders. Of course, it ended their alliance with Wu,* and it made them all

* But it did not end his credit in Moscow. On March 25, 1926, the Politburo's Committee on China resolved that the alliance with Wu should be renewed in case he recovered military hegemony in the north. See a report of the committee entitled "Voprosy nashei politiki v otnoshenii Kitaya i Yaponii" in the Trotsky Archives.

the more willing — even eager, which they had not been before — to enter the ranks of the Kuomintang. They had lost their proletarian base in the north, lost it standing by helplessly; and they had lost confidence in their own strength, their ability to cope with the warlords. The Kuomintang would protect their flanks if they operated inside it; it would hold off the warlords while they would be free to build up their workers' following. Thus Wu P'ei-fu and his riflemen succeeded better than Maring in convincing the Communists that they stood to gain from membership in the Kuomintang.[20]

Maring had taken the first step toward effecting two-party unity when he visited Sun in November 1921 at Kweilin in Kwangsi Province. There, at his headquarters, Sun was engrossed in planning a march to Peking, undeterred by his lack of any armed force nearly adequate for this purpose.* His visitor did not bring him word of forthcoming material assistance; but the word he did bring confirmed Sun's belief that history was his ally. What Maring told him of the Soviet experiment confirmed him in his conviction that his own brand of socialism was the best, both in theory and in practice.

This is how Sun himself put the matter when, on returning to Canton, he informed his close comrade, Liao Chung-k'ai, of what had transpired at Kweilin.

> I had been very skeptical that Marxism — pure communism — could be carried out after the Soviet revolution, because the world is now in a period of capitalist high-tide, Russian industry and commerce are not very developed, and communism, unable to succeed in isolation, still has a long way to go to be realized. Now I have just learned from Maring that Soviet Russia, after having a go at communism, ran

* To remedy this lack, Sun was raising a new army under the command of Hsü Ch'ung-chih, an old party comrade and, as it turned out, the only general who would fight on his side when he finally broke with Ch'en Chiung-ming. In 1922, Hsü's forces took the field against Ch'en's and were completely defeated.

into deep difficulties and therefore switched to the New Economic Policy. The spirit of this New Economic Policy coincides with the Principle of People's Livelihood which I advocate. I am very glad that Soviet Russia has embarked on a policy which corresponds to my principle and am strengthened in the belief that my principle can be entirely realized and must ultimately succeed.[21]

Thus Sun came away from his first meeting with a Comintern emissary firmly convinced that Russian communism in practice resembled what he himself taught. No specific agreement resulted from the Kweilin talks; but shortly afterwards, a Kuomintang delegation went to Moscow to take part in the First Congress of the Toilers of the Far East.

In January 1922 the Kuomintang made its debut before the international brotherhood in Moscow. But its reception can scarcely be called fraternal, except in the sense of an elder brother admonishing the younger. The congress gave it far more advice than praise, and censured its chief delegate, Tao Sheng-tek,* for talking radical bombast.

The mood of the congress was less sanguine than that which had pervaded the Second Congress of the Comintern a year and a half before. It is true that the Comintern's chairman, Zinoviev, still spoke in confident tones; the entire Far East, he proclaimed, was "ripe for the soviet system." But as soon as Tao Sheng-tek ventured to say the same, he was severely rebuked; for although Zinoviev was chairman of the Comintern, its chief spokesman on Asian affairs, Safarov, did not share his confident outlook. "I do not know," he said, "who could profit by the statement that the Chinese masses are already ripe for . . . the soviet system." As to Tao's claim that the Kuomintang had advocated soviet principles for twenty years, Safarov

* According to Mr. Chang Kuo-t'ao, who attended the congress, the name of the chief Kuomintang delegate was Chang Ch'iu-pai. "Tao Sheng-tek" may have been a badly garbled form of this name, or a pseudonym.

said scornfully that "we are not so naïve as to imagine that this party is a revolutionary communist party." [22]

Zinoviev was not naïve either when it came to appraising the Kuomintang as a partner in world revolution. "Among the adherents of Sun Yat-sen," he complained, "there are those who look, not without benevolence, to the side of America . . . thinking that it will be from there that the blessings of democracy and progress will flow on revolutionary China." The Kuomintang's attitude toward the presence of Soviet troops in Outer Mongolia also disturbed Zinoviev. "It would strike me as very sad," he said, "if among the 'aktivs' * of revolutionary South China there should be some who took the doctrinaire approach to the Mongolian question and started talk about returning Mongolia to China." [23] Actually, of course, he had reason to feel sad already.

But it was for its domestic program that the Kuomintang incurred the most criticism. It proposed to nationalize the land, said its delegate; but only after national unity had been restored. Why not earlier? asked Safarov. He also accused the Kuomintang of preaching "harmony between labor and capital" in order to keep the workers' movement "in diapers." On the other hand, he conceded that "sharp conflicts" between the two were unlikely and undesirable in the immediate future.[24]

Thus Safarov, a moderate on the question of Chinese soviets, took an intransigent stand on the question of class collaboration in China. This is surprising; for when the Chinese Communists took the same stand half a year later, Moscow made them relinquish it. Also surprising, in retrospect, is the subordinate role which the congress assigned to revolution in China. "The Japanese proletariat is the principal force which

* This is an untranslatable Soviet term denoting the active members of an organization, party, or movement.

will solve the Far Eastern problem," said Safarov to the consternation of the Kuomintang delegate. In his concluding speech, distributed to all delegates, he expressly identified this viewpoint with Zinoviev's.[25]

How the Chinese Communists reacted to the prospect of having their problems solved by their Japanese comrades is not a matter of record. But in regard to the Kuomintang, they seemed to agree with Safarov. Their *First Manifesto on the Current Situation*, issued in June 1922, condemned the Kuomintang by faint praise. It admitted that the Kuomintang was revolutionary, but only in a relative sense. It summoned the Chinese proletariat to "act jointly" with the Kuomintang in a "united front of democratic revolution"; but it left no doubt by whom this united front was to be led. The "struggle for democracy" remained, in the best Marxist tradition, the "struggle of one class." [26]

Exactly what the Communists meant by "united front" became clear in the *Manifesto of the Second National Congress*, issued in July 1922. To overthrow feudalism and accomplish the "democratic revolution," the workers were to join hands with the petty bourgeoisie: the poor peasants, shopkeepers and artisans. This would stop the class struggle on one front but would step it up on another. The struggle against the native capitalists, or national bourgeoisie, would grow intense as soon as the breakdown of feudal barriers left labor and capital facing only each other. Proletarian support of the "democratic revolution" was therefore no "surrender to the capitalists": it was a move to array the two classes along their historical lines of battle. The alliance with the petty bourgeoisie served the sole purpose of securing the flanks of the proletariat while it laid the groundwork for soviets. Such a "united front" had obviously no place for capitalists: these belonged to the camp of the enemy.[27]

The *form* of united front envisaged in the manifesto was clearly the "bloc without": a horizontal alignment *alongside* the Kuomintang. But what actually emerged in the end was a "bloc within": a vertical alignment *inside* the Kuomintang. The records of the Second Congress contain no suggestion of this later development.

The manifesto expressly identifies the Chinese Communists as members of the Comintern.[28] In fact, their affiliation with the Comintern had just been ratified by the Second Congress.[29] It is therefore surprising that no available record of the congress mentions the presence of a single Comintern agent.* Maring, for one, did not arrive in Central China until shortly after the congress, and then for the express purpose of changing the course it had set.[30]

In August 1922 — one month after the Second Congress — a plenum of the Central Committee convened at Hangchow and resolved to convert the "bloc without" into a "bloc within." Eyewitness accounts of this crucial event contradict each other. According to Ch'en Tu-hsiu, Maring compelled the plenum, under pressure of Comintern discipline, to endorse his plan for the entry of Communist Party members into the ranks of the Kuomintang. To justify this unprecedented move, he argued that the Kuomintang represented not merely the bourgeoisie but all classes opposed to imperialism. However, Ch'en and four others† strongly objected to his plan, which they held to be incompatible with the party's proletarian mission.[31]

Maring contradicts Ch'en on two points. He admits some opposition to his proposal — notably from Chang Kuo-t'ao —

* Some sources claim that Maring attended the congress, which they locate at Hangchow. Actually, the congress met in Shanghai. It is therefore quite obvious that these sources confuse the congress with the Hangchow plenum, which took place shortly afterwards.

† Li Ta-chao, Chang Kuo-t'ao, Ts'ai Ho-shen, Kao Yü-han.

but claims that Ch'en and the majority of the Central Committee upheld him. He also denies having invoked Comintern discipline to impose his will.[32]

Chang Kuo-t'ao's own testimony reconciles the most glaring discrepancies between Maring's and Ch'en Tu-hiu's.[33] It seems that the Chinese Communist leaders agreed provisionally to Maring's plan, hoping that an appeal to Moscow would yet secure its modification or withdrawal.*

This hope rested on the suspicion, later confirmed by Maring himself, that he had "no specific instructions" and hence no express authority to weld the two parties together.[34] Moscow did, to be sure, back him up in the end, but apparently not till months later. In January 1923, it still spoke of "coordinating the activities" of the two parties without hinting at a closer union.[35] Was it still unwilling to commit itself irrevocably? We cannot tell, but it had reason to waver. The unorthodoxy of Maring's scheme was disturbing, and so were the facts of its origin. For actually Maring had only been its promoter: its father was Sun Yat-sen.

In 1922 — Ch'en Tu-hsiu relates — an emissary of the Communist Youth International, Dalin, suggested a regular two-party alliance to Sun. But "Sun categorically refused this. He would permit members of the Chinese Communist Party and of the Youth Corps only to join the Kuomintang and obey it. He would not accept any combination outside of the party."[36]

Sun himself has confirmed this account indirectly. According to him, the Communists "hoped to monopolize Russian aid and to compete with our party as an independent unit"; but the Soviet leaders "corrected them on my behalf."[37] Considering that Sun had favored one-party government ever since

* Evidence that such an appeal was actually made — directly from Ch'en to Lenin — appears in a Japanese account. See Hatano Kanichi in *Shina seiji soshiki no kenkyū*, p. 88.

1914, it would have been strange indeed had be preferred a two-party bloc to outright absorption of the Communists.

Hangchow was a first step in the direction that history was to take; but it was only a faltering step, tentative and indecisive. Neither Sun nor the Communists looked on their *entente* as a definite, final commitment. Both continued to search for alternatives, to prevaricate and maneuver. They might well have drifted apart again but for certain subsequent happenings.

At the time of the Hangchow plenum, Sun's political fortune stood at an all-time low. He had been compelled to seek refuge in Shanghai, because General Ch'en Chiung-ming, rather than support his expansionist schemes, had forcibly expelled him from Canton. The local Communists had denied him their aid; he had lost much liberal sympathy; and now even friends thought they served him best by advising him to leave politics.[38] Thus the Communist leaders could argue with reason — and did in fact argue at Hangchow — that by joining the Kuomintang they would join a party that was already moribund.[39]

In this sorry predicament, Sun had no choice but to seek an immediate alliance with anyone who offered him help, on almost any conditions. Thus he was eager to enroll the Communists even though one of their leaders took pains to inform him that they would continue to give prior allegiance to Moscow.[40] But Sun's attitude stiffened when his luck improved; for soon he found himself able to strike a bargain with two southern warlords, enemies of Ch'en Chiung-ming. Ch'en was ousted from Canton; and Sun returned in January 1923, rid of his rival and hence, overnight, in a stronger position than previously. Now the Communists found him so hard to deal with that they called on Maring to mediate; but Maring succeeded no better than they in making him more amenable. "If the

Communist Party enters the Kuomintang," Sun told him in a summary manner, "it must submit to discipline and not criticize the Kuomintang openly. If the Communists do not submit to the Kuomintang, I shall expel them; and if Soviet Russia should give them secret protection, I shall oppose Soviet Russia." [41] Sun did not live to carry out this threat; and those who finally did so found it wiser to disavow any intent of opposing Soviet Russia.

Sun, still uncertain of Moscow's reaction, continued to look for allies who, in case of necessity, might take the place of the Soviets. When the United States Minister to China came to Canton a few months later, he approached Sun with a far-reaching plan for Western assistance to China. Civil and military advisers from the United States and Europe were to supervise China's administration for a five-year period of tutelage.[42] Zinoviev's nightmare had thus come true: the Kuomintang's guiding spirit was guiding it toward American ways of "democracy and progress." And this although he had just put his name under a manifesto that seemed to place him, once and for all, on the side of Soviet Russia.

In January 1923, Sun had met Adolph A. Joffe, an experienced negotiator and intimate friend of the still powerful Trotsky. Together they drafted a joint declaration that settled, at least ostensibly, all major issues in dispute between Moscow and the Kuomintang government. Moscow renounced any intention of exporting soviets to China: an intention which, in actual fact, it had given up a year earlier. It promised to help in the restoration of China's national unity; yet it insisted on its right to keep troops in Outer Mongolia. At the same time it withdrew its demand for Mongolia's independence; in return, Sun agreed to accept the *status quo* in that country.[43]

By the end of the year (1923), Sun had firmly concluded that China did not have a friend in the world apart from Soviet

Russia.[44] What would have happened if the United States and the other Western powers had not brushed aside his overture to the American Minister? As it was, they ignored it and—far worse—paraded their naval power to stop him from asserting his claim to the Canton customs surplus.* Thus prevented from seizing a source of revenue that he needed badly, Sun finally cast in his lot with those who approached him with gifts, not with gunboats.

While Sun thus determined to go through with his plan to absorb the Communists, how did the Communist rank and file react in face of this prospect? Some young party members simply refused to resign themselves to it in silence and switched their allegiance to the Socialist Youth Corps, where resistance to it was strongest. Then the dissidents threatened unitedly to run the Socialist Youth Corps as "another party, along different lines from those of the Communist Party." [45] To counter this threat, the party leaders forced every Youth Corps member over the age of 26 to return to the ranks of the party.†

However, the party leaders themselves had also been slow to conquer their original scruples about tying themselves so closely to their Kuomintang ally. At the Fourth Congress of the Comintern, in November 1922, the Chinese delegates, led by Ch'en Tu-hsiu, had been teased for their "youthful convictions." Karl Radek, a Comintern luminary who dealt often with Asian matters, had urged them with stinging irony to leave their "Confucian study chambers." To rally the working class and to array it on an anti-imperialist battle front, next to

* The Canton customs surplus—that part of customs revenue not set aside for Boxer indemnity payments—went, under foreign direction, to the "legal" government in Peking, which opposed Sun.

† The statutory age limit for membership in the Youth Corps was 28; but this limit had not always been observed, especially not in the case of high-ranking members.

the nationalist bourgeoisie, was all they could do for the present. Neither socialism nor a soviet republic, he reminded them sharply, were objectives that they could hope to attain in the immediate future.[46]

The Chinese Communists changed their minds, but less in response to this lecture than to the lesson which they learned soon from Wu P'ei-fu and his riflemen. "The February 7 incident," says a party historian, "taught the Chinese workers to take part in the national revolution."[47] This is confirmed by Ts'ai Ho-shen, who was then a high party leader, and who has given us an account of Ch'en Tu-hsiu's response to the incident. According to Ts'ai, the massacre destroyed Ch'en's previous conviction that the Chinese workers were strong enough to make their way independently.[48] Thus he and the others who had resisted entry into the Kuomintang were henceforth quite willing to go along with the Comintern in this matter.

But they were still at variance with Moscow and at odds with each other as to the exact length to which they should go in surrendering their independence. When the Third Party Congress convened in June 1923, it styled the Kuomintang the "central force in the national revolution."[49] But it did not specify how far this force was to reach in practice; for on this issue the congress had split, revealing a deep-seated conflict.

Ch'en Tu-hsiu's role at the congress has been grossly distorted by party scribes eager to vilify him after his fall from power. These picture him as a right-wing extremist toadying to his allies and making sure that the Communists surrendered "all work to the Kuomintang."[50] In actual fact, he still insisted (as he had at the last party congress) that the party should at all costs avoid a "surrender to the capitalists." Even the year after, when the multi-class bloc had actually been established, he remained adamant on this point and re-emphasized it as follows. "The oppressors of the world can only be overthrown by advancing the revolution of the world's oppressed toilers (the Communist revolution) *in conjunction with* that of the world's oppressed nations (the nationalist revolution)" (emphasis mine). These words of Ch'en's belie the contention of his later detractors that, to preserve the multi-class bloc, he tried to stop the class struggle.[51]

How, then, are we to explain the fact that Ch'en proposed to the congress that even the labor unions should be controlled by both allied parties equally? How shall we reconcile it with his previous as well as his subsequent efforts to keep the unions "independent" — that is, out of the Kuomintang's orbit? He would never have urged the opposite except under orders to do so; and it is not difficult to guess who probably gave him such orders. Standing behind him at the Third Party Congress was the Comintern delegate, Maring: the sponsor and warmest advocate of closer two-party relations.[52]

One faction at the Third Party Congress supported Ch'en's strange proposal; another one, almost equal in strength, put up a stiff fight against it. The defenders of trade-union "independence" rallied around Chang Kuo-t'ao, the head of the party's orgburo (department of organization). When the question was finally put to the vote, Ch'en's proposal was carried; but it obtained only one vote more than that of the opposition. However, this margin increased to two when a delegate from Hunan Province who had cast his vote with the minority asked to have it switched to the other side. Thus Mao Tse-tung — for this was the name of the renegade oppositionist — made himself eligible for the rewards that lie in store for the orthodox.[53]

Presently he was chosen to succeed Chang Kuo-t'ao as head of the ørgburo in Shanghai. He himself has described his duties in that post as "coordinating the measures of the Communist

Party and the Kuomintang." [54] To this end he had to work closely with Hu Han-min, the representative of the Kuomintang Executive Committee in Shanghai. Mao himself was elected to the Kuomintang Executive in January 1924, taking his seat in its Shanghai branch, next to Hu.[55]

After that, Mao's relations with the Kuomintang became so close that his standing as a Communist suffered. In the party branches at Peking, Hankow, and Ch'angsha, his administration of the ørgburo came under sharp attack. The actual target of these attacks was not so much Mao himself as the policy he represented; but personal animus found its vent too; for he had made enemies at the Third Congress. Those whom he had deserted there now paid him back by deriding him as "Hu Han-min's secretary." * Within a year he found his post so uncomfortable that he resigned it on the pretext of illness.[56]

Of course, this inglorious episode has not found its way into the party's hagiographies. In these we see Mao the steadfast helmsman steering an unsteady party along its predestined middle course between two pernicious deviations. On the right lies surrender to the bourgeoisie (supposedly urged by Ch'en Tu-hsiu); on the left, isolation of the working class (supposedly urged by Chang Kuo-t'ao). The party did in actual fact find a middle way between these evils, but not under Mao Tse-tung's leadership nor even at his suggestion. Instead, it finally took the course which Chang Kuo-t'ao and his faction had first proposed to the Third Party Congress, and which had then been rejected.†

Only two months after the congress, in August 1923, the

* This epithet had been coined by Li Li-san, a labor organizer and strong supporter of the minority viewpoint at the Third Congress. No love has been lost between Li and Mao ever since. Though Li is still a member of the party's Central Committee, he has lost every other post that he held in the early years of the Chinese Communist regime.

† It should be noted here that even where I have made heavy use of data supplied by Mr. Chang, I have always interpreted them in my own fashion.

Central Committee resolved to keep organized labor "independent," exactly as Chang had proposed.[57] Why the reversal? Coming shortly after Maring's recall to Moscow, it may have been prompted by official displeasure with his role at the congress. For instance, N. I. Bukharin — then the Comintern's leading theoretician — apparently felt that concessions to the Kuomintang had gone too far.[58] Since many Chinese Communists felt the same, they may also have had a hand in this. True, the majority at the Third Congress had bowed to Maring's authority; but they had also done so at Hangchow without accepting his decision as final. At that time their hope for a reversal had been disappointed; but now it was not. Maring never returned to China; and those who had opposed him at the congress found themselves specially favored by his successor, Voitinsky.[59]

The Third Party Congress marked out the course along which the Communists sought to win power during the following years. The Kuomintang was to be conquered by the occupation of key positions from within and by pressure of mass organizations from without. Both of these methods succeeded — up to a point. Infiltration from within proceeded smoothly until Chiang Kai-shek stopped it by force in early 1926. Pressure from without, in the form of workers' and peasants' risings, reached its height — and collapsed — the year after.

The success of Communist (as well as Fascist) subversion is more remarkable for the publicity than for the secrecy that surrounds it. We do not have to guess what the Chinese Communists meant to do to the Kuomintang, because they clearly stated their aim at a Comintern Congress. In 1922 (at the Fourth Congress), one of them openly boasted that they were out to "rally the masses . . . and to split the Kuomintang."[60] The way to do this was left obscure; but less than a year later, the Socialist Youth Corps shed light on it in one of its resolutions.

In August 1923, the Second Congress of the Youth Corps passed a resolution stipulating that "Corps members who have entered the Kuomintang shall take their orders from Corps executive committees [which in turn] shall receive their orders from the Central Committee of the Chinese Communist Party. . . . Our Corps must preserve the independence and tightness of its organization." This resolution came to the attention of the Kuomintang Supervisory Committee, which sent it on to Sun Yat-sen as one of *Two Cases for Impeaching the Communist Party*.[61]

In reply Sun conceded the obvious: the Communists were joining the Kuomintang not singly but as a faction. But this was not, in his view, a reason to refuse them admission—especially not since their admission had only recently become one of his three key policies.* He felt confident that the Kuomintang would retain full control of its members even if they formed factions and that, in case of necessity, the Soviets would help it to do so. "As long as Russia wishes to collaborate with China, she can only work with our party," he wrote. "If Ch'en Tu-hsiu does not obey our party, I shall certainly expel him." [62]

Sun also advanced a theoretical argument in support of his stand. He had earlier become convinced that the Soviets had in effect adopted his principle of people's livelihood. Now he carried this synthesis even further. Not only was there "really no difference" between communism and people's livelihood, but his other two principles—people's rights and

* The other two were "alliance with Russia" and "support of the workers and peasants." After Sun's death, the Kuomintang enshrined these policies as the Three Great Policies.

nationalism — were also part of the Soviet system. "In its beginning stage, the Russian revolution only carried out the principles of people's rights and people's livelihood," Sun wrote. "But after fighting with the foreign powers for six years, it discovered that the principle of nationalism really required its utmost efforts." [63] Thus it seemed to Sun that the Soviet leaders after years of bitter experience had finally reached the starting-point of his own teaching and practice.

The Soviets, for their part, looked on this jugglery of ideas without the slightest illusion. The Fourth Congress of the Comintern had repeated Lenin's warning against bourgeois nationalists under a "communist coloring." Citing the Kuomintang as an example, the congress had complained that "frequently . . . representatives of bourgeois nationalism . . . cloak their . . . efforts in 'socialist' or 'communist' forms." [64] Later, in May 1923, the Comintern had issued another warning, this time directly to Sun. It served him notice that Moscow opposed his "combinations with warlords . . . which threaten the Kuomintang with degeneration into a movement of one militarist clique against another." [65] To counter this threat, Moscow sent a mission to Canton; but its fears could hardly have been allayed by what that mission reported. The Kuomintang leader — wrote the chief of mission soon after his arrival — was an "enlightened little satrap," to be used but not to be trusted.[66]

Why, then, did Moscow insist that the Chinese Communist Party should voluntarily submit to this "little satrap's" authority? We know the long-range considerations that lay behind this insistence; but these had meanwhile become more concrete and, therefore, also more urgent. The February 7 massacre had weakened the Chinese Communists; the workers responded skeptically to cadres who came to rally them.[67] The Kuomintang, on the other hand, had managed to spread its influence over the trade-unions in the south, where the labor movement was strongest. During a strike, in 1922, of the seamen in Hongkong and Canton it had gained further labor support by giving aid to the strikers. Maring had been a witness to this and had come away from Canton deeply — perhaps unduly — impressed by the Kuomintang's hold on the workers. In fact, it was largely because of this that he became so eager to see the Chinese Communists enter the ranks of the Kuomintang. Only by joining it, he maintained (and this became a stock argument), would they be able to save the workers who had fallen under its influence.[68]

Another reason why the Communists finally joined the Kuomintang was that it was weak, and hence vulnerable, in point of organization. Because of its weakness, it is true, the Communist leaders at Hangchow had argued that it was only a clique which it would be pointless to enter. But now that they *had* entered it, they could hope that thanks to this very weakness, they would succeed the more easily in finally winning control of it. They could hope to "instill a communist soul into the Kuomintang body" until the body itself would be theirs in all but outer appearance.[69] So good seemed the prospects of this scheme, especially with Soviet backing, that nearly all of its erstwhile opponents wound up as its warm supporters.

To put this scheme into operation became the responsibility of one of the shrewdest and most experienced field agents of the Comintern. Michael Borodin (once a school principal in Chicago) had already attended to Comintern business in five different countries.[70] Now, in September 1923, he arrived in Canton as personal adviser to Sun Yat-sen and chief of a large Soviet mission.* He, too, found the Kuomintang more akin

* His only official title, however, was that of correspondent for the *Rosta* News Agency.

to a clique than to a true party;[71] so he set about remolding it after the Bolshevik pattern. In so far as the Communists hoped to profit from the Kuomintang's weakness, they thus deprived themselves, by their own act, of the basis on which their hope rested.

Yet what else could they do? To fulfil the "bourgeois" task of unifying the nation, the Kuomintang had to become strong politically and militarily. Hence Borodin provided it with all the means that it needed to forge its mercenary bands into a modern army. His efforts bore fruit: China became almost united; the Kuomintang generals proved equal to the task that he had set before them. But they proved also equal to the task that Sun Yat-sen had bequeathed them: that of suppressing the Communists as soon as they tried to seize power. Thus Borodin became, helplessly, a victim of his own triumph, while the revolution he had guided upset the schema of its schematizers, leaving them stranded with their plans.

CHAPTER III

THE COMMUNISTS IN THE KUOMINTANG: AN ALLIANCE IN OPERATION

When the Chinese Communists entered the Kuomintang, a theoretical impossibility became a practical fact. With the Kuomintang reorganized on the Bolshevik model, both parties now adhered to a concept of organization which pictures "members" in the original sense of the word, as limbs of a body united in will and action. The notion that the Communists joined the Kuomintang as individuals therefore conflicted with the fact of their membership in either party.

It was a fiction lending a gloss of logic to the paradox underneath. How consciously it was so used is a matter for conjecture. Some Kuomintang leaders feared from the start that the Communists would prove unassimilable. A reasonable fear, but not one that could shake Sun Yat-sen's colossal self-confidence. Sun tried to lay his comrades' misgivings, while his Communist allies, speaking through the amiable Li Ta-chao, echoed his reassurances. "We cannot be said to have a party within a party," Li told the reorganized Kuomintang at its First Congress. The Communists adhered to the "general principles" of the Kuomintang; by adhering to Marxist principles also, they formed the needed link between the Chinese nationalist and the world revolution.[1]

Li's argument may be dismissed as conscious deceit intended to lull the Kuomintang into complacency. Its logic was indeed that of "double-think";* but "double-think" does not always prove duplicity. The Communist endows contradictions with

* This, it will be recalled, is the term which George Orwell coined in his novel *1984* to describe the degenerate form of dialectical thinking.

the immanent unity of the dialectic; he sees them dissolving as history moves up another stage — which it does whenever the party so pleases. Thus the dual allegiance of the Chinese Communists was bound to turn into a single one in the coming merger of the Chinese nationalist with the world revolution.

However, this merger would not be the ultimate synthesis through which the historical dialectic comes to rest.* It would end the exploitation of China by foreigners, but not the exploitation of Chinese workers by their own bourgeoisie. Hence the nationalist revolution, once successfully accomplished, would have to be followed immediately by the struggle for socialism.

The workers would thus have to see to it that the onrush of revolution would not be arrested by the bourgeoisie once it had achieved its own aims. They would have to rally the masses behind them in order to become strong enough to push their bourgeois allies aside at the moment of common victory.

On the other hand, they would have to beware of provoking a rift with their allies as long as the feudalists and imperialists remained a danger to both of them. They had no hope of defeating these enemies in the foreseeable future if they also made war on the bourgeoisie and, worse still, on the Kuomintang.† Thus the Kuomintang, like the bourgeoisie, had to be strongly supported and, at the same time, undermined — helped into, and kept out of, power.

How was this to be done in practice? A party bulletin gave the answer:

> We who have joined the Kuomintang must give our united attention to effective work in the lower echelons. We must by all means avoid

* The Marxian dialectic ends in communism, just as Hegel's ended in the Prussian state. Marxism thus abandons its philosophical premise — progress through conflict — in its vision of a static world brotherhood.

† The distinction between the two would have seemed unreal to Trotsky, who considered the Kuomintang a bourgeois party.

harmful competition for posts in the upper Kuomintang echelons. . . . All our efforts should go into the city and district party branches. . . . As regards the various organizations under the Kuomintang, our comrades should concentrate on winning their sympathy.[2]

In other words, the Communists were to win a position of strength at the base of the Kuomintang and then apply leverage, as in mechanics, from the bottom up. But could such leverage be made to apply to a political body so constituted that the power to move it worked from its apex downward?

Pressure from below had never gone far in the Russian Communist Party, in whose image (as Moscow could scarcely forget) the Kuomintang had been fashioned. But the more intractable Stalin found the leadership of the Kuomintang, the harder he tried to intimidate it by precisely such pressure. How could this attempt be reconciled with his concurrent efforts to strengthen the hand of the Kuomintang leaders, even against the masses?

It could not be so reconciled, save by one of those miracles which happen in practical politics; but in this case, no miracle intervened, and Stalin's policy foundered. One might even say that it *had* to fail, but only at the risk of forgetting that, over a period of roughly three years, it also scored brilliant successes. Thus "harmful competition" for high Kuomintang posts turned out to be wholly unneeded: the Communists were *given* such posts and, till 1926, retained them. Even after that, they proved to be able, in the course of the Northern Expedition, to spread and to strengthen their influence in the lower ranks of the Kuomintang. By this, they virtually cut it in two; for most of its local branches, especially in the newly-won areas, fell under their domination.[3] Hence, when the Kuomintang leaders resolved to reassert their authority, they could no longer do so through the party itself but only with help from the army.

This, strange to say, proved how correct the Communists had been on one point: their Kuomintang allies could not match their skill in running party machinery. Sun Yat-sen had been aware of this, too, but had counted on using their talent, harnessed and rendered innocuous, for the Kuomintang's benefit. Thus, when his party combined with theirs, he had been perfectly happy to see its key offices left in charge of various prominent Communists. Its department of organization, for instance, had been assigned to T'an P'ing-shan, the guiding light of the Communist Party in the Canton area. Its department of peasants went to one Lin Tsu-han,* while those of propaganda and labor, though nominally under Kuomintang chiefs, were soon run by Communist secretaries.[4] This had been accomplished with little effort: a committee for reorganization, of which Ch'en Tu-hsiu and Li Ta-chao were members, had endorsed the appointments readily. All the more readily because Borodin, who was nominally its adviser, had actually been entrusted by Sun with guiding it through its proceedings. The Chinese Communists acted, in turn, as Borodin's advisers, but so inconspicuously that Sun, for one, did not suspect them of meddling.[5]

Thus Sun himself helped the Communists to infiltrate his party, and this against the urgent advice of some of his oldest comrades.[6] He simply assumed that his leadership would never be disputed, that he could exploit the infiltrators and then, at his pleasure, dismiss them.[7] Was he unwise? In judging him it is well to remember that the gift of leadership rests on strong — and often excessive — self-confidence.

Sun agreed with the Communists that the Kuomintang should have a mass base, and that they, past masters in agi-

* Lin, it is true, was soon replaced by Ch'en Kung-po; but Communists — chiefly the peasant leader P'eng Pai — continued to dominate the department.

tation, were the ones to provide it. He had been deeply impressed by the work of the Socialist Youth Corps, because its members went to the slums and rubbed elbows with the proletariat.[8] Henceforward, he referred to the Communists as "youngsters" or as "young students," partly because many of them were young and partly for a deeper reason. He knew how closely they were connected with the radical students; and he regarded this, wisely indeed, as one of their principal strong points. In fact, he desired their collaboration partly because of this strong point — because he understood youth's leavening role in the process of mass fermentation.[9]

All Communist movements in the East must win support from the student class in order to carry their message to the illiterate masses. Thus there was a Socialist Youth Corps in China* before there was a Communist Party — and a Youth Corps that dominated the stage even after the party's entry.[10] It continued to move ahead of the party into small towns and villages, where it would remain the sole Communist unit over extended periods. As late as October 1922, Ch'en Tu-hsiu frankly admitted that the Youth Corps had "much greater influence" than the regular party.[11] Moreover, the Corps often took a tack somewhat to the left of the party, its youthful spirit disposing it to take party programs too literally. It could afford such deviations because it managed to retain some autonomy (a very unusual state of affairs) until the late 1920's.[12] Its great prestige reflected itself in the prestige of its leaders: men like Chang T'ai-lei and Yün Tai-ying ranked high in the party also. And they had risen to high party posts on the strength of their proven ability to catch the imagination of youth within and without the party.[13] In this connection, it should be recalled that Ch'en Tu-hsiu and Li Ta-chao, the

* The Chinese Socialist Youth Corps changed its name to Chinese Communist Youth Corps at its Third Congress in February 1925.

party leaders with the most prestige, had risen in similar fashion. They had been drawn into politics by espousing the cause of their students in the May 4 Movement of 1919, when they were professors at Peking.*

Henceforward, agitation by students gave an ever more powerful impetus to the release, slow or violent, of the forces of change in China. For instance, the first labor unions in Shanghai — precursors of a large federation — were those of the printers and of the machinists, both formed on the Youth Corps' initiative.[14] In Canton the Corps took full advantage of the favor with which Sun Yat-sen viewed it to gain a foothold inside the trade-unions under Kuomintang influence.[15] The party, of course, upon seeing these moves could not but wish to control them; and control them it did, from its First Congress onward, through a trade-union secretariat. Among the members of this secretariat, only one was of working-class origin; the others were young men who had studied abroad, "returned students" in Chinese parlance.[16] These were not much older — and in some cases younger — than the "youngsters" of the Socialist Youth Corps whose efforts to rally the working-class they had been appointed to supervise.

Again, it was the Youth Corps (chiefly in Canton) which did all of the pioneering in the colossal enterprise of mobilizing the peasants. Its agitators — students on vacation — swarmed out into the countryside to explain to the peasants that by banding together they could redress their grievances.[17] The party took due note of these activities and gave them some central guidance; but not until late 1925 did it organize them more thoroughly. At that time, it established a training school for professional peasant agitators and brought Mao

* The May 4 Movement began with demonstrations of protest against the peace negotiations at Paris, where the Allied powers had agreed to the virtual cession of Shantung Province to Japan.

Tse-tung out of semi-retirement to make him the school's first director.*

However, a year later, in 1926, the amateurs of the Youth Corps became even more active than before as cadres of rural revolution. The Kuomintang armies were by then advancing rapidly northward, destroying the warlords' petty domains, and sowing the seeds of freedom. The seeds fell on rich soil; the peasants rose up; but their rising was so vast, so sudden, that the handful of cadres trained at Mao's school was far from sufficient to guide it. Again, the "youngsters" rose to the occasion; the Youth Corps rushed into the villages; and there its units became overnight the nuclei of peasant unions.[18] "It was the students who first aroused and organized the peasants," wrote an American eyewitness.[19]

No wonder, then, that the Communists had come to regard the youth movement as a domain to be jealously guarded against trespassing by the Kuomintang. An attempt by the latter, in 1925, to establish its own youth corps thus ran afoul of resolute Communist opposition.[20] One may doubt that this opposition found full support in Moscow, which so often censured "separatist" stands by the party leaders in China. This much is certain: in its own approach to the radical youth of China, Moscow drew only a very thin line between Kuomintang members and Communists. Thus nearly four-fifths of the entering class at a training school for Chinese cadres which it established later that year† consisted of Kuomintang members.[21]

* Mao had returned to his native province of Hunan after resigning from the Kuomintang Central Executive Committee in late 1924. His temporary retreat, of which we shall say more below, became, as such retreats often do, a personal — and historical — turning point.

† This was the Sun Yat-sen University for the Working People of China. Another training school for Asian cadres, the Communist University for Toilers of the East, had been in operation since 1921; but as far as is known, this school did not admit members of the Kuomintang.

The training of Chinese students in Moscow only hastened the process by which Chinese nationalism became, both in thought and in action, Leninist. Hitherto, it had flared up in flashes without being sustained systematically, as in the May 4 Movement of 1919, whose flames had burnt brightly but briefly. But as a controlled, concerted effort, Chinese nationalism did not make history until the year 1925 and the May 30 Movement.

This movement was marked, like the earlier one, by student riots and rallies; but this time there was method—Leninist method—in the emotions behind it. Not that it lacked spontaneity; again, long-standing resentment of China's treatment at foreign hands burst out under provocation. However, by now there were young Chinese who understood, thanks to Lenin, how to control, direct, and exploit all eruptions of spontaneity.

This vanguard had also learned by now how to gather an army behind it: how to win followers among the workers by knowing their needs and their temper. In 1919, sympathy strikes had supported protesting students; this time, workers protested first and students rushed in to aid them. The May 30 Movement began with a strike in the textile mills of Shanghai—a strike by abused Chinese workingmen against their foreign employers. The mills affected were Japanese-owned as well as Japanese-managed; therefore the strike aroused not only class hate but patriotic passion.[22]

On May 24, 1925, the strikers had held a rally to honor the memory of a comrade shot dead by a Japanese foreman. Students had come to address the meeting and had been promptly arrested by the foreign police, who enforced respect for the rights of foreign investors. It was in protest against these arrests that a massive column of students paraded through Shanghai on May 30 — the day that thus became famous.

Famous because when the student marchers stopped in front of a police station, flaunting their slogans and shouting defiance, the policemen inside opened fire. The British police officer in charge had given the order to fire, imagining in a moment of panic that the students would storm his station. But for this error and the blood it cost, the rallies and demonstrations that had accompanied the mill-workers' strike would not have become a great movement.

Yet even the bloodshed of May 30 would not have led to this movement if the Communist Party had not been prepared to make the most of such incidents. As it was, it had already spent years training the student cadres on whom it depended at this point to rally the people of Shanghai. Most of these cadres had been trained at Shanghai University, which had been founded two years before by a group of high party leaders.* Here the young radicals had learned to associate with true proletarians, part-time students selected for training by party cells in the factories. Additional channels of Communist influence over the masses of Shanghai had been developed by party leaders doubling as Kuomintang functionaries. Thus the Communist youth leader Yün Tai-ying, a teacher at Shanghai University, served also as chief of the workers' department in the Shanghai branch of the Kuomintang.[23]

Because of the wide popular appeal of the May 30 Movement, Communist sources tend to exaggerate the role that the party played in it. But it is certain that this role was great and that, in so far as the movement was launched by the efforts

* Most notable among these were the Russian-trained scholar Ch'ü Ch'iu-pai and the labor leader Teng Chung-hsia.

of any one group, this group was the Communist leadership.

Two of the Communist leaders stand out from among the others for the alacrity with which they pounced on each chance to develop the movement. The first of these was Ts'ai Ho-shen, a member of the Central Committee and editor in chief of the party journal, the *Hsiang-tao chou-pao* or "Guide Weekly." It was Ts'ai who proposed on May 28, after the mill-workers' rally, that their "economic struggle should be expanded into a national effort." [24] The student parade of May 30 sprang directly from this proposal, so that Ts'ai deserves much of the credit — or blame — for the upheaval that followed.*

Again, it was on Ts'ai's initiative that the Central Committee, meeting on the evening of May 30, formed an action committee. This body organized a general strike and rallied support for the strikers from every sector, whether rich or poor, of the city's Chinese community.[25] It inspired the formation, on May 31, of a new labor federation, the Shanghai General Labor Union, under purely Communist leadership.[26] Chairman of the Union and leader of the strike became the dynamic Li Li-san, then only 29 years old and the party's best public speaker. Li gained more stature in the movement than did any of its other leaders, and henceforth acted in party councils as chief spokesman for the workers. In fact, it was through the May 30 Movement, and thanks to Li Li-san's energy, that the party acquired its first real taste of leading a workers' struggle. Moscow exulted; even the Profintern (Trade Union International), hitherto gloomy in its outlook on China,[27] became suddenly enthusiastic. At last China's workers sat in the saddle, crowed a Profintern spokesman; the petty-bourgeois

* Ts'ai's career ended under mysterious circumstances. In 1931 he fled to Hongkong, where the British police arrested him. Subsequently, he returned to the Chinese mainland — we do not know when or why — and was executed by the Kuomintang police.

intelligentsia had "completely forfeited" its leadership.[28] But had it really? As we look more closely at Communist labor leaders who played important roles in the movement, we see a different picture. Only two of these leaders — Liu Hua and Hsiang Ying* — had ever been real workers; and even these two came from impoverished bourgeois, not from proletarian, families.[29]

Moreover, the role of organized labor in the May 30 Movement became proportionally less important as other groups joined the struggle. The Communists could therefore maintain after the movement's failure that organized business, not organized labor, had actually stood at the head of it. Thus they alleged that the "backward workers, steeped in patriarchal mentality," had easily been taken in tow by the Chinese Chamber of Commerce.[30] A strange verdict coming from those who, in fact, had themselves been the most successful in taking the Shanghai workers in tow and leading them into the movement.

The Chamber of Commerce had, it is true, aligned itself with the workers and given them unstinting support as long as their cause seemed hopeful. The Communists had even invited it to join the action committee through which they and the General Labor Union directed the strike operations. The Chamber had declined to join this committee but had furnished it with aid funds which, as a highly respectable group, it could raise from the moneyed classes.[31] Important as these contributions were, they do not signify, however, that the Chamber had actually led and controlled the entire May 30 Movement.

Those who *had* led the movement, the Communists, had

* Hsiang Ying did not arrive in Shanghai until after the movement had been launched. The two Communist labor leaders of genuinely proletarian descent — Su Chao-cheng and Hsiang Chung-fa — took no part in the movement at all.

turned it to their advantage: they had emerged on the national scene with mass sentiment behind them. They had trebled their following and, more important, expanded their sphere of influence far beyond the circle, still amazingly small,[32] of party and Youth Corps members. This increase in strength had strained their relations with their Kuomintang ally; for each side in the two-party bloc viewed the other's gains with misgivings.

For all the successes the alliance had won during the May 30 Movement, it had failed to bring unity to the land and to oust the foreign "imperialists." * These had in the end been able to split it by pouncing upon its right wing from the "commanding heights" that they held in Shanghai's industrial complex. The Chinese manufacturers who had backed the movement had done so on the understanding that the strike would be limited to foreign firms, so that they themselves would not suffer. But the foreigners owned Shanghai's power plant and could thus force the Chinese-owned factories, simply by stopping their supply of current, to suspend operations. The Chinese manufacturers, rather than shoulder a mounting load of relief payments without any income from production, decided to seek a settlement.[33]

By this they surrendered, in the eyes of the workers, to the imperialist enemy; and now the strike movement turned against *them*, its nationalist fervor subsiding.[34] The common struggle against the imperialists gave way to divisive class war, not because the foreigners had suffered defeat but because they had won a battle. This was quite contrary to the schema

* But it did stimulate feelings of national solidarity: even the northern warlords gave it financial assistance. It also induced the foreigners to make some minor concessions. The Shanghai Municipal Council, hitherto their exclusive preserve, voted to admit representatives of the Chinese business community. In addition, a conference on Chinese tariff autonomy opened in October 1925, partly in response to the movement. Not until five years later, however, did China actually regain her tariff autonomy.

of nationalist revolution; but the schema was saved, its warped frame straightened out, by subsequent schematization. The organic image of revolution showed the retreat of the capitalists as a seasonal shedding of dead tissue, of a class layer that had rotted.[35] By the same token, another such layer may be said to have sloughed off soon after: the mill workers went back to their jobs in return for minor concessions.[36] But this event did not find a place in the organic image, because such images always exclude whatever might mar their perfection.

In spite of these signs of growing weakness in the May 30 Movement, it gave the Communist rank and file an intoxicating sense of power. Talk of insurrection started up in the lower ranks of the party just as the strike wave began to recede and the workers began to talk compromise.[37] The high party leaders were not, to be sure, as hot-headed as their followers; but even they felt the need to move left, toward greater class independence. This feeling grew all the intenser because, since Sun Yat-sen's death three months earlier, hostility to his "great policies" was mounting inside the Kuomintang.

The strongest link between the two parties had been Sun's prestige as a leader; yet his prestige had sometimes sunk low, especially with the Communists. They had always distrusted his tendency to seek allies among the warlords by striking bargains that were very Chinese, but not very revolutionary. Thus they openly censured him when he left for Peking in late 1924 to negotiate with Marshal Tuan Ch'i-jui,[38] the new head of the northern government.[39] Tuan was notoriously pro-Japanese; and Sun, on his way to meet him, stopped in Japan and delivered a speech extolling Sino-Japanese friendship.[40] His Communist allies at home were disturbed; some wished to disavow him; of these, the most prominent was Ts'ai Ho-shen, who has left an account of this episode. It seemed to Ts'ai that Sun was about to go over to the enemy, that "the aim of [his] trip was to seek an *entente* with the militarists and with imperialism." But for his subsequent death — Ts'ai concludes — Sun might have accomplished his purpose and come to terms with imperialism and with its Chinese puppets.[41]

Ts'ai is quite right to this extent: had Sun lived a year or two longer, he might well have expelled the Communists and abandoned the Soviet alliance. Some Kuomintang rightists thought so, too; hence, acting on their own authority, they announced in November 1925 that they were ousting the Communists.* But they could not oust them in fact, for the rest of the Kuomintang leaders — the legitimate party leadership — stood faithfully by their allies. The Communists therefore had nothing to fear from this fringe of right-wing extremists; but from closer quarters they faced a threat that was subtler and, therefore, graver.

Sun had been dead a bare five months; his three "great policies" were revered as holy scripture, when the man who did the most to carry them out — Liao Chung-k'ai — was suddenly murdered. Who had employed the murderer (himself an insignificant person) to do away with the foremost leftist in the Kuomintang leadership? Circuitous threads of investigation led to the door of Hu Han-min, the man to whom Sun, before going north, had delegated his authority. The Canton government was perplexed; Borodin, after taking Hu's measure, suggested that it "deal strictly" with him, but Hu's comrades preferred to be lenient. Chiang and Wang Ching-wei suggested that Hu should be sent off to Moscow; the pilgrimage would make him atone and remove him to a safe distance.[42]

* Their faction became known as the "Western Hills group" because it had assembled in the Western Hills near Peking. It included not only inveterate anti-Communists but also ambiguous figures like Chang Chi, who had been among the first to advocate closer two-party relations.

Hu went, and Moscow received him — but as an honored confederate, not as a penitent pilgrim. Whatever information had been sent ahead on the background of his visit had either been put away in some file or reasoned away effectively. The illustrious ambassador of the Chinese revolution demanded more aid for his party and (incredible as it seems now) a place for it in the Comintern.* The Comintern functionary who looked after him wrote later that "Hu Han-min cursed Kautsky and talked about world revolution during his whole stay in Moscow." [43]

Hu's success in enlisting Satan's aid the better to cast out Satan was paralleled by a similar feat in Kuomintang political theory. A party theorist named Tai Chi-t'ao had learned from his own experience how to affirm as well as deny the Marxist-Leninist doctrine. Having felt "spiritually at one" with its adherents in China, he had helped them to found the Communist Party without, it appears, ever joining it.[44] He still subscribed to much more of Marxism than Sun had ever accepted; not merely an admirer of Leninist methods, he believed in dialectic materialism. Yet he was a firmer opponent than Sun of the class struggle in China — and this on the basis of his belief in the doctrine of imperialism. He used Lenin's doctrine to transform the class struggle into a war between nations, between the oppressed peoples and their oppressors, the imperialist powers. To wage this war, the subject peoples needed internal class harmony: Tai's version — his caricature — of what Lenin had meant by "temporary alliances." Thus Tai's image of the class struggle resembled that of the Fascists: the poor, as in Marx, come to grips with the rich, but as nations, no longer as classes.[45]

* The Executive Committee of the Comintern voted to admit the Kuomintang as a "sympathizing party" in March 1926. This affiliation was never formally dissolved.

A perversion, of course, but the usual by-product of the selective process by which the inheritors of any doctrine reduce it to self-consistency. In truncating the body of Lenin's precepts, Tai made them less paradoxical; a choice between class strife and united-front concord had to be made at some point. Sun's teaching had to be truncated too; Tai opposed the continued membership in a party that stood for class harmony of those who promoted class war. He saw more clearly than anyone else that this unity between the two parties united the edges of an abyss between different aims and assumptions. To avoid a collapse, he proposed a solution that was very far from Fascist: make the Communists leave the Kuomintang; then form an alliance with them. Once the two parties were free of each other, they were to form a committee of composite party membership to coordinate future policies.[46] Tai thus envisaged a peaceful divorce, not a violent rupture such as Chiang Kai-shek provoked in the end in order to shake off the Communists.

Still, Chiang took from Tai, a very old friend,* the framework for his own outlook: for that high-minded haze in which Lenin's shade blends into that of Confucius. National unity was their chief aim, and world revolution but a peripheral process through which this aim was to be achieved with the least internal commotion.[47] Sun, it is true, had pursued the same aim with the same single-minded persistence; moreover, he too had sought to achieve it by high-level machination. But his encouragement of Communist efforts to rally the workers and peasants shows that he had meant to release, not repress, the latent strength of the masses. His Soviet advisers had helped him to see that a modern political movement, though led and inspired by a very few, derives its strength

* The two had been intimate friends — it is said, sworn blood-brothers — ever since 1907, when both of them lived in Japan.

from the many.* This lesson was not wholly lost on his heirs; they applied it very successfully when they embarked, the year after his death, on the Northern Expedition. But as national unity was being restored under Chiang Kai-shek's ascendancy, the popular movements launched in its support were quickly repressed as disruptive. Since these movements were entirely Communist-led, this may have been unavoidable; but as a result, the popular base of national unity crumbled. The idea of unity, with Chiang as with Tai, had become such a prepossession that Chinese society took in their eyes the shape of a Confucian monolith. If there were cracks in this monolith, benevolent rule would repair them, granting to each class what was its due while holding it to its duties. The people at large were not encouraged to participate in their salvation;[48] those above them manipulated their own peers, but never popular sentiment. The Communists, meanwhile, became adept at taking up popular causes, at giving voice to mute discontent, at supporting just aspirations. Because of this, the Communist armies would one day sweep across China as swiftly, as smoothly, and as weakly opposed as had those of the Northern Expedition.

But we must go back to 1925 and to Tai Chi-t'ao's emergence as the outstanding theoretical spokesman for the cause of national unity. Among the Communists, at least Ch'en Tu-hsiu was quick to read the omen: with national unity the supreme law, the class struggle would become outlawry. Tai's emergence — Ch'en warned the Central Committee when it convened in October — portended the onset of the reaction and called for a shift in the party line. He recommended "immediate preparations for a withdrawal from the Kuomintang"

* Sun had felt this even before his Soviet advisers drove the point home to him; otherwise, he would not have been so impressed with the agitation carried on by the Communist "youngsters."

— or at least so he said four years after the event, at the time of his break with the Comintern.[49]

He also said then (in a public letter addressed to his party comrades) that the Central Committee and its Comintern mentor had flatly rejected his motion. We know for a fact that the Central Committee complained at its subsequent session of certain comrades who still urged a break — a *total* break — with the Kuomintang.[50] But Ch'en, for one, had made no such proposal; he had not urged a total rupture but merely *preparations* for one: a difference that may seem trivial. Yet the distinction is important, because prior to his dismissal, Ch'en himself had acknowledged that such preparations had in fact received due approval.[51] Not, it is true, from the Comintern delegate; he, in this earlier version, appears in the role of a Pontius Pilate, taking no position whatever.* Thus it becomes evident that Ch'en, after his break with the party, inflated some of the differences that he had had with it previously.

There is further proof that in 1925, Ch'en and the Central Committee agreed in substance on what should be done, though they differed, perhaps, on timing. The resolution which the Central Committee adopted in October called on the party to "manifest more political independence." [52] This meant in effect that it was to loosen its existing ties with the Kuomintang, to start — exactly as Ch'en had proposed — "preparations for a withdrawal." It meant that the party was to resume the proletarian offensive which it had launched a few months before, in the May 30 Movement. In fact, agitation to prepare the workers for an intenser class struggle had been under way since January, when the Fourth Party Congress had called for it. The congress had resolved that

* It seems likely that this delegate was Voitinsky, who is known to have felt ambivalently toward the two-party bloc.

party propaganda directed at the proletariat should henceforth preach communism pure and simple instead of Kuomintang doctrine.[53] Now, in October, the Central Committee sharply reminded the party that it could not hope to further its cause unless it enrolled more workers. The petty bourgeoisie, on the other hand, had its proper place in the Kuomintang; there — it was hoped — it would form a left wing amenable to Communist leadership.[54]

This hope was the strongest, and lasted the longest, among the leaders in Moscow; but the Chinese Communists nurtured it too, or at least professed to be doing so. They sounded confident that the Kuomintang left wing would sooner break with the right wing, and even with the "center" around Tai Chi-t'ao, than forsake its alliance with them. They only feared that, in backing the left, their own comrades in the Kuomintang would feel strongly tempted to take its place, to push it aside impatiently. This they wished to avoid: their party comrades in the ranks of the Kuomintang were to manipulate and lead, not to *become*, its left wing.[55] They were to wage a factional war without showing their true colors, without letting it become obvious that they were themselves a faction.[56]

This plan was wise; for any attempt to *become* the Kuomintang left wing would (as subsequent history proved) have led to an open rupture. It would have converted the factional struggle into a war between parties, a war which the Communists could not hope to win until they had grown much stronger. Their hope of victory lay, instead, in the sharpening of the class struggle, in the mounting strength of the working class and of its ally, the peasantry.

The Communists made it perfectly clear (without saying so directly) that leading the peasants, like leading the workers, was to be their exclusive prerogative. Though the peasants formed part of the petty bourgeoisie for which the Communist schema provided a place in the Kuomintang left, their own place was not to be in it. The petty bourgeoisie that had been marked out for membership in the Kuomintang seems to have been chiefly that in the towns: shopkeepers and intellectuals.[57]

Thus, drawing ever sharper lines between themselves and the Kuomintang, the Communists drifted back toward the stand that they had taken at Hangchow. Their renascent purism, itself a sign of returning self-confidence, had doubtless been stimulated by their gains in the May 30 Movement. But it had not been *caused* by these gains; we have seen that already in January, they had decided (at the Fourth Party Congress) to arouse the workers more openly. On the other hand, we have also seen that not until after May 30 did they show a greater and growing concern about winning over the peasants. To what extent this deeper concern can be ascribed to the movement (itself a purely urban affair) is difficult to determine. The revolutionary euphoria emanating from Shanghai does seem to have had one important effect upon the peasant movement. Under its influence, Mao Tse-tung, then in his native Hunan, set out for the first time — momentous occasion! — to rally the local peasants.[58] This was a new departure for Mao; but for P'eng Pai, another Communist, the son of a wealthy landlord in Kwangtung, it was an old experience.[59] P'eng had been rallying *his* local peasants for over three years already, so that by now a strong peasant union — the first of its kind — stood behind him.[60] Yet it was not P'eng, the pioneer, but Mao, the comparative novice, who soon became in high party councils the chief spokesman for the peasants.[61]

From now on the party redoubled its efforts to win the peasants' allegiance; but we do not know to what extent it intended to enlist them as members.[62] It aimed at winning control of the peasants through control of their unions without giving these a Communist stamp, without actually annexing them.[63] This was in accord with what Lenin had taught the proletariat in Russia: unite with the peasants in common action but not in a common party.[64] Lenin had always (as far as is known) remained too believing a Marxist to embrace as heterodox a concept as that of the multiclass party. And nowhere had the Marxist tradition of proletarian class purity found stauncher, more religious defenders than among the Chinese Communists. They had shown this at Hangchow; and the Hangchow spirit had remained latent in them, as its revival in 1925, which we have just noted, demonstrates. Now the question arises: did this revival rearouse the dissension which their original stand at Hangchow had caused between them and Moscow?

At first sight, this may seem to have been the case; for Stalin's approach to the Kuomintang did differ on two conspicuous points from that of the Chinese Communists. He hailed it, in May 1925, as a "party of workers and peasants" [65] — a formula which they declined to adopt, and not only for the reason just cited. The formula could be taken to mean, since they "represented" the workers, that the Kuomintang had been granted the right of "representing" the peasants. In fact, some months later, a Kuomintang delegate, the many-sided Hu Han-min, secured it a place on the presidium of the Peasants' International.[66] He himself took his seat there, a long-gowned scholar "representing" the Chinese peasants, surrounded by European peasant leaders chiefly from Balkan countries. One may doubt that the Chinese Communists were amused by this spectacle; they had, after all, made it perfectly clear that *they* meant to speak for the peasants. Though they had probably no desire to enlist them *en masse* in the party, they did want to draw them, through peasant unions, into its exclusive orbit. In fact, they succeeded before long in bringing the peasant unions under still more thorough one-party rule than even organized labor.*

Afterwards, Moscow found this wrong: the Kuomintang left wing, it argued, could have coped better with the right if workers and peasants had entered it.[67] Nor was this wholly a hindsight verdict; from mid-1926 onward, the Comintern line allowed less and less room for Chinese Communist "separatism." However, in mid-1925, the news of the strikes in Shanghai had caused even Stalin to become quite "separatist" in his thinking. Hence this was the time in the "Great Revolution" of 1924–27 when he and the Chinese Communists stood in fact the most closely united.

The evidence — strange as this may seem — lies in the same speech by Stalin in which he referred to the Kuomintang as a workers' and peasants' party. He delivered this speech on May 18, at a time when the strike wave in Shanghai had already reached an impressive height, though not yet the peak of its power.† The prospect in front of the Chinese workers looked suddenly so much brighter that Stalin thought they could now reduce their dependence on other classes. Away with the national united front, with the bourgeoisie as an ally; a smaller revolutionary bloc would now serve the workers better. And not the workers of China only: they formed part of a global picture; Stalin spoke of several countries at once, bracketing China with — Egypt! These two exemplified in his eyes all the dependent countries which, although backward, were not totally so, having industry and a proletariat.[68]

* The Kuomintang failed to win control of one single peasant union; but in Canton, where it had been the first to organize labor, its influence with the trade-unions remained strong.

† The strikes which culminated in the May 30 Movement had begun as early as February 1925.

Yet the policy which he prescribed for those countries was clearly a mere projection of that which the heartening news from Shanghai had led him to map out for China.

What was this policy, what kind of bloc did Stalin propose to substitute for the broader alliances which, in his view, had now become an encumbrance? Henceforth the workers were to unite with the petty bourgeoisie only, in a bloc to which they might give the form of a *workers' and peasants' party*. Now the Kuomintang — Stalin opined from afar — was such a party already; how it could seem so, in face of the facts, we shall try to make clearer presently. Stalin regarded it, in any case, as a model to be used elsewhere, provided, however, that it and its likes met certain basic conditions.

The first of these, underlying the others, was that such a "peculiar" party should actually be two parties in one, a bloc of two distinct classes. It should link the workers to the petty bourgeoisie for a common stand against imperialism without joining them so closely together as to merge their respective parties. It should leave the Communists perfectly free to carry on their own mission: to extend their exclusive sway over the workers and to spread their own propaganda. It should allow them to win control not of the workers only but of their nationalist allies as well, of the whole revolutionary movement. Unless it fulfilled all of these conditions, the Communists would have to break with it or else risk the loss — a fatal one — of their "proletarian army." [69]

Now these were at bottom the same conditions that Lenin, in 1920, had declared essential to any alliance with the nationalists of the Orient. That Stalin enumerated them again may hence seem like routine repetition; but actually it was not his wont to mention, let alone dwell, on them. They did, after all (at least as first stated), raise doubts as to whether Lenin had ever approved — or would have approved — of the two-party bloc in China. Their sudden re-emphasis by Stalin hence indicates that at this juncture he himself was leaning exceptionally far toward a "separatist" position.

It indicates that he was reverting — though, as it turned out, only briefly — to the purer, more class-conscious "Leninism" of the year 1920. His concept of a workers' and peasants' party was, to be sure, a monstrosity — both from the strictly Leninist and, more still, from the Marxist viewpoint.[70] But then, by reducing the number of classes in the multiclass party, it marked at the same time a reversion toward a smaller, more orthodox class base. It did, after all, directly reflect an orthodox development: the sudden emergence of the Chinese proletariat into militant maturity. By comparison, the Chinese peasant movement was still in its adolescence; we have seen that the period of its great advance began only after May 30. How then could it, as the peasant component of the "workers' and peasants' party," be equated to the bulk of the Kuomintang, even if only implicitly?

The Kuomintang was scarcely a peasant party either in make-up or outlook; it did favor agrarian reforms, but had not yet carried out any. On the other hand, it doubtless embodied the force of Chinese nationalism; and nationalism, according to Stalin, derived its strength from the peasants. They made up most of its popular base or, as he said, its "main army"; without them there could be no national movement of genuine depth and vigor. He had propounded this remarkable thesis only a few weeks earlier (on March 30, 1925) while rebuking a Yugoslav comrade. Yugoslavia he had put down as a country "not fully independent" because "tied up with certain imperialist groups" — very much as was China. But even without this parallel, it would be clear that his thesis had not been meant to apply to one country or to one area only.[71]

What, then, was the general advantage of transferring to

the peasants the historical function which, by the book, should have been bourgeois-nationalist? Why this stealthy replacement of an orthodox canon by the bizarre idea that the founts of nationalist sentiment lie principally in the villages? The answer is that Communist parties could now support nationalist causes even where an alliance with the bourgeoisie was not, or no longer, desired.* The mere fact of being aligned with the peasants (as they *had* to be in backward countries) now gave them, on doctrinal grounds alone, a place in nationalist movements.

Thus, when Stalin came to believe that in China a bloc with the bourgeoisie was no longer useful or needed, he simply renamed the Kuomintang a "party of workers and peasants." Of workers — if only for the reason that part of it was in fact Communist; of peasants — for a simpler reason still: by virtue of its being nationalist. For with "nationalism" stamped on the peasantry, a party of that description could in turn, by the logic of class imputation, receive a "peasant" imprint. To derive the class nature of a party from its political outlook did, it is true, turn Marx upside down; but then, Lenin had done so already.

We saw an instance of this in his notion that the Labour Party in Britain was in fact a "bourgeois party through and through" even though it consisted of workers. Class, with Lenin, had thus become almost a moral concept: a matter of political choice, not simply of social origin. Yet neither with Lenin nor with Stalin did class become *wholly* political: a workers' party remained for them a party with workers in it. They did not foresee that one day, in China, the workers

* Strictly speaking, they could do so already thanks to the replacement of the term "bourgeois-democratic" by "national-revolutionary" at the Second Comintern Congress (see Chapter I). But that change of adjectives had not had nearly as deep implications as the change of class labels undertaken now.

would be "represented" by a Communist party subsisting, sealed-off, in remote corners of the hinterland. They did not — *could* not — foresee what twist Mao Tse-tung would give to their precepts any more than Marx had foreseen how they, in quoting him, would change his meaning.

Of course, if either Lenin or Stalin had been faced with the situation to which Mao Tse-tung responded as he did, they might well have responded likewise. But as it was, they never confronted a choice between political suicide and total withdrawal from the cities — from all contact with the workers. True, when Lenin had looked toward the East in 1919–20, he had seen that the working class there was weak, far too weak to seize power unaided. He had seen how heavily it depended on support from the peasants; and he had expected such support to be won through a network of rural soviets. He had also expected that the struggle in the East would soon be aided and guided by a victorious proletariat in the West, by European soviet governments. On both counts, it had turned out since then, he had been far too hopeful; but in one sense, prospects had since improved, at least with regard to China. The sudden display of working-class strength in the May 30 Movement held out a promise which, five years before, had been but a distant vision. Lenin had never dealt in China with as orthodox a situation as that which the militant Shanghai workers now created for Stalin. The Chinese revolution seemed at long last to follow the Marxist pattern; no wonder that Stalin, in dealing with it, became also more rigidly Marxist.

More rigid a believer, that is, in the tenet that revolution, whether in China or anywhere else, must come under working-class leadership. Stalin could afford to apply this tenet to the Chinese revolution with a fullness of faith for which Lenin, in his day, would have lacked a base in reality. Lenin had perforce, in his program for the East, given to rural soviets so big a supporting role that they might in fact have ended up in the leading one. If his program had proven workable and soviets had been established, a trend in the "Maoist" direction might thus have resulted from it. As it was, the trend of events since then — and, with it, that of Stalin's thinking — had run in the opposite direction, farther away from "Maoism." One might think that this would have ceased to be true after the May 30 Movement, which, as we saw, set Mao on his path and which ended in a setback for labor. But actually such was not the case: the belief that the Chinese proletariat would yet fulfill its historical task remained stronger than it had been with Lenin. Lenin had called for peasant soviets as an immediate necessity; Stalin opposed them; one could not — he said — "leave out the industrial centers." * For a long time (how long, we shall see below), Stalin kept on insisting that the Chinese revolution would conform to type, that "inevitably" it would be worker-led.[72]

Yet the outcome of the May 30 Movement, unfavorable to the workers, could not but damp the excessive hopes which its upsurge had raised in Stalin. Class strife in China had died down instead of gaining momentum; the foreign imperialists had held their ground; bigger forces would be needed to oust them. The national united front, which Stalin had been ready to terminate, would, after all, have to be preserved if the struggle was to be completed. "Separatist" sentiment in favor of pulling away from the Kuomintang, such as Stalin himself had begun to feel, seemed again like idle idealism.

Therefore, in late 1925, Stalin returned to his policy of seeking the closest cooperation with his Kuomintang ally. The response he received was encouraging: at the Second Kuomintang Congress, held in January 1926, the left won a three-

* See Chapter V.

fifths' majority. Communists remained in control of the Kuomintang secretariat and of its department of organization: the gateways to its lower hierarchy.[73] Professions of complete solidarity with Moscow and the Chinese Communists filled the air at the congress, and they came from the lips of its most prominent speakers. "If we wish to fight the imperialists, we must not turn against the Communists," cried the chairman, Wang Ching-wei. China marched with the Soviets toward world revolution, according to Chiang Kai-shek.[74] The prospect that the Kuomintang would bend to the Communist will seemed good.

CHAPTER IV

THE COMMUNISTS IN THE KUOMINTANG: TO WHOM THE HEGEMONY?

Moscow felt safe with the Kuomintang because it had fashioned it in its own image and imbued it with its own spirit, and because it had seen the power of Sun Yat-sen pass to heirs whom it thought it could trust. At the head of the party stood Wang Ching-wei, the flamboyant idol of the left, and the chief intermediary between Borodin and the government in Canton.[1] At the head of the army stood Chiang Kai-shek, known also as the "Red General," at least to some of the treaty-port press, which wrote of him with a shudder. Chiang's speeches alone might have earned him this name; but he had also gone to Russia with special orders from Dr. Sun to study Red Army methods. While there, he had visited Leon Trotsky, who, as the Red Army's founder and also as Commissar for War, could advise him as no one else could. These consultations stood him in good stead when, on returning to China early in 1924, he tackled the task awaiting him. He became the director, at Whampoa near Canton, of a military academy which the Kuomintang was just setting up to train its own army officers. There he created, on the Soviet model and with Soviet funds and advisers, the nucleus of what became soon the strongest army in China.[2]

But Chiang did not return many favors for the help that he thus received; on the contrary, as his power grew, he felt less need to show himself grateful. At last, on March 20, 1926, he demonstrated his intention to become the sole master of his house, whoever had helped him to build it. All of a sudden, he arrested the commissars (mostly Communists) attached to his troops, confined his Soviet advisers to their quarters, and disarmed the strike committee which had halted foreign business in South China since the Cantonese "May 30." [3] Canton firmly in hand, he claimed to have prevented its seizure by a Communist gunboat captain, and asked for punishment by the civil authorities whom he had "rescued" without prior consultation.[4] But the head of the civil government, Wang Ching-wei, found the time propitious for a cure abroad, so that Chiang, left in full control, could safely exonerate the gunboat captain to whom he had imputed his own plot.[5]

He could afford such magnanimity because he had already removed the Communists from all positions of influence in the Canton branch of the Kuomintang. The Canton branch of the Communist Party was therefore the first to react to his coup, and it reacted sharply. "In the opinion of our Cantonese party workers . . . and of Borodin also, an offensive tactic should have been adopted," Ch'en Tu-hsiu reported later. "They held that we should not put up with the March 20 coup but stage our own March 20." [6] At least some proponents of this countercoup thought that it should lead to a total break with the Kuomintang.[7]

But in Shanghai, distance made for a calmer appraisal of the events in Canton. Only a minority of the Central Committee demanded a break with the Kuomintang.[8] The majority agreed with Ch'en Tu-hsiu that the Communist forces were "insufficient for the suppression of Chiang Kai-shek." [9] But Ch'en did not propose to sit still; he wrote the Comintern of his "personal opinion that cooperation with the Kuomintang through joint work within should be changed into outside cooperation." [10] This personal opinion was to become soon the official stand of the party.

It failed, however, to make any impression on the policy-makers in Moscow, who saw graver dangers on the Eastern horizon than that posed by Chiang in Canton.* Not that their interest in China had flagged; on the contrary, it had risen — so much so, in fact, that China policy was now made by the Politburo. For that matter, the Politburo had appointed a special committee (not all of whose members came from its own midst) to deal solely with China policy. This committee convened on March 25, with Trotsky acting as chairman; but apparently it concerned itself little with the new situation in Canton.[11] Instead, it grappled with the bogy of a possible new alliance (the old one having lapsed four years previously) between Japan and Great Britain. It feared that both of these powers combined might strangle the Chinese revolution and that — worse still — they would pose a threat to the safety of Soviet Russia.[12]

The committee proposed to avert this threat by offering Japan concessions that would make her forgo the advantages which a new pact with Britain might give her. The Japanese were to be bought off, and at no expense to the Soviets; the Chinese alone were to pay the price, in the form of Chinese territory. They were to agree that "South Manchuria [should], for the present, remain in the hands of Nippon"; and they were to accept Manchurian "autonomy," almost certain to follow.[13] The committee knew that the Chinese public would resist this surrender; but it counted on the Kuomintang and the Chinese Communists to overcome this resistance. The Chinese revolutionaries would, of course, have to be themselves persuaded that the sacrifice demanded of them as Chinese would help them as revolutionaries. Once they understood the advantages of giving away Manchuria, they would have to make themselves heard through the press

* Moscow had a special emissary in Canton at the time: Andrei S. Bubnov, a member of the Central Committee. In contrast to Borodin, Bubnov exerted his influence to restrain the Cantonese Communists. Trotsky, *Problems of the Chinese Revolution*, p. 271.

— if necessary, by founding new journals. It all seemed as simple as that in the eyes of the experts in Moscow: a little persuasion, a little pressure, and the Chinese people would follow them.[14]

How, in this instance, they were undeceived is not a matter of record; but one reason why they abandoned their plan was doubtless Chinese resistance. Neither the Kuomintang nor the Chinese Communists were as pliant as Moscow imagined; with regard to the Kuomintang, this had been made clear by Chiang Kai-shek's coup of March 20. Yet even when Moscow was fully apprized of what had occurred in Canton, it continued to think of Chiang as its tool, because he encouraged such thinking.

Once secure in the power that he had seized, Chiang apologized very humbly for the "inconvenience" which his Russian advisers had suffered while confined to their quarters. He reinstated most of them;* the ousted political commissars he placed in a "Higher Training Detachment" especially formed for the purpose.[15] As to the workers who had been disarmed, they received as sole compensation the assurance that what had happened to them had been a regrettable error. The raid on their strike headquarters, said Chiang, had been staged without his permission; the commander of the Canton garrison was dismissed as the person responsible.[16] To dispel all doubts as to where he stood, Chiang reaffirmed in April, with greater verve than ever before, his submission to Comintern discipline.[17]

At the same time, he saw to it that his party adopted a series of measures designed to enforce the utter submission of its Communist members. On May 15, 1926, he summoned a

* Notable exceptions were Andrei S. Bubnov ("Kisanko") and General Victor Rogachev, the second-in-command of the Soviet military mission. These two, with a small group of other advisers, left Canton at the end of March. *Documents on Communism, Nationalism, and Soviet Advisers in China*, pp. 220, 250, 509.

plenum of the Kuomintang Central Executive in order to lay these measures before it and to have them adopted. A "Resolution Adjusting Party Affairs" excluded Communists from all higher posts in the Kuomintang and limited them to one third of the seats on all party committees but local ones. In addition, they were to take their orders no longer from their own leaders but from a joint two-party committee with a Comintern delegate on it. They were not to criticize Kuomintang doctrine as embodied in the Three People's Principles; in effect, they thus forfeited the right to propagate their own teaching. Lastly, they were to hand over a list of their party members, so that the Kuomintang would know against whom to enforce the projected "adjustment."[18]

What then remained after May 15 of the Communists' independence, of their freedom to agitate and to recruit, on which Lenin had insisted so firmly? Had he not made it perfectly clear that unless they enjoyed this freedom, Communists should never belong to any coalition whatever? He had laid down this rule to safeguard their freedom to rally the masses behind them; hence the question arises whether, in China, they still remained able to do so.

At first sight, this does not seem to be the case; the new "adjustment," on paper, seemed to reduce the Communists to a mean auxiliary status. Gone was their opportunity to divide and conquer vertically, to subdue the Kuomintang from above, by control of some of its key posts. Even below, their only prospect seemed to be the very dismal one of exercising their energies for the sole benefit of the Kuomintang. Who could have foretold that but three months later the Northern Expedition would free their hand on the local level and make them masters of millions?

They themselves did not look this far ahead; stricter Leninists than Lenin's successor, they regarded the "adjustment" as a signal for leaving the ranks of the Kuomintang. The party leaders seem to have expressed the sentiment of the membership when they called for a bloc of two separate parties to replace the existing alliance.[19] On June 9, the Communist Central Committee informed its Kuomintang counterpart that it did not feel bound by the rules of the interparty "adjustment." The Communist letter is worth quoting because it took it for granted that the "bloc within" had already been scrapped, that each party was again independent.

> Your decision to adjust party affairs [wrote the Communist leaders] is an internal matter . . . in which other parties do not have the right to meddle. Members of your party must obey your party, but *organizations outside the Kuomintang* do not have this obligation. . . . Regarding the problem of future collaboration . . . our parties should enter negotiations *on the basis of their own resolutions* (emphasis mine).[20]

Thus the Communists proclaimed their autonomy while exercising due caution not to provoke an immediate break with an ally who had the upper hand. At the same time, they felt that the break could not be put off much longer and that, if the party was to survive, they had to arm it immediately. Therefore they resolved — Ch'en Tu-hsiu disclosed this later[21] — to "train independent military forces" for use against those of the Kuomintang. But this brave resolution ran afoul of Borodin's cold refusal to release any weapons from the stores intended for Chiang Kai-shek's armies. To arm now, he maintained, would weaken Chiang in face of the hostile warlords and thus delay or even prevent the unification of China. Hence the Communists would have to go on doing "coolie service for the Kuomintang" — a disagreeable task, to be sure, but a necessary one historically.[22]

Clearly, Borodin had changed his mind since in the flush of excitement following the March 20 coup he had advocated a countercoup. He had been in Peking at the time, allegedly to plan strategy with the "Christian general," Feng Yü-hsiang, who was then on the Soviet payroll.[23] Actually, his meetings with Feng may have been quite incidental: he may have gone north to plan strategy with a visiting Comintern mission.[24] If so, his initial opposition to Chiang may possibly have been inspired by some of the Comintern's experts on China who favored a harder policy. Conversely, his surrender to Chiang only a few weeks later may indicate that the hapless experts had been "corrected" by Stalin. In any event, Borodin emerged as the most zealous promoter of all-out assistance to Chiang Kai-shek — of the gamble that finally ruined him. His change of mind should not be ascribed to Moscow's dictation only; Chiang himself did his best to bring it about by his persuasive diplomacy.

He sent a personal emissary — Shao Li-tzu, a former Communist — to Peking in order to ask Borodin to return to his post in Canton. At the same time, he ordered the arrest of some of his recent accomplices — army officers and Kuomintang rightists — for their part in the March conspiracy. Borodin was delighted;[25] Chiang seemed to be back on the side of the angels; but what completed the reconciliation was military necessity. The most powerful warlord, Wu P'ei-fu, soon launched a great southern offensive, which, nearing Kwangtung, bade fair to eject the Kuomintang from the country. Aid to Chiang now became the equivalent of supporting the Chinese revolution against the reactionary forces that were trying to extinguish it.

Yet there remained, in spite of this, some Comintern agents in China who still felt that March 20 and May 15 called for Communist countermeasures. This group advised Moscow of its opinion that the Chinese Communist Party should be permitted to stretch the rules that the Kuomintang had lately imposed on it.[26] Without formally leaving the Kuomintang, the Communists should in practice "progress by stages" from the "bloc within" to one of two separate parties.[27] This, as we saw, was the very course which their leaders desired to follow; hence it appears that these had made converts among their Soviet mentors.

But Moscow would not be easily swayed; though the proposal before it was already cautious and vague enough, it wanted to be still more so. When the Comintern received telegraphic news of the May 15 Plenum, the chief of its Far Eastern Division, Voitinsky, took the matter to the Politburo. The Politburo met in special session; and Voitinsky, appearing before it, submitted the following proposals, which it adopted unanimously:

1. The Chinese Communists were to try, "in case of absolute necessity," to discuss with the Kuomintang the "possibility of a certain separation of functions";

2. The "best known Communists" were to be removed from "all Kuomintang institutions," but those "not yet known to the Kuomintang" were not, or not yet, to leave them;

3. The "possible separation" of the two allied parties might, "in case of emergency," be worthy of consideration.

However, to avoid a misunderstanding, the Politburo went on record with the view that to leave the Kuomintang now was definitely undesirable.[28]

This last directive at least was clear — more than one can say for the others which Voitinsky had drafted with such perfect knowledge of what his superiors wanted. But his knowledge of the new situation in Canton was incomparably poorer; this becomes evident as we look closely at the first three directives. How could the "best known Communists" give up posts in the Kuomintang which in fact they no longer occupied since the coup of March 20? How could those "not yet known to the Kuomintang" hope to remain anonymous if the party complied with the new "adjustment" and released a list of its members? Just what was a "case of emergency" or of "absolute necessity" if the coup of March 20 was not one but, somehow, a lighter matter? In short, how could the Politburo deal with the crisis in Canton almost as if it had never occurred or as if it had been without consequence?

The simplest answer that comes to mind, and the one that seems most plausible, is that the Politburo was too ill-informed to judge the situation correctly. Complaints that news from Canton was scarce could often be heard in this period;[29] indeed, one wonders why Borodin informed his superiors so badly. Did he deliberately hush up the worst features of the "adjustment" for fear that Moscow might cut off or reduce the assistance it gave to the Kuomintang? Possibly so; for he did, it seems, promise Moscow's assistance to Chiang's projected drive to the north before Moscow itself would support it.[30] But whatever impeded the flow of intelligence between Canton and Moscow, bad information explains only in part why Stalin viewed Canton distortedly. Even if he had been better informed (as he did in fact become later), he would hardly have looked at Chinese events in their properly Chinese perspective.

The reason for this is that China policy became involved in the struggle which gradually split the Bolsheviks into opposing factions. It thus became a domestic issue ever more unrelated to actual changes on the Chinese scene, which sank into the far background. China as such all but disappeared behind China, object of policy, object to be handled this way or that, according to Moscow's decision. The dispute about how to handle this object did not reach its height till spring 1927, when the power to decide China's fate had in fact returned wholly to her own leaders.

In 1926, on the other hand, when Moscow might still have changed the course of events in China, it did not concern itself nearly so much with questions of China policy. Even Trotsky, leader of the Opposition, paid but scant attention to China; he left most of the talking on this subject to his half-hearted ally, Zinoviev. Zinoviev found himself in the Opposition without having really joined it; Stalin had pushed him into it by turning slowly against him. He had lost his power in the party machine because Stalin, the great *apparatchik*, was systematically making sure that only *he* kept such power.[31] But Zinoviev did not like to be cast loose; adrift in the Opposition, he always attempted, through compromise, to regain the Stalinist harbor. Though feeling with Trotsky that the Chinese Communists should withdraw from the Kuomintang, he refused to come out for their withdrawal except through "transitional formulae." [32] By this he meant formulae such as those which his right-hand man, Voitinsky, had devised in May 1926 for submission to the Politburo. But if compromise had been the true intent behind these ambiguous formulae, the Stalinists had agreed to them with a different motive. In July, they accused the Opposition of desiring a break with the Kuomintang[33] — a charge which Zinoviev promptly denied but which was at bottom justified.[34]

The widening gulf between the two factions did not deter Zinoviev from trying for almost another year to throw a bridge across it. On his insistence, the Opposition continued to speak about China in harmless "transitional formulae" designed to meet Stalin halfway. But Stalin refused to be thus obliged; he would not meet his critics halfway; at stake was the right to wield absolute power; and he was stronger than they were.

Hence, when they attacked his alliance with Chiang, they only made Stalin defend him all the more firmly and blindly;

he became as dependent on Chiang's allegiance as Chiang was on his assistance. Chiang knew how to use this situation; the factional struggle in Russia allowed him to call the turns, as it were, in his dance with his Soviet partner.[35] The Russians were helpless without Chiang, Borodin lamented later; and Chiang, at this juncture, was equally helpless without his Russian allies.[36]

He needed their military aid, if only to repel the forces by which Wu P'ei-fu hoped to conquer the south and to destroy the Kuomintang. It soon turned out that the strength of these forces had been much overrated; their southward advance was easily stopped, their fighting capacity shattered. Chiang pursued his advantage and drove on north, though some of his Soviet advisers, headed by Bubnov, known as Kisanko,* had tried for months to restrain him.[37] Bubnov's objections, as we shall see, merely echoed the Kremlin's; they might have been raised by Borodin too, had Borodin been in Canton. As it was, he had been away in Peking, escaping the painful necessity of giving Chiang unwelcome advice and making himself unwelcome.[38] He had thus regained the general's favor, even earned a promotion: he was now adviser to the Kuomintang *party* as well as to the Kuomintang government. Chiang could afford to admit him more freely into the party's councils; holding all six of its highest posts, he did not have to fear foreign influence.[39]

Never did Chiang prove more astute as a political leader than during the Northern Expedition, when he used—and outwitted—the Communists. Arms alone, he knew well at that time, could not win as swiftly and surely as arms preceded by propagandists bearing a popular message. By leaving

* Bubnov and Chiang are known to have been on bad terms. In March 1926, Chiang asked for Bubnov's recall and obtained it. Whether their enmity was cause or result of their disagreement on strategy remains an open question.

the Communists a free hand in the lower Kuomintang echelons, he secured for his armies the mass support which the "youngsters" knew best how to rally.

Thus shrewd calculation lay behind the consummate hypocrisy with which Chiang pretended after May 15 that nothing whatever had happened. On May 25, he told a meeting of local Kuomintang functionaries that he, for one, had not lost his faith in the loyalty of the Communists.

> As the Communist Party has already joined our party [he said] there should be no special regulations to restrict them. Recently it was reported that our party was being encroached upon by the Communist Party. I do not believe this at all. . . . Both the Communist Party and the Kuomintang are fighting against imperialism, and if the Kuomintang left the Communist Party alone [sic], not only would the Communist revolution not succeed but the Kuomintang's revolution would also be a failure. . . .[40]

Chiang may have intended these words for the Kremlin more than for those who heard them; for they achieved the desired effect through their effect on Moscow. The Chinese Communists duly went on doing "coolie service" for the Kuomintang, but only because their Soviet superiors sided with Chiang against them. They for their part contrasted his soothing words with the rough tenor of his action — and concluded that it would still be best to rid themselves of his company.

To this end, a plenum of their Central Committee* adopted a resolution demanding a thorough transformation of the entire Kuomintang. The Kuomintang was to "relax its statutes" so that its Bolshevik structure might be replaced by a looser one allowing of group affiliation. Then it would be possible to "broaden its base" by converting it into a network of "mass

* Held in July 1926, this plenum is often misdated June 1926 in Western (including Comintern) sources.

organizations of the left," "political clubs," etc. The new Kuomintang — this becomes clear, though it was not made explicit — was to be patterned after the model of the Labour Party in Britain.[41]

Thus the Communists hoped to regain nearly all of their independence without disobeying Moscow's command that they remain in the Kuomintang. Their proposal was both a subterfuge and an attempt at compromise, comparable to the "transitional formulae" of the Opposition in Russia. But because it was more transparent than these, less capable of various readings, it lived only long enough to be killed by a summary Stalinist veto. The entire resolution of the Central Committee was simply annulled by Moscow in the most crude application so far of discipline instead of persuasion.[42]

That the whole resolution was thus thrown out should not be attributed solely to its demand for the creation of a federated Kuomintang. An undercurrent of unorthodox thinking ran visibly below its surface — visibly enough to draw Moscow's attention and to cause its annulment.[43]

There was, for instance, a clear intimation that the Kuomintang, unless reorganized, would soon serve the interest of one class alone — not that of the workers, unfortunately. One class, entrenching itself at the top, would gain control of the party unless the party structure were changed, its center of gravity lowered. Instead of competitive collaboration between several classes — instead of the Kuomintang as it was now — there would be a one-class party. An "authoritarian one-class party," with a hostile class in authority, was scarcely the type of organization that the Communists wished to belong to.[44]

Which, then, was the class that they feared might emerge in control of the Kuomintang? They failed to name it in their resolution, and the omission was prudent. They obviously meant the bourgeoisie; but to say so would have been dangerous, seeing that Trotsky said much the same: the bourgeoisie ran the Kuomintang. This was the classical Marxist premise, the solid orthodox granite, on which Trotsky based his entire case against Stalin's tactics in China.[45]

It was the premise on which Ch'en Tu-hsiu had taken his stand at Hangchow, and which he had only slowly abandoned under pressure from Moscow. Or had he merely abandoned his stand without really changing his premise? The new resolution of the Central Committee may well have aroused this suspicion.

Some lines in it — this much at least is clear — expressed an unhealthy skepticism (unhealthy by Stalin's hygienic standards) of Chiang Kai-shek's good intentions. It was easier to forgive and forget from a distance, in Moscow, than from nearer by, where the coup of last March had left more tangible imprints. Moscow and Chiang had soon made it up after the recent "incident"; but the Chinese Communists lagged behind: they still felt immediately threatened. Instead of thinking the incident closed, they viewed it as a beginning, as only the start of a grand offensive still under way against them.[46]

True, those who had launched it, Chiang and his men, still seemed to be men of the middle; they had not moved nearly as far to the right as the ultraist Western Hills group. They might even decide to move back toward the left to keep their support from that quarter; the Communists certainly hoped that they would and proceeded on that assumption. What else could they do, given Stalin's conviction that Chiang should be kept as an ally and that it was up to himself, not to Chiang, to decide at what point to part company. They undertook to "handle" Chiang; but reading their resolution, one feels that they did so with graver misgivings than Stalin considered legitimate. To speak of "counterrevolutionary forces . . . directed by the [Kuomintang] center" — the center being

Chiang's men of the middle—was not, at the time, good Stalinism.[47]

The Chinese Communists tried, of course—tried hard—to be faithful Stalinists; they tried to work through the Kuomintang in order to take it over. But much of their effort in this direction had been frustrated—and they knew it—by their contrary effort to work on their own, to save the party's identity. They had failed, because of their very success in saving their independence, to win as much influence as they needed in the lower ranks of the Kuomintang. They had therefore lacked effective support from the Kuomintang membership when some of its leaders—the "right" and the "center"—had launched their offensive against them.[48]

Moreover, for fear of losing themselves in the surrounding Kuomintang, they had lost sight, or almost lost sight, of one of their own objectives. They had forgotten (so that by now the point had to be re-emphasized) that they were to *guide* the Kuomintang left, not to supplant, to *become* it. Perhaps this had been too subtle a task to be accomplished successfully; but it would now become easier if the Kuomintang were reorganized. A federate Kuomintang largely made up of public organizations already safely in Communist hands would surely prove more amenable.

This much for the Communist plan, forged at the very juncture when history presented the party with its great opportunity. The Northern Expedition had just begun; and in the sweep of its armies, the restraints of May 15, which had seemed like fetters, no longer seemed to weigh heavily. The Communists promptly made the most of their sudden opportunity, but had they been able to have their own way, it would not even have arisen.

In the same resolution of their Central Committee which we have only just quoted, they had denied that the Northern

Expedition could be genuinely revolutionary. It was "only a defensive campaign" for the protection of Kwangtung — a move to halt Wu P'ei-fu's advance, not one to unify China.[49] Of all the points in the resolution, this happens to be the only one on which the Chinese Communist leaders were completely attuned to Moscow. There Stalin and his ally Bukharin (we are told by Zinoviev) "opposed the Northern Expedition doggedly and unremittingly." Only, of course, until its success was no longer to be doubted; then they promptly "forgot who led the campaign" in order to applaud it.[50]

Had he who led the campaign — Chiang Kai-shek — not yet regained their confidence? Unlikely, though later it was given out that they had never trusted him.[51] A better explanation of why they were slow to give the campaign their blessings may be found in connection with their fear of the Anglo-Japanese bogyman.

We have noted how the imaginary threat of Anglo-Japanese aggression had prompted the Politburo's Committee on China to propose certain countermeasures. Now we find attached to its report a brief amendment which Stalin, though not a member of the committee, is supposed to have drafted:

"For the time being, the Canton Government must abstain from armed expeditions of an aggressive nature and from all actions that may push the imperialists on the road of armed intervention."[52]

To understand what Stalin meant, let us see what position the warlords — to him mere cards in the imperialist game — were occupying at that juncture. Wu P'ei-fu, who had not yet begun his drive south, had combined with Marshal Chang Tso-lin to eject the forces of Feng Yü-hsiang from the capital, Peking. Feng, as we saw, was in Soviet pay and therefore a "revolutionary," whereas Wu and Chang represented to Moscow the two powers that it most dreaded. Wu it considered a British puppet since this fitted its over-all picture, and Chang it put down as a servant of Japan since he dealt with her in Manchuria.

Moreover, Britain presented a threat to the Chinese revolution long before Wu, her putative puppet, began to move south to quell it. It should be recalled that in this period the Kuomintang and its government supported a strike which effectively throttled British trade out of Hongkong. But for the restraining hand of Borodin, acting on Moscow's orders, the Kuomintang might have gone to the extreme of starting a war with Britain.[53]

Thus Wu P'ei-fu's sudden lunge toward the south only added one more touch of horror to Moscow's nightmare of two imperialists carving up prostrate China. Everything seemed to become clear: Wu and Britain taking South China, while to the north Chang Tso-lin and Japan busily widened their own sphere. For the Chinese revolution to survive, the Kuomintang would have to concentrate entirely on its self-defense — the defense of its base in Kwangtung.

Rational in every detail as are so many nightmares, this one also collapsed at the first loud knock by someone outside and not dreaming. Chiang Kai-shek launched the Northern Expedition and, by its easy victories, dispelled the fears which his patrons in Moscow had nurtured with tens of reasons. Now Stalin, himself fully awake, seized upon Chiang Kai-shek's triumph to vindicate his own course in China and even his claim to foresight. With success on his side, he easily silenced his critics in the party, so that by the end of 1926 he argued only with henchmen.*

* At the crucial Seventh Plenum of the Comintern Executive, the Opposition did not, as far as the records show, attack Stalin's China policy. On the other hand, the records show Stalin sharply at odds with his own China experts, Mif, Petrov, and Rafes. See Chapter V.

Indeed, until early in the next year, one could reasonably hold the opinion that the Chinese Communists had gained the most from the Northern Expedition. It is true that the number of party members had increased by only one thousand, but their following had increased by the million and their influence grown immeasurably.[54] Thus, though their position inside the Kuomintang might have made Lenin shudder, it yet enabled them to rally the masses precisely as he had envisaged.

This convinced Stalin that all further advances by the Kuomintang armies would continue to be of benefit to the Chinese Communist Party. The Kuomintang generals — he told fellow Bolsheviks who seem to have been slightly skeptical — were "old jades" that should not be "driven away" while they pulled the Communist wagon.[55] The Chinese Communists, who sat on the wagon, could not feel quite so superior: they knew that the driver, who held the whip, did not obey their directions.

They also knew that although they had comrades among the Kuomintang officers, not one of these held a major command in the Northern Expedition.[56] True enough, on every command level down to the regimental one served political commissars whom they had trained and who still remained their adherents.* By statute, the commissars held higher authority than the military commanders; but actually relations between the two were seldom governed by statute. Especially since March 20, the military commanders had regained such authority that, at times, they would even name their own commissars.[57] In a "significant portion" of the army — a Communist writer admitted — the regular officers had thus assumed even political leadership.[58] The significant portion, it turns out upon

* The commissars were trained by the Political Department at Whampoa, a Communist preserve since the opening of the academy. In charge of the department was Chou En-lai, the present Chinese Communist premier.

closer examination, was very significant indeed: the bulk, no less, of the army.

The National Revolutionary — that is, Kuomintang — Army comprised at first only six army corps of which five had their special history. These five were by origin warlord armies which the Kuomintang had "reorganized" not by changing their structure or personnel but simply by giving them numbers. The remaining unit — the only one that had been newly created — was an elite corps whose officers were Whampoa graduates only. This was the so-called Whampoa Army which Chiang had commanded in person until the beginning of the northern campaign, when a close associate succeeded him.* But the six army corps which began the campaign were actually only a nucleus to which accreted the motley troops of one warlord after another. By the time the Kuomintang army arrived on the banks of the Yangtse, thirty-four warlords had joined its side to share its hour of triumph.[59]

Thirty-four warlords and their troops raised the strength of the Kuomintang army to a sum total of forty corps: an increase that was almost sevenfold. But in this mighty array there was only one single regiment (commanded by a Colonel Yeh T'ing) that the Communists could count as friendly.[60] Thus they were weakest exactly where the Kuomintang was strongest: in their ability, in case of need, to use force in support of their argument.[61]

But how about their ability to win over the soldiers — soldiers of peasant origin — by promises and propaganda? Had not the Russian Bolsheviks coped with the tsarist army by shaking the loyalty of its soldiers — also, for the most

* This was General Ho Ying-ch'in. With Chiang in supreme command of the Kuomintang forces, his immediate subordinates were now the following generals: 1st corps — Ho Ying-ch'in; 2nd corps — T'an Yen-k'ai; 3rd corps — Chu Pei-teh; 4th corps — Li Chi-shen; 5th corps — Li Fu-lin; 6th corps – Ch'en Ch'eng.

part, peasants? They had indeed, but with this difference: they had dealt with a *beaten* army, and their aim had been not to wage a war but to end one as quickly as possible.* The Chinese Communists, on the other hand, could not undermine an army on which they relied to defeat their own foes, the feudalists and imperialists.

They could not — and knew it — incite the soldiers against the land-owning officers and expect the officers to keep still, to keep faith with the revolution. Therefore they had formally decreed that in the Kuomintang army, the party should spread only Kuomintang, not Communist, propaganda.[62] How faithfully this was actually done emerges from the plaintive passages of a compendium of military wisdom which the party put out three years later. The soldiers, we learn, either did not know that the Communist Party existed or, if they knew, were unable to tell how it differed from its ally, the Kuomintang.[63]

How indeed should they have told them apart? There was not a Communist Party cell in all of the Kuomintang army, at least not till December 1926, when a few were formed in a hurry. And these few were not for the common soldiers but for officers only: the officers, unlike the illiterate soldiers, could read secret tracts and circulars.[64]

As much as their weakness in the army impaired the Communists' prospects, it could not have been remedied while they followed the policy laid down by Moscow. Knowing this, Moscow fully approved the self-restraint and circumspection with which they approached the delicate tasks confronting them in the army.[65] But there were those in the Comintern, particularly China specialists, who in their hearts did not

* Instead of "they," it would be more accurate to say: Lenin and a few followers; for there was a strong war party within the Bolshevik leadership. Whenever we digress into Russian history, we cannot but oversimplify.

approve — who, in fact, wished to change — the whole policy.

Already in July 1926 — the chairman of the Comintern tells us — its "best connoisseurs of the Chinese movement" felt such a change to be needed.[66] Its chief of Far Eastern affairs, Voitinsky, ranked the highest among these; we have seen how in May the Politburo took counsel with him about China. Though ill-informed about Chinese affairs, Voitinsky enjoyed the sheltered state of the expert: being adviser to those in power without entering into their struggles. This gave him an air of neutrality in spite of his links to Zinoviev, so much so that Stalin still trusted him and presently sent him to China. He left for China early in June to "correct the separatist tendency" of the Chinese comrades — to cure the disease of which he himself carried the germs in his system.

Soon after his arrival in Shanghai, Voitinsky showed so much sympathy with those he had come to censure that they regarded him as an ally among their alien mentors. All the more cruel was their disappointment when at a decisive moment he refused to side with them against the Kremlin and, instead, enforced its instructions. Thus Stalin had not misplaced his trust when sending him out to China: wherever his actual sympathies lay, he did carry out his orders.[67]

Voitinsky's *volte-face* (to which we shall return at a later point in this chapter) was a common act of bureaucratic submission under uncommon pressure. A Soviet functionary of the time could not show sympathy with the Chinese Communist viewpoint without becoming immediately suspect as a probable Trotskyite. It so happened that the Opposition in Russia and the Chinese Communist Party actually did see eye to eye on a number of crucial issues. But this concurrence of views did not grow out of collusion: Trotsky knew little of Ch'en Tu-hsiu, and Ch'en just as little of Trotsky.

It is true that much later, in 1929, when Ch'en was expelled from the party, he did found a rival group giving allegiance to Trotsky's ideals and leadership. This made it easier for Communist writers whose task it now was to discredit him to reinterpret his whole career as that of an inveterate Trotskyist.[68] A thin thread of truth invariably runs through the fabric of slander; in this instance, too, the slanderers had a fact or two to go on. Ch'en's Marxist objections to the multiclass party, first raised at the Hangchow Plenum, were indeed very similar to those raised subsequently by Trotsky. Moreover, the May 30 Movement seemed both to him and to Trotsky the proper occasion for reasserting Communist independence. Yet all told, Ch'en remained to his last day in office obedient to Comintern orders or to (what had almost become the same) the personal orders of Stalin. He himself admitted this afterwards, when, as an oppositionist, he might, if less honest, have tried to deny that he served Stalin well while in office.[69] But there is no need to take his own word for it; Trotsky, who watched him from Moscow, never thought him to be anything else than a loyal henchman of Stalin's. So little did Trotsky know of Ch'en that in 1927 he still wondered if Ch'en would ever agree to break away from the Kuomintang.*

Moreover, the Stalinists themselves have unwittingly given evidence of how innocent Ch'en was of Trotskyism while at the head of his party. When they overruled him, they did so in secret, without heaping all the abuse on him that they invariably heap on a comrade who has really lost their confidence. When at last they did abuse him in public to conceal their own failures, they accused him of crimes which, taken together, contradict and cancel each other. They charged him not only with Trotskyism, which is a left deviation, but with opportunism as well: an unduly rightist proclivity.

* See Chapter VI.

This though he had followed so straight a path that on at least one occasion he had found it necessary to tell his own party why he remained loyal to Moscow. Some surge of dissent had left him no choice but to explain in public why revolutionaries in China should accept any aid from Russia. Ch'en's apologia is the more remarkable because of the time when he wrote it: in the autumn of 1926, at the height of the Northern Expedition. Never were the benefits of Soviet aid more obvious than at this juncture; yet Ch'en felt compelled to vindicate them as though they were still unproven.

> There is a group of persons — he wrote in the party weekly, *Hsiang-tao* — who think that we should achieve our revolution by our own strength, without counting on Soviet aid. [This] view . . . is not false, and we should act accordingly as best we can. . . . But if Soviet aid enables us to accelerate our revolutionary development, there seems to be no reason why we should refuse it or oppose Soviet Russia.[70]

Oppose Soviet Russia? Did the demand for an end of Russian assistance have overtones of outright hostility to the Russian presence in China? Apparently so, since Ch'en felt the need to battle against the notion that Moscow's concern for the freedom of China hid "imperialist aspirations."[71] How, he protested, could this be so considering that the Russians, unlike the real imperialists, did not prop up Chinese feudalism? Instead of supporting feudal warlords like Wu P'ei-fu and Chang Tso-lin, they helped only champions of revolution: Feng Yü-hsiang and, of course, the Kuomintang.[72]

Such were the facts that Ch'en adduced in support of his prior assumption, though he would have seen, if not blinded by dogma, that actually they contradicted it. True enough, the Soviets did not support either Wu P'ei-fu or Chang Tso-lin; but then they had courted favor with each until each had at last rebuffed them. Of their dealings with Wu we have treated already; of their dealings with Chang, the ruler of Manchuria, suffice it to say that they paid him court till Japan proved the stronger wooer.*

The distrust which Soviet generosity inspired in some Chinese Communists was doubtless sharpened by their dislike of Soviet aid to the Kuomintang. Even though the Kuomintang was fast becoming the ruling party of China, there were still a good many Communists who did not relish being in it. The Communist high command in Peking — the Northern District Committee — continued to advocate a break in spite of all contrary pressure.[73] Even on the Central Committee in Shanghai, dissident voices grew louder: drop the Kuomintang like a "rotten corpse," advised a poetic member. "Stand on the side of the masses," cried a like-minded comrade, "and oppose the National Government" — the government, that is, of the Kuomintang.[74]

The masses on one side and government on the other: the image was a commonplace of Marxist rhetoric, but it did not lack reality. As the generals of the Northern Expedition became surer and surer of victory, they also bore down harder and harder on workers' and peasants' unions. Government in the liberated areas — especially in Kiangsi Province — had thus, by the autumn of 1926, become openly reactionary. Communists who held office as magistrates tried to stem the reaction; but with all real power in the hands of the army, they could accomplish nothing.

The Central Committee therefore concluded that party members in government would discredit the party in the eyes of the people if they continued in office. To avert this danger

* In 1924, when the Soviets concluded their first treaty with the Republic of China, they signed a separate, almost identical treaty with the government of Manchuria. By thus recognizing Chang's separate rule over the Chinese Northeast, they lent legal support to what they would call Chinese feudalism.

where it seemed most acute, the committee sent orders to Kiangsi that every Communist magistrate should immediately quit his position.[75] But scarcely had these orders gone out when others arrived from Moscow: have party members *enter* government organs, make them share the rule of the Kuomintang.[76]

These orders came from the Seventh Plenum of the Comintern Executive, at which Stalin achieved the height of his glory as an expert on China. The plenum convened in late November, flushed with a sense of triumph: the Communist cause still seemed to advance with every advance of the Kuomintang. Now Stalin's friendship with Chiang Kai-shek underwent its apotheosis, not least because of the eloquence of Chiang's spokesman in the assembly. On behalf of "Comrade Chiang Kai-shek," Shao Li-tzu, the Kuomintang delegate,* swore yet another oath of allegiance to the Comintern leaders.[77]

The plenum was duly enthusiastic; but the trust it reposed in the Kuomintang did not evoke any enthusiasm in the Chinese Communist Party. In fact, the party leaders were shocked: the Comintern's spokesmen in Moscow did not speak the same language as Voitinsky, the chief of its mission in Shanghai.† Voitinsky had only just advised *against* joining any government; let the Kuomintang govern alone, he had said, without making us its accomplices. But now that his superiors in Moscow had ordered the very opposite, he quickly conformed and even rebuked the laggards who argued

* Originally a Communist, Shao has since returned to the fold by taking service with the Peking government. He is now a member of the Standing Committee of the National People's Congress.

† One might say: chief of its mission in China; for he was nominally the senior Comintern agent in the entire country. The actual chief of mission was, of course, Borodin; but in order to safeguard Borodin's position with the Kuomintang, this was never admitted. Eudin and North, *Soviet Russia and the East,* pp. 368–69.

as he had. His cold-blooded turnabout enraged Ch'en Tu-hsiu, who, though a disciplined Communist, could not quite adjust himself to Moscow's whims as though they were Marxist world laws.[78]

But this core of integrity in Ch'en did not tempt him into rebellion: he always submitted in the end, even though under protest. At times, however, he found it possible to resist by procrastination, the favorite weapon of the weaker side, especially in the Orient. When, as in this case, both he and the Kuomintang wielded that pliant weapon, it had much greater effect, of course, than if one of them only had used it. They both used it because they agreed — even if only tacitly — that a two-party government such as Moscow demanded would not serve their mutual interest. Thus it took them half a year to comply: not till May 1927 (the very end of May, in fact) did they form a common government. The central government of the Kuomintang had meanwhile moved north from Canton and established itself on the banks of the Yangtse in three neighboring towns known as "Wuhan." * Thus it was at Wuhan that two Communist ministers were finally sworn into office, receiving portfolios in which their party had doubtless expressed great interest. The ministry of labor went to Su Chao-cheng, a professional trade-unionist, and that of agriculture — at least as important — to the party leader T'an P'ing-shan.[79]

T'an was to become both symbol and victim of the abortive effort to "push the Kuomintang to the left" by governing jointly with it. Yet it had been he who, not long before, had tried to convince the Comintern that to work with the Kuomintang as it was now could only lead to disaster. As the principal spokesman of the Chinese Communists at the Seventh

* An abbreviation of Wuch'ang, Hankow, Hanyang.

Plenum, he had declared himself for a "line" which skirted the brink of heresy.

This line was not new: only recently — five months before the plenum — the Central Committee of the party had announced its intention to follow it. T'an merely reworded the proposal which the Central Committee had made in July 1926 — and which Moscow had brusquely rejected.

This, as we saw, had been a proposal to reorganize the Kuomintang so as to give it a federate structure like that of the Labour Party. T'an revived the idea with similar arguments as had been put forward previously, again from a premise which it was wise not to make too explicit. But the implication was no less clear than it had been five months earlier: the Kuomintang served the bourgeoisie, and it alone, as a vehicle. The workers and peasants who also belonged to it could not use it for their own ends; its rigid Bolshevik discipline only helped to keep them in bondage. This discipline threatened them with "alienation from their [proper] class interests" and with "progressive assimilation" — to which class, though unsaid, was obvious.[80]

These were dire prospects that T'an conjured up; yet they failed to frighten the plenum: as once before, the scheme he proposed was curtly and quietly vetoed. Was this because Stalin anticipated that the Kuomintang leaders would not allow themselves to be trapped and would reject the proposal? Hardly so; for in May 1927, when he had far more reason to anticipate its rejection, he suddenly hauled it down from the shelf and presented it as his own policy.

No, at the time of the Seventh Plenum, Stalin was still full of confidence that the Kuomintang would do almost anything that he might require of it. The Chinese bourgeoisie, he thought, was weak (what else could he think, since Trotsky believed the opposite?); in any case, it did not have the strength to dominate all of the Kuomintang. "Certain strata" of it would therefore "continue to march with the revolution," even though their place at the head of the column would "inevitably" go to the working class.[81]

"Certain strata"—Stalin was wise to be vague; for who could prove to him afterwards that he had thought of Chiang Kai-shek under this general heading? Yet he had doubtless thought of him thus; for he suffered from an illusion to which powerful statesmen—not only tyrants—frequently prove susceptible. He mistook acceptance of his government's aid and openness to its influence for readiness to follow its lead, or at least for extreme tractability. He erred the more gravely in this respect because, on another level, he judged the Kuomintang and its leaders altogether correctly. He saw that their nationalism transcended narrow class aspiration, that it was not merely "bourgeois," as Trotsky, quoting scripture, contended.[82] In fact, since their nationalism sprang in the main from hatred of the imperialists, it formed the most solid and genuine link between them and their Communist allies. Trotsky did not appreciate this because of a blind spot in his political vision: he did not see, because he did not feel, the power of modern nationalism.[83] He could not explain the strength of the Kuomintang except by grossly inflating the strength which the Chinese bourgeoisie had gained in "its" revolution. Perhaps it was safer to exaggerate thus than to overrate, as did Stalin, the strength of the so-called Kuomintang left and the depth of its friendship for Moscow. But simply because Trotsky did not commit this cardinal error of Stalin's, it should not be concluded that he knew more of Chinese conditions and feelings.

Quite the contrary: Stalin at least stood prepared to stretch a Marxist principle the better to deal with the Kuomintang as the party of Chinese nationalism. But his comprehension of nationalism was obscured in actual practice by the strongest instinct of which he was possessed: that for wielding absolute power. In Russia, he was achieving such power by consummate skill in the manipulation of persons; only thus did he finally become able to manipulate social forces. But in China, he started at the opposite end, manipulating social forces on the tacit assumption that the Kuomintang leaders would have to submit to their action. One may argue that in the course of decades this assumption gained some validity; but during the years with which we deal here it proved foolish as well as disastrous. Stalin, the master-maneuverer of men, was outmaneuvered in China not because the Chinese were more cunning than he but because he ignored them as humans.

More than that, he ignored all reports from China that did not fit into his schema: he would not let an untoward event disturb the calm of his vision. This became especially obvious at the Seventh Plenum, to which T'an P'ing-shan reported at length about conditions in China. Between T'an's report and Stalin's "Theses on the Chinese Situation" [84] yawns an abyss by which we may gauge Stalin's distance from noisome data. It is hard to convey the sense of an abyss, of absolute unrelatedness, but the following dialogue in *non sequiturs* may possibly serve the purpose:

T'an: Since the establishment of the National Government in Canton . . . nominally a left-wing government, power actually rests with the right wing — as shown, for instance, by the fact that five out of six government commissars belong to the right wing . . . After the March action [March 20, 1926], a military dictatorship of the center was set up, while political power remained in the hands of the right wing.[85]

Stalin: Latest events have shown that the Communists must enter the Canton government in order to support the revolutionary left wing in its struggle against the weak and vacillating policy of the right.[86]

T'an: The demands of the peasants . . . have not been fulfilled . . . by the government. When a conflict developed between the large landlords and the poor peasants, the government always sided with the former.[87]

Stalin: The apparatus of the National Revolutionary Government provides a very effective way to reach the peasantry. The Communist Party must use this way.[88]

T'an: The landowning class forms the basis of the Chinese military system. In order to put an end to the militarists, we must solve the agrarian question.[89]

Stalin: The Communists . . . must take all possible measures to neutralize the elements in the army which are hostile to the peasants, to preserve the revolutionary spirit in the army and to direct things in such a way that the army helps the peasants and mobilizes them for revolution.[90]

The army mobilizing the peasants—did Stalin, after all, have the vision to foresee how the Chinese Communists would eventually come to power? By no means; from what else he said at the plenum it emerges quite clearly that the only army which he had in mind was the army of the Kuomintang. No doubt on this score is possible for the simplest of reasons: he expressly forbade the Chinese comrades to form a separate army. A proposal to form separate units had been made by the daring T'an P'ing-shan, at that time not in the least afraid of swimming against the current.* He virtually asked the Comintern to reverse a previous decision; for it had rejected his present proposal at an earlier juncture. We have seen already that such rebuffs left T'an and his comrades undaunted: their proposal to loosen the Kuomintang structure had also been previously vetoed. Were they audacious or desperate? T'an spoke of armed insurrection; and we may assume that

* T'an was expelled from the party in November 1927. But when it seized power two decades later, he found his way back into its midst, serving the Peking government in various minor capacities. He died in 1956.

he spoke for those who had sent him to Moscow.[91] Stalin rejected his recommendation firmly but without vehemence; he agreed that some Chinese Communists should study the art of warfare. But only, he said, to "advance step by step," to win "some leading post or other in the revolutionary army" — the army, that is, of the Kuomintang.[92]

Stalin did not dote on his ally but believed, and believed with reason, that only the Kuomintang could complete the unification of China. So far, it ruled over half of the country, up to the Yangtse River; the whole northern half with the capital, Peking, still remained to be conquered. Who knew what resistance it might yet encounter? The warlords might very well rally and stop its advance or even defeat it if its army was now disrupted. And so it would be if the Communists tried to form separate units; the more successful their attempt, the more they would weaken the Kuomintang. Stalin would not take so grave a risk; "in China armed revolution [was] fighting armed counterrevolution," he explained to the plenum.[93] He was addressing himself less to T'an and to those for whom T'an had spoken than to a group of his own advisers, who inclined toward a similar viewpoint. These advisers (as we shall see presently) disagreed with his thesis that the progress of the Kuomintang armies was the same as "armed revolution." It was while rebuking them that he coined his phrase, unaware that many years later he would be able to dig it up and to have it quoted as prophecy. In 1949, Chinese Communism finally attained to power — exactly, it seemed, as Stalin had said: by means of armed revolution. Who remembered that what he had actually meant when using that phrase originally had been the army of Chiang Kai-shek, the army now cut to pieces? Not his hagiographers, of course, nor those of his foreign critics who, though abhorring him, accepted the myth of his foresight and of his omniscience.

CHAPTER V

A DEFEAT OUT OF VICTORY AND A DEVIL OUT OF THE MACHINE

Scattered quotations, strung together, composed Stalin's record of prophecy, tracing a unilinear past back from the accomplished present. Communism seemed to come out of this past unmindful of divergent alternatives, undivided by human cross-purposes, undeviating from self-fulfillment. The by-passed alternative, the defeated purpose, the unattained goal fell into forced oblivion or sank, under imprecations, into a hell of frustrated devilry. Stalin constantly repainted the past in order to find, in retrospect, the image he made of himself.

Such repainting continues under his successors, but with this important difference: no longer is one man made out the author of Communist victories everywhere. Now party leaders outside of Russia who have attained to power may share in the glory of having done, and of doing, the will of history.

It is true that they share in this glory only as it is apportioned by Moscow, and that the size of their share varies widely, according to their power and influence. It is also true that the strongest of them, the leader of Communist China, had to be granted a moderate share already in Stalin's lifetime. But while Stalin lived, he saw to it that the credit for Mao Tse-tung's victory went ultimately back to himself — himself as vicar of history.

That Mao had only been Stalin's pupil, though admittedly one of great talent, was easily proved with the help of judiciously chosen quotations. What was there to "Maoism," after all, but the dual manner of conquest which Stalin had once called "armed revolution" and "revolution in the village"? To a combination of these two Mao owed his ultimate victory — to the very strategy, it appeared, of which Stalin had spoken much earlier.

He had spoken of it at the Seventh Plenum of the Comintern Executive, and he had spoken of it in a context which we must now elucidate. For what he said at the Seventh Plenum provided ample quotations to those bent on proving that Mao carried out the long-range design of his master. Through one of those strange alliances which history delights in creating, the Stalinists and their fiercest enemies vied with each other in proving this.[1]

Much of what Stalin told the Plenum was intended as a rebuttal of views propounded by his own "experts," Mif, Petrov, and Rafes.* Mif had been commissioned by the plenum to draft its theses on China; but he did not know what Stalin wanted: his draft met severe disapproval. In the course of rejecting it, Stalin set forth a notion of "armed revolution" and of "revolution in the village" which conflicted with that of his experts.[2]

Mif and his colleagues would hardly admit that there *was* a revolution in China; the Northern Expedition, in any case, did not strike them as revolutionary. They denied that the Kuomintang generals differed in kind from the warlords: the struggle between them was one between cliques, not between social forces.

This viewpoint coincided with that of the Chinese Com-

* Pavel Mif was the guiding light of this trio; but we know little about him. Not even his true name: "Mif" — which is Russian for "myth" — was obviously a pseudonym. In spite of the criticism which Stalin heaped on him at the plenum, he did not fall into disfavor for many years to come. In 1927, he replaced Radek as rector of the Sun Yat-sen University; and in 1930, he was sent to China on important Comintern business.

munist leaders; in fact, there is reason to assume that it had been borrowed from them. The Chinese Communists had, as we saw, an instinct for making converts among those in the Soviet apparatus who were supposed to guide them.

Their own view of the Northern Expedition remained skeptical, if not hostile, in spite of the gains which they had made thanks to its rapid progress. In September, the party journal, *Hsiang-tao*, had restated their view on the subject in an article written by P'eng Shu-chih, the voice of the party leader. The Northern Expedition, according to P'eng, was not propelled by the masses; nor was the Kuomintang government a government of the people. It was merely the "special organ" of a cabal of generals, designed to serve their "personal ends," to help them expand their dominions.[3]

Now Mif said virtually the same in the draft that he had submitted: he did not consider the Northern Expedition a "growth of the Chinese revolution." It was merely a "struggle of Canton generals against Wu P'ei-fu and Sun Ch'uan-fang* . . . a fight for supremacy of one group of generals against another group of generals." [4]

Stalin knew at once that if this view were allowed to become legitimate, his gamble in China would appear futile or — even worse — ridiculous. What sense would it make to support Chiang Kai-shek against the feudal warlords if he was really one of them, if his aims were equally narrow? No, such misgivings had to be laid; Chiang stood for "armed revolution" and his enemies stood for the opposite: armed reaction on the defensive.

Having made his pronouncement on "armed revolution" to correct Mif's dangerous error, Stalin discussed "revolution in the village," also to rebuke his adviser. Mif had urged that

* A warlord of the Peiyang clique, who was then in control of Shanghai and the southeastern provinces.

the Chinese peasants be permitted to form their own soviets, and he had done so without insisting that urban workers should lead them. Though this spoke very well for his foresight, it did not recommend him to Stalin: he was guilty of "underrating the role and significance of the working class." It was entirely "out of the question to form soviets in the country and to leave out the industrial centers," as he had rashly suggested. A "radical agrarian policy" would naturally be required to promote — and, even more, to complete — the revolution in China. But only trained proletarian cadres could carry out such a policy; and so far there were too few of these to "permeate this ocean of peasantry." Hence the Chinese Communists would have to lean upon their Kuomintang ally — upon the government now at Wuhan — if they were to "reach" the peasants.[5]

Stalin himself counted ever more firmly on the government at Wuhan to act as his chosen instrument in the struggle for China. He had some reason to believe that this government could be trusted: it did represent a more radical trend than had ever prevailed in Canton. In fact, it soon came to represent the Kuomintang left wing exclusively — the faction that followed Wang Ching-wei, who had been forced into exile. Chiang Kai-shek parted company with this faction when, early in 1927, he established a government of his own at Nanch'ang in Kiangsi Province. The air at Wuhan seemed all the clearer on account of this rupture; Borodin, surrounded only by leftists, seemed all the more influential. Wang Ching-wei was returning from exile in Europe to take the helm at Wuhan; on the way, he stopped dutifully in Moscow to consult with the Comintern leaders. No wonder that Stalin looked fondly on Wuhan as a "revolutionary center" through which he could handle or, as he said, "reach" even the Chinese peasants.

No wonder — and yet how strange it is that all the cold-blooded realists to whom history-making is a sport deceive themselves almost romantically. Stalin was right: the Wuhan Government could effectively "reach" the peasants; but he forgot that the purpose of reaching them would be the collection of taxes. This lapse was serious, because Wuhan depended for its very survival on its ability to extract revenue from the surrounding countryside. The revenue that it was able to raise from taxes on commerce and industry was rapidly dwindling to a trickle: business in Wuhan was paralyzed. The river shipping that linked it to Shanghai had virtually come to a standstill; Chiang Kai-shek bestrode the Yangtse downstream and saw to it that Wuhan felt it. Rail traffic to Peking and other points north had also been interrupted; there was, after all, a state of war between Wuhan and the northern warlords. To make matters worse, the seizure, by a mob, of the British concession in Hankow had led to the closure of vital businesses owned and managed by foreigners.[6]

While Wuhan had thus lost sources of revenue, its outlays had steadily mounted because, to survive, it had to enlarge its military establishment. To meet its expenses, it had to rely increasingly on such taxes as it could collect in the province of Hunan, the most fertile in all of China. But already by the end of 1926, its revenue from that quarter barely exceeded one fourth of its outlay for military purposes only.[7]

The land tax would normally have yielded more, but those who paid it, the landlords, had become difficult to "reach" since their tenants had risen against them. Many of them had fled to the towns, while others maintained, not unjustly, that since they had lost their usual rent, they could not pay the usual taxes. Rent had been high: more than half of the crops; but out of it came the moneys that paid not only for the whims of the gentry but also for those of government. The peasants, by keeping all of their crops, threatened to ruin the government through which Stalin had only just proposed to administer their revolution.

Under the circumstances, it was inevitable that Wuhan should sooner or later take steps to restrain or even repress the turbulence in the countryside. The Chinese Communists would be compelled, as soon as they joined the government, to side with lawful authority against the law-breaking peasants.

True, by delaying, as they did, their entry into the government, they could escape this necessity at least for a few months longer. But they could not make a stand against Wuhan in favor of the peasants unless they were willing to risk a breach with their superiors in Moscow.

One of them demanded nevertheless that they should side with the peasants, openly and unequivocally, against those who were trying to curb them. The chief of the party's peasant department pleaded for unrestrained violence in a report — outwardly routine — on the peasant movement in Hunan. For the first time in his career, Mao Tse-tung, the official in question, put himself on record with a view that conflicted sharply with Moscow's.

Did Mao have the courage of his convictions or was he, perhaps, quite ignorant of the unorthodoxy, and hence of the dangers, hidden within his argument? We do not know but may venture the guess that he scarcely suspected how sharp a deviation from Moscow's path the course he proposed represented.

He submitted his report to the Central Committee in February 1927, after having spent roughly six weeks touring through Hunanese villages.[8] He had thus left Shanghai not very long — no longer than a fortnight — after the Seventh Plenum in Moscow had concluded its business. He could scarcely have seen, let alone studied, the plenum's theses on China in this brief interval before his departure into the distant interior.

But even if he had read the theses, he might well have assumed — by reading them from his own standpoint — that Moscow was no less eager than he to unleash the Chinese peasants. It certainly lent them verbal support, applauding them no less warmly than it applauded the government whose authority they were flouting. On whose side it stood in actual fact could not be easily gathered from oracular sayings which, like all of their kind, applied to every contingency.

Because of this catholicity of Moscow's pronouncements on China, even Mao's report appeared to fit in: superficially, it seemed orthodox. Hence it could be published in the Communist press without any critical comment: who, after all, was not in favor of unshackling the peasants? [9]

Moreover, it could be published because, though protesting against the measures that were being taken to curb the peasants, it put no blame at all on the party. Mao did not say — perhaps did not know — that the "erroneous decisions" which he believed should be "quickly corrected" were enforced with Communist backing.* When he wrote his report, it was still quite possible to be vague in this matter: the party had not yet entered the government, hence did not yet support it actively. Only later, when it had taken charge of the ministry of agriculture, did it quite openly do its bit toward suppressing the peasants.

By that time, Mao himself had changed front, having, it

* In October 1926, the Chinese Communists had received orders from Moscow — in fact, from the Politburo itself—not to "force" the agrarian revolution (Stalin, *Marxism and the National and Colonial Question*, p. 237). If, as Stalin has claimed (*ibid.*), this order was soon rescinded, Mao may have thought that the policy which it embodied had been abandoned for good. Subsequent events were to prove that this was not the case.

seems, discovered that he could not persist in his course and also advance in the party. Although his report had been well received, Mao was not long in perceiving that by acting upon it at this time he would have risked his career.

Not that he pursued a different end than was pursued by Stalin; the question of *means* was the only one over which they might have collided. The issue was one between revolution *for* the peasants, through government, and revolution *by* the peasants: Mao's contribution to Marxism. His novel view that the peasantry could take the place of the working class in the van of a "proletarian" movement had now been given expression. In fact, he was never again to state it with the boldness and frankness with which he stated it this first time, in his plea for the Hunanese peasants.

And this though the Chinese proletariat was then still far from defeated: in Shanghai, it was actually on the point of taking control of the city. Yet Mao was already of the opinion that as compared to the peasants, the urban workers were unimportant to the Chinese revolution. "If we allot ten points to the accomplishments of the democratic revolution," he wrote, "then . . . the urban dwellers and military units rate only three points, while the remaining seven points should go to the peasants. . . ." [10] Three points altogether for "urban dwellers" — not workers only but also much of the middle class — and for the "military units" as well: presumably the troops of the Kuomintang. Roughly one point for the proletarians who, in the opinion of Stalin, would quite "inevitably" take command of the revolution in China. Likewise, only a point or so for the army which, to Stalin, was the "most important factor" of all in freeing the Chinese masses.[11] Metaphoric as Mao's mathematics were, they revealed with mathematical clearness how sharply his view of the struggle in China differed from that of Stalin. They revealed more, in any case, than he cared to show to the public once he was in power and, for reasons of state, determined to give Stalin no umbrage. New editions of his report on the peasant movement in Hunan therefore omit the formula which conveyed its meaning too clearly.[12]

True, its meaning had not been clear to its original readers; but then it had not seemed very important when originally published. The data it cited attracted more interest than did its general message; and thus, like many another report, it was no sooner praised than buried. It caused no stir nor any revision of the party line then being followed; the Hunanese villagers remained for Stalin something less than the workers of Shanghai. He had no reason to give up hope for the Chinese proletariat; growing stronger, it would yet show its full-grown strength once the warlords had been defeated. Until then, the "most important factor" in the Chinese revolution remained the troops of the Kuomintang, the army of unification.

By now there were actually two such armies: Wuhan's, advancing northward, and Chiang Kai-shek's, advancing due east with Shanghai for its objective. The Kuomintang forces had been split when Chiang had broken with Wuhan and established a capital of his own down the Yangtse River at Nanch'ang. Borodin had tried to dissuade him from this and had thus forfeited his favor — perhaps the more quickly because Chiang knew a Russian who stood prepared to support him.[13] A common antipathy — few bonds are stronger — united Chiang and Voitinsky: they both bore a grudge against Borodin; they both wished him out of the country. Chiang would not forgive him for siding with Wuhan (he seldom forgave opposition); Voitinsky resented him because they were rivals by virtue of their positions. One the nominal chief of the Comintern mission, the other in actual charge of it:

one suspects that Moscow *meant* them to fight, and thus to control, each other.

It was not very long before Borodin gave his enemies an opportunity to lodge a complaint against him in Moscow and to demand his dismissal. When he heard of Chiang's plan to drive east on Shanghai, he again tried to dissuade him: Shanghai could wait; Chiang should drive North, thus concerting his effort with Wuhan's.[14] Borodin knew that the capture of Shanghai would give Chiang a tremendous advantage;* but Chiang knew it too and would not be talked out of the victory that awaited him.

Instead, he decided to put up no longer with Borodin's opposition; he wired Moscow and asked it to rid him of his unwanted adviser. Voitinsky seconded his request (if, indeed, he had not inspired it): should Shanghai remain under warlord rule because of Borodin's spitefulness? But Stalin would not recall Borodin; his emissary in China seemed useful to him as long as Wuhan seemed to repose its trust in him. Also, Borodin stood not alone in opposing the drive on Shanghai: the chief of the Soviet military mission, General Blücher,† stood by him. Not only this: the Chinese Communists, who had learned to distrust Voitinsky, now threw their support to Borodin, making his victory certain.[15]

Chiang took his defeat with very good grace; his quarrel, he told the public, had been with individual Russians, not with the Soviet Union.[16] He remained friends with the world revolution and with its organ, the Comintern; in fact, just now he

* He had no reason to hope that it would weaken Chiang or even "break his neck," as a group of dissident Comintern agents claimed in a "Letter from Shanghai" (see Appendix of Trotsky's *Problems of the Chinese Revolution*, p. 409). Borodin could be wrong, but he was never silly.

† While in China, Blücher went under the pseudonym of Galen. Even Blücher may have been a pseudonym.

was playing host to a group of Comintern visitors.* They were being conducted through his domain, where, going from banquet to banquet, they glimpsed signs of a terror that gave them no joy: it was not the *right* kind of terror. They talked to workers' and peasants' leaders who had barely escaped the firing squad; Chiang left no doubt that in *his* revolution the masses should remain quiet.[17]

It was easy to see this but hard to say it; the visiting Comintern mission did not report what it really saw; to do so would have been foolhardy. Criticism of Chiang Kai-shek, in Moscow's political climate, was almost sure to be made out as treason, as proof of Trotskyite sympathies. Those who liked their peace — and who liked their careers — therefore echoed the party line: while Chiang fought the warlords and the imperialists, he remained an indispensable ally.

He in turn found his ally if not indispensable, at the very least useful: as long as Moscow supported him, he could count on the Chinese Communists. While in Stalin's favor, he could be certain that they would continue to help him, to render him excellent "coolie service," however much they disliked it. He could be certain that they would help him in the battle for Shanghai; indeed, there might be no battle at all if they seized the city from inside.

Their power in Shanghai derived from their hold on the General Labor Union, which had soon recovered from its defeat in the May 30 Movement. Though outlawed since that time, it had gained new strength and launched strike after strike to test it; above all, it had laid up stores of arms to be equal to any occasion. At the approach of Kuomintang troops, in February 1927, the union proclaimed a general strike and mobilized its armed pickets. Chiang waited patiently by the

* The group consisted of Earl Browder, Jacques Doriot, Tom Mann, and Sydor Stoler.

gates while the workers inside gave battle to the troops of the Shanghai garrison, who would have resisted his entry. By the end of March, the workers had won; the city was in their possession; now the question arose: should they open its gates and surrender it to their "ally"?

The question had been posed earlier by the Communists' chief propagandist, who had answered it in the negative — pending a verdict from Moscow. To P'eng Shu-chih, an inveterate critic of the Kuomintang generals, it seemed only natural that Chiang and his cohort should be kept out of Shanghai.[18] Chiang had, after all, declared himself: he had announced in the papers that he would dissolve any trade-union found in possession of firearms.[19] Did Moscow know this? why did it cling to an image of Chiang the Liberator which most of its own observers in China felt to be false and dangerous? P'eng was disturbed; he had to find out; he had to convince the Russians that by postponing resistance to Chiang they would finally make it impossible. He traveled to Hankow to see Borodin, who turned out to be sympathetic; the case of the Chinese Communists would be referred to Moscow. But Moscow dismissed it out of hand; let Chiang enter Shanghai, it ordered; be sure to "avoid any clashes" with him; have the workers bury their weapons.[20]

Chiang entered the city unopposed; *he* had no cause to fear "clashes"; having the upper hand, why should he wait till he might no longer have it? By striking now he could strike decisively without any fear of the outcome; hence he struck at dawn on April 12 — not, one would think, unexpectedly.* Yet actually he effected surprise; the workers were in confusion; was he their enemy or their friend? Their leaders said one, then the other. He himself had to show just where he

* His troops had staged sporadic raids on Communist centers in Shanghai ever since early April.

stood, and show it he did in all honesty as his "revolutionary" troops closed in on the workers' pickets. Fighting ensued, but not for long; when it stopped, began the terror; the soldiers became executioners, riddling the ranks of the workers. They shot down Communists, real and suspect, as well as their friends and helpers; when they had done, there was not much left of China's proletarian vanguard.[21]

There was not much left of the Chinese revolution as planned and guided by Stalin; but would Stalin therefore abandon Chiang? He had always forgiven him everything. Chiang himself was determined to keep friends: why should his magnanimous ally, who had all but ignored the fracas in Canton, feel upset by the rumpus in Shanghai? He reassured him: now as then, his quarrel was not with Moscow: he was merely correcting its meddlesome agents and undisciplined pupils in China. He knew fully well that when Borodin and his henchmen caused any trouble, the blame was wholly and solely theirs — not, as some people thought, the Kremlin's.[22]

Chiang meant what he said; he had no intention of ending the Russian alliance; in fact, he would not give it up for lost even when it lay clearly in ruins. At the end of June, he made one more attempt to persuade the Soviet government that the shootings in Shanghai were surely no reason why it should cease to trust him.

A good occasion to deliver this message through diplomatic channels arose when the Soviet consul in Shanghai was ordered home to Moscow. One of Chiang's diplomats, C. C. Wu, bidding farewell to the consul, gave him a number of oral assurances to take back to his government. The purge of the Kuomintang had not been intended as a blow at the Soviets, nor did it signify any compromise with the imperialist enemy. With the Soviets, General Chiang desired to restore the "traditional" friendship; with the imperialists, there could only be war till he had expelled them from China. How could it be otherwise? Russia and China, Wu reminded the consul, occupied a "similar position in the family of nations." [23]

Stalin would have liked to agree;* but he could not pass in silence over the mass executions in Shanghai — and the nonsense they made of his prophecies. He had been fooled and now had to face the "I told you so's" of his critics; in reply, he could only say that he too had foreseen that Chiang would betray him. After all, he *had* said that the Chinese comrades would continue to be supported by "certain strata" of the bourgeoisie; other strata, of course, would desert them. His meaning — as he expounded it now — had been perfectly patent: Chiang belonged to one of the *other* strata, one of those which he had distrusted.[24]

Why, if such had indeed been his meaning, no one had understood him, why it had been thought that he meant the opposite, Stalin took care not to mention. And for good reason: he *had* meant the opposite; the journals which took their cue from him had always spoken of Chiang as a member of the most trustworthy "stratum." [25] Reports of his approaching defection had been dismissed disdainfully as baseless rumors spread by the imperialists to sow discord inside the Kuomintang.[26] Only a few days before April 12, the highest Bolshevik leaders had received an autographed portrait of Chiang, distributed by the Comintern. In its covering letter, the Comintern had asked the distinguished recipients (including a very indignant Trotsky!) to return their own autographed portraits.[27] Moreover, Stalin had just told a meeting of Muscovite

* And did agree to the extent of not breaking diplomatic relations with Chiang's government at Nanking. This forbearance seems to have disturbed some of the more purist Bolsheviks. In any case, Stalin's ally, Bukharin, made excuses for it in the *Pravda*. Diplomatic recognition of Chiang — he explained — did not imply approval of Chiang's regime; and the Soviet government, unlike the Comintern, simply *had* to deal with reactionaries. Eudin and North, *Soviet Russia and the East*, p. 376.

party workers that Chiang was not only tractable but even "submitting to discipline." He would be "squeezed out like a lemon" as long as he fought the warlords and then "flung away" without further ado into history's spacious garbage can.[28]

Stalin's figure of speech was not his own: nearly twenty years earlier, a left Bolshevik by the name of Lashevich had used the identical image. The original "lemons" had also been soldiers, professional army officers; but their resemblance to Stalin's lemon did not extend beyond this. Lashevich had spoken of officers who had served in the tsarist army and whom the Bolsheviks, in need of their skill, were drawing into their service. He had spoken of men who, while being used, could be effectively supervised and who, politically impotent, could be dismissed at pleasure.[29]

To these men Stalin compared Chiang Kai-shek, not directly but none the less clearly; his choice of a metaphor, hardly fortuitous, showed how he thought of his ally. He thought of him as an officer whose skill was temporarily needed: an expert without political weight; historically, a cipher. He knew that Chiang was truly devoted to the struggle against imperialism; why ask for more? His mission completed, he would be done away with.

He would be crushed in the machine of which Stalin held all the levers, crushed and ejected by the apparatus of international communism. The wheels of the Kuomintang meshed at the top with Comintern wheels in Moscow; down below, they would scarcely have turned at all but for the Communist "youngsters." Stalin felt safe; he knew his machine, knew how it ran in China; a part might occasionally wear out, but he stood ready with spare parts.

Also, he had vision while those who advised him — specialists — merely had knowledge: a General Blücher might warn against Chiang; he, the great Stalin, knew better. Blücher, it was true, saw much of Chiang; as his military adviser, he had more occasion to deal with him than any other Russian. But then this was doubtless one of the reasons why he had come to detest him: contact as frequent and close as theirs was bound to generate friction. It had been obvious for years that such friction existed: already in 1925, Blücher had shown vexation.* He had complained of Chiang's stubbornness and warned his superiors in Moscow that it might soon prove necessary to find another ally. "Other units" of the Kuomintang army — other Kuomintang generals — might prove to be more deserving than Chiang of aid and advice from Moscow.[30] A year later, in 1926, Blücher had become blunter: appraising Chiang's character for Moscow's benefit, he had almost become abusive.[31]

But even this bluntness had had no effect; Stalin had laid down his policy and followed it pertinaciously until April 12 upset it. The upset was a shock; but once it had happened, it could be explained "objectively"; a Marxist could find a host of reasons why it had, after all, been inevitable. Stalin adduced them one by one, suddenly eager to demonstrate that Chinese history ran its own course, whatever he did or did not do. He could not prevent the Chinese bourgeoisie from betraying the revolution; afraid for its property, it *had* to make peace with feudalism and imperialism. That stratum of it of which Chiang was the tool had now changed sides as expected; such was the meaning of April 12; any Marxist could see that.

In fact, no Marxist could *fail* to see it; the logic of class analysis pointed compellingly toward a view such as Stalin was

* Blücher succeeded, however, in concealing his feelings from Chiang. Thirty years later, Chiang fondly remembered him as an "outstanding Russian general as well as a reasonable man and a good friend." Chiang Kai-shek, *Soviet Russia in China*, p. 51.

taking. Of course, one could hold, as the Trotskyites did, that if only the Chinese Communists had been permitted to anticipate Chiang, the break would have been less bloody. But in explaining the *fait accompli* and Chiang's motives for turning traitor, Trotsky and Stalin were at one: after all, they read the same bible.[32]

In their simple world, made up of two camps, Chiang, having deserted one camp, could only have joined the other one: he was now on the side of the warlords. He had joined hands with Chang Tso-lin, *Pravda* informed its readers; the Northern Expedition had thus been abandoned by its former commander.[33] His reason seemed obvious: he needed money; and imperialism and its underlings, receiving him into their citadel, had made it available to him.

This was how a solid Marxist materialist had to explain Chiang's defection; but how seldom materialist images conform to material data! Chiang had not abandoned his drive to the north; before very long, even Moscow could not help admitting that, after all, he continued to fight the warlords.[34] And for that matter the imperialists too: it very soon became obvious that if they had opened their coffers to him he requited them ill for their kindness. Actually, there is no evidence apart from tendentious gossip that he received any money at all from foreign sources in Shanghai. Or else he would scarcely have felt so much need to squeeze money out of his compatriots, out of the Chinese businessmen to whom Moscow thought him subservient. He pressed them hard because they would not pay — because, contrary to Moscow's assumption, they balked at financing the operations of their reputed agent. Only by threatening them with jail and by carrying out his threat in a few prominent instances did he finally raise the full amount which he had asked them to furnish.[35]

Thus he assured himself of the means with which to continue the struggle not only against the northern warlords but also against his rivals. To these — the leftists ruling at Wuhan — his loss of the Soviets' favor had brought the commensurate advantage of enjoying it undivided. Their chief, Wang Ching-wei, was at last back home, fresh from consultations in Moscow; soon after returning, he had seen Ch'en Tu-hsiu; the result was a joint manifesto.[36] Though only a routine affirmation of two-party solidarity, the manifesto did make it clear that Wang had Stalin behind him.[37] But he could not fill the place which Chiang had occupied in Stalin's thinking: he could not be the champion of "armed revolution" because he was not a soldier. Being unable to take the field against the northern warlords, he needed a military *alter ego* to lead his armies for him. This he found in General T'ang Sheng-chih, an officer who had turned "leftist" in the sense that he had turned against Chiang in order to supplant him.

With Wang at the head of the Wuhan Government and T'ang in command of its armies, Stalin felt snugly reassured: he could go on with his program. The Chinese revolution remained the same even though Chiang had betrayed it; it was moving on through its present stage but had not yet passed to a higher one. As yet there was therefore no occasion to revise, let alone abandon, the program set forth by the Seventh Plenum in its theses on China. On the contrary, it was imperative to give full effect to the theses; they had not, up to now, been given effect with all the requisite vigor. The man who had drafted them, M. N. Roy, was therefore dispatched to China to inculcate the need for prompter compliance upon the Chinese comrades.

Arriving in Wuhan toward the middle of April, Roy found that the Chinese comrades knew even less about the theses than had been feared in Moscow. Of three representatives of the Central Committee whom he encountered at Wuhan, only one came out clearly for the theses; the other two scrupled and cavilled. Unfortunately, it was these two, not their more docile comrade, who spoke — as Roy himself noted soon — for most of the Central Committee.[38]

Roy had an idea: if he laid the theses before a party congress, the obstructionists would perforce let them pass: they could not risk open defiance. Accordingly, Roy approached Ch'en Tu-hsiu with the urgent suggestion that the Fifth Party Congress, the next one due, should be convoked immediately. Not easily trapped, Ch'en refused, but then gave in under pressure; he always submitted in the end: his loyalty was his weakness.[39] Thus he called his party comrades together for a national congress; it met in Hankow on April 28, giving Roy the desired forum.

Roy's calculation had been correct: the congress adopted the theses; but he knew (because even a stranger could feel it) that it doubted their wisdom. In its "prevailing opinion," he reported later, "their applicability to Chinese conditions yet remained to be proven." [40]

Its "prevailing opinion" was not merely that of Ch'en Tu-hsiu and his followers, as party historians were to maintain after Ch'en's removal from office. Li Li-san, for example, a rival of Ch'en's who aspired to his position, did not — to use his own delicate phrase — "understand the whole line of the Comintern." [41]

To understand the Comintern would not have been quite so difficult if both of its leading spokesmen in Hankow had taken the same position. As it was, Roy said this and Borodin that, each with an air of authority, so that the congress could only guess which one of them *did* speak for Stalin.

Over the principal issue before it — whether or not to support T'ang Sheng-chih, the new champion of "armed revolution" — two factions, one for Borodin, one for Roy, arose at the party congress. T'ang wished to commit all of Wuhan's forces to a resolute lunge toward Peking in order to take the capital before Chiang, his rival, could do so. Borodin spoke in favor of T'ang's plan, not to further the general's fortunes but for reasons entirely his own, which will be mentioned presently. Roy, on the other hand, disapproved: why encourage T'ang to push northward before the party had tightened its hold on Wuhan's existing dominions? In fact, it might lose such a hold as it had; if it did, a retreat toward Canton, to its original base in the south, might prove its only salvation. The argument gained ready adherents among southerners at the congress: Roy's firmest ally became T'an P'ing-shan, who spoke for the Cantonese delegates. But for all the support which he rallied behind him, Roy could not cope with his rival; Borodin, in alliance with Ch'en Tu-hsiu, remained in control of the congress.[42] Now there was only one way for Roy to win the case for his own side, and that was by quickly appealing it to his superiors in Moscow.

Thus Roy appealed — by telegram — and the verdict was not long in coming: a verdict like that of an oracle, contradictory and ambiguous. You are right, said the oracle, the Chinese Communists would do well to deepen their influence; but then they would also do well to widen it when opportunity offered. Such an opportunity was at hand; the Communists had only to seize it; they would be foolish not to move in behind Wuhan's advancing armies. Borodin was therefore as much in the right as Roy who argued against him; by siding with both, Moscow sided with none; success would decide the issue.[43]

Meanwhile, T'ang Sheng-chih did not, of course, wait for Communist approval to launch his offensive in the North, his attempt to push through to Peking. By the middle of May, his campaign had progressed to a point where it seemed to

Stalin that it was fairly sure to succeed and that, therefore, he could safely applaud it. So applaud it he did, giving reasons why, arguing — it seemed on the surface — exactly as Borodin had done at the party congress in Hankow. He pointed out, as had Borodin, that here was an opportunity to join hands with General Feng Yü-hsiang, who hovered about north of Wuhan. Feng had established himself in an area stretching through Honan northwestward; his troops had received their weapons from Russia; surely he would show himself grateful? Stalin as well as Borodin now looked to him for assistance; but each entertained a different notion of what sort of help he should furnish. Stalin expected him to lend support to the government at Wuhan, to bolster it up militarily once its army and his were in contact. Wuhan remained the central factor in Stalin's whole calculation: from there, he believed, the Communist power would be established in China.

Borodin, on the other hand, had his doubts; for instance, he knew already that "nothing could force the Left Kuomintang to promote agrarian revolution." [44] He placed little confidence in T'ang Sheng-chih; in fact, he had come to regard him as a potential Chiang Kai-shek, who might soon turn against the Communists. These would therefore do well to move out of his reach into a safer area: to the northwest, where Feng Yü-hsiang seemed ready to give them shelter.[45] Their leader had agreed to his plan: at the Fifth Congress of the party, Ch'en Tu-hsiu had presented it in the form of a *Northwestern theory*. He spoke of it theoretically, because, had he been more explicit, he would have provoked an immediate clash with T'ang Sheng-chih and his backers. Yet it is precisely in this form — as his, or Borodin's, theory — that the proposal to move northwest is now of the greatest interest. We quote a summary of it by Mif, written, it should be noted, to prove that Borodin had been wrong, that he had misled the party.

The theory assumed, according to Mif, that "the revolution could not develop in Canton nor in Shanghai nor in Tientsin nor in Hankow nor in any of those regions where industry was most developed, because there imperialism and the Chinese bourgeoisie held the stronger positions." Hence "the revolution was to retire to the northwest provinces where the influence of imperialism was weaker and where the revolution could more easily concentrate its forces for a later attack on the imperialist strongholds." [46]

Mif goes on to relate that the party congress "decisively rejected" this argument: an act of defiance that would not have been possible unless higher quarters had called for it. The party could not have said 'no' to its leader and to his Russian adviser unless Moscow had previously passed down the word that 'no' was the proper answer. Moscow was probably well aware that the unfortunate theory was the work of its agent, Borodin, afflicted with a bout of defeatism. Even if Borodin had tried to hush up his authorship of it, there were comrades about him who would have been quick to establish his responsibility. Roy and Voitinsky, both of them eager to see him recalled to Russia, would scarcely have failed to inform his superiors of his defeatist affliction. Indeed, one can hardly account for the speed with which his plan was rejected except by assuming that one of his rivals had wired a protest to Moscow. The fate of his plan is scarcely surprising: after all, it disparaged the chances of having a nicely orthodox, a *workers'* revolution in China. Stalin still thought that these chances were good; in fact, he felt so very sure of it that he could afford to be tolerant of those who maintained the opposite. Neither Borodin nor Ch'en Tu-hsiu had as yet forfeited his favor; they could stay at their posts as long as they obeyed — and as long as they suffered no failure.[47] Only when they had irremediably failed — failed to make Wuhan come up to Stalin's great expectations — were they dismissed and pilloried for "opportunist" errors. The Northwestern theory was one of these; for to stray from the path of the doctrine and to bog down on the alternate path is the essence of "opportunism." Accordingly, Borodin's theory only ceased to be "opportunist" when it was applied, with full success, almost a decade later.

The Long March which the Chinese Communists undertook in the mid-1930's was a hegira to the northwest, a flight to escape destruction. It enabled them to sit down and wait, as Borodin had envisaged, for a chance to swoop down on their enemy whenever he seemed the weakest. Their flight to the hills and its final reward, their triumphal return to the cities, fulfilled the prophecy which Borodin had made in the face of catastrophe.

But all fulfillment in human affairs is fulfillment *with a difference;* and the present example goes to show that this difference can be crucial. We must recall that the theory by which Borodin proved his foresight was only a vehicle for his plan to join hands with his favorite warlord. To him, the northwest meant Feng Yü-hsiang; and Feng, it turned out soon after, was just as slippery an ally as Chiang Kai-shek and the others. Thus Borodin's vision came to him in the train of a speculation which, by itself, proved totally false — and which might have proven disastrous.

True enough, he *had* to seek armed protection from one general or another since, at the time, there was no such thing as a Chinese Communist army. In this lay the crucial difference between his own position and that of the men who inherited — and successfully solved — his problem. By the time the party moved to the northwest, it had its separate army; or else, it could not have moved very far — except, as before, in theory.

The fatal weakness of Borodin's plan as originally put forward was therefore the same kind of false assumption as that which Stalin was making. Like Stalin, he trusted in his ability to manipulate a Kuomintang general and to accomplish, by dint of it, nothing short of "armed revolution." True, "armed revolution" had proven its value in the Northern Expedition; but its value to the Chinese Communist Party was rapidly dwindling to nothing. The Kuomintang generals behaved less and less like "old jades" pulling Stalin's wagon; the wagon, they knew, would roll heavily over their family property. Most officers in the Kuomintang army came from the landed gentry; they would therefore have liked a world revolution without unrest in the countryside. Stalin tried to oblige, since for the time being they continued to serve his purpose; thus he ended by virtually taking their side against that of the turbulent peasants. Their landed property and that of their kinsmen came under his protection: the Chinese Communists declared it exempt from their program of confiscation. This was a big exemption indeed; for the greater number of landlords living in Kuomintang territory had a kinsman in Kuomintang uniform. Wherever their land had been taken away by their indiscriminate tenants, its seizure had therefore been illegal, even under Communist statutes. True enough, indiscriminate expropriation of the entire gentry continued to be preached at party assemblies as a "basic [Communist] principle." Thus the Fifth Party Congress upheld the principle with intransigeant rhetoric, while at the same time it killed a proposal to uphold it in practice. In fact, this proposal (which set out in detail how the land was to be reapportioned) did not even reach the floor of the congress, being left to die in committee.[48]

To its author, this might have seemed like a betrayal since, when it came to principle, he had, after all, been far more consistent than those who had overruled him. As it was, Mao Tse-tung, the author of the untimely proposal, understood very well that in case of conflict, policy comes before principle. In fact, he resigned himself with such ease to the limitations of principle that in no time at all he was lending support to the policy which he had criticized.

He became chairman of an organization whose openly stated purpose was to give the party better control of its followers in the countryside. The All-China Peasants' League had been formed in May 1927 out of the existing peasant unions or, to be exact, *on top* of them. The task of the league, as defined by the party, was to afford protection to the army officers' families whose "welfare" was being threatened. There were a "few peasants" who frightened these families by trespassing on their property; they would have to be stopped from disturbing the peace in the camp of the revolution.[49] (These few would be hailed at other times as the almighty masses: in Communist usage, even arithmetic follows the twists of the party line.)

Considering, then, what kind of task Mao Tse-tung had agreed to accomplish, it is not surprising what kind of name he earned among some of his comrades. It is not surprising that M. N. Roy, after listening to his informants, concluded that Mao belonged to the right wing — the *extreme* right wing — of the party.[50] For the time being, Mao had indeed made his peace with the "opportunists," so that it remained for humbler folk to plead the cause of the peasants.

The young men of the Chinese Communist Youth Corps who had started the rural upheaval saw no good reason why it should be stopped and why they, of all people, should stop it. They annoyed their seniors by demanding to know, with the terrible logic of children, how the party could preach agrarian revolution and cooperate in its suppression. The party leaders explained and explained, but the subtlety of their argument was lost on the young idealists, who could well afford to be adamant. The "youngsters" were in a sense the stronger, what with their hold on the peasants and what with their hold on the *party itself* almost everywhere in the countryside.[51]

Party branches in villages and in the smaller market towns were commonly former Youth Corps units that had been graded upward. Their composition had seldom changed: the pioneers of the Youth Corps had simply continued at their posts as functionaries of the party.[52] In most such cases, their deepest loyalty still belonged to the Youth Corps; hence they declined, like the Corps itself, to make peace with the landed gentry.

How could humble functionaries down at the bottom of a Communist party — normally puppets of those at the top — decline to obey their superiors? They could never have blocked the execution of a policy handed down to them unless the usual chains of command had been loosened or even broken. This is precisely what had occurred: the Chinese Communist Party, expanding rapidly at the base, had all but lost its cohesion.

The precipitate rush into every area freed by the Kuomintang army had thrown the forces of revolution into creative chaos. Wherever the "youngsters" had set up command posts — here in a school, there in the peace of a temple — they had naturally paid very little attention to tables of organization. Kuomintang or Communist, party or Youth Corps, Youth Corps or peasant union: what did it matter which was which: they all had a cause in common. The common tasks that they faced in the village blurred the distinctions between them; here they became, not in name but in fact, a single organization.

The loser in this was the Kuomintang, which the Communists threatened to truncate by taking hold of it "from below" and cutting it off from its leaders. But their preponderance at the base — the very success of their "youngsters" in asserting local autonomy — wrought havoc with *all* party discipline. At the summit, in Wuhan, *all* party leaders, including the clever Communists, felt the ground receding under their feet: their followers no longer followed them.

The Chinese Communist Party machine — designed, like all of its counterparts, to function as an integrate whole — was actually falling to pieces. Ch'en Tu-hsiu, who should have been master of it, admitted in open assembly that he was rapidly losing control of its constituent units. Regional branches of the party were supplanting its Central Committee; there would soon be only "provincial parties," each following its own counsel. The warning was meant for guilty ears: Ch'en sounded it from the rostrum of the National Party Congress in Hankow, before many provincial delegates.[53] Did he exaggerate the drift into chaos in order to frighten his listeners? A report by Voitinsky leads one to think that he did *not* exaggerate. It seems, on the contrary (if Voitinsky is right), that he dared not admit to the congress how deeply the poison of localism had eaten into the party. Even the "provincial parties" themselves no longer hung together: their own local branches — Voitinsky reported — were often "completely autonomous." [54]

Autonomous and — he might have added — therefore in a position to go their own way when those higher up turned suddenly against the peasants. Those at the summit of the party looked on the rural turmoil with all the horror and helplessness of the sorcerer's apprentice. Ch'ü Ch'iu-pai, the successor of Mao Tse-tung as head of the peasants' department, made futile attempts to calm the emotions which Mao had whipped up so effectively.[55] The minister of agriculture, T'an P'ing-shan — Ch'ü's counterpart in the government — found himself equally impotent in his ministerial dignity. One month after being sworn into office, he asked for a leave of absence, having failed to put the peasants "on the right track," as he said in his public apology.[56]

The task of putting the peasants right had been tackled much more aggressively by the hounded landowners' loyal kin in the officers' corps of the army (nine tenths of the corps came from Hunan Province, the scene of the greatest violence and the "Prussia" of China, as Mao Tse-tung, himself a "Prussian," has boasted). On May 21, the Ch'angsha garrison — Ch'angsha is Hunan's capital — had "cleaned up" the city with that passion for purity to which Chiang Kai-shek owed his power. The provincial committee of the Communist Party somehow slipped through the dragnet; but its simple followers somehow got caught, perishing by the thousands. In the surrounding countryside, the peasants still wielded power; but they were like troops without officers: no match for even a garrison.[57]

The Ch'angsha coup caught the Communists in a familiar dilemma: should they obey the Comintern or the dictates of their situation? Their Politburo held an emergency meeting to decide one way or the other, and their leader seized eagerly upon the chance to restate his inveterate prejudice. "Break with the Kuomintang," Ch'en proposed more insistently than ever — and more audaciously; for in effect he proposed a showdown with Moscow. Moscow's representative, Borodin, understood this immediately; "I quite agree with you," he declared, "but Moscow will never permit it." Everyone present felt the same and therefore felt apathetic; only a spokesman for the Youth Corps, Jen Pi-shih, came to Ch'en's assistance. A void opened up, a shiftless void marked by uneasy silence; at last, Chou En-lai, always the diplomatist, jumped in with a happy formula. A break with the Kuomintang, he observed, would not help the workers and peasants; but the "military movement" — the campaign in the north — would surely "suffer great setbacks." On this all agreed: a verbal solution of an insoluble problem seemed better than no solution at all — better than sitting in silence.[58]

Or was there still some ground for hope that a *true* solution, a settlement by more than words, might in the end prove feasible? Might Stalin's confidence in Wuhan still prove to be justified, and Wuhan more reliable than its provincial satraps? Kuomintang headquarters in Wuhan seemed loyal to the Communists; at least, it spared no friendly gesture to convey that notion. It had appointed a commission to go down to Ch'angsha and settle all "misunderstandings" in that troubled city. It had instructed the commander of the Ch'angsha garrison to return confiscated weapons to their former owners.[59] Pending the outcome of these moves, any use of violence — unpromising in any case — seemed totally gratuitous.

At least it seemed gratuitous to higher party leaders who could look down from a distance on the scene of trouble. Local leaders of the party in the Ch'angsha area took more emotional a view of the recent "incident." They would strike back, retake the city, save the revolution; they had already all the men they needed for this mission. A force of several thousands — survivors of the "incident" combined with local peasantry — stood ready for the counterthrust.

This force had just begun to move when orders came to halt it: there would be no attack on Ch'angsha, either now or later. A Politburo member, Li Wei-han, passing through the area, had vetoed the proposed attack the moment that he heard of it.[60] This was entirely in keeping with the party's policy of doing nothing to provoke a rupture with the

Kuomintang. The party leaders at the top had yielded to the Russians: again they leaned, though knowing better, on their friends at Wuhan. They had instructed their adherents in the Ch'angsha area—those who had managed to survive—to "avoid further friction." [61] The Ch'angsha garrison commander was naturally glad of this: having to fear not even friction, he could do what suited him.

He therefore felt no need at all to accept mediation by the untrustworthy commission coming down from Wuhan. Its chairman was T'an P'ing-shan, a Communist stalwart; was *this* the man to decide who should rule at Ch'angsha? Certainly not; when the commission reached the Ch'angsha city wall, it was turned back under threat of being sent to prison.[62]

To gain admittance to the city would obviously require an army somewhere at one's back to underline one's argument. Themselves unwilling to risk battle, the Communist Party chiefs looked for a "leftist" general to fight out their quarrel. The commander in chief of Wuhan's forces had voiced his indignation at the unauthorized behavior of his Ch'angsha garrison. General T'ang, some people said, was actually a Communist: he served the party all the better by serving it in secret. The party leaders knew that T'ang was nowhere on their roster; but some of them fondly believed that he was a sympathizer. Ts'ai Ho-shen trusted him the most; and Ts'ai's intuition had proven to be excellent in a previous crisis.* Hence he had very little trouble persuading the Politburo that T'ang Sheng-chih was the man to break the Ch'angsha deadlock.[63] A formal appeal to T'ang (through the Wuhan Government) asked for a punitive campaign against the Ch'angsha army clique.[64] T'ang for his part stood quite prepared to go down to Ch'angsha, but only to investigate, not to mete out punishment. He did go to investigate and pres-

* See Chapter III.

ently concluded that all the shooting in the city had been just and proper. The garrison had started it merely to defend itself — to protect soldiers' families against extremist trespasses.[65]

What had caused T'ang to change his mind? * Perhaps some information that he collected on the scene? One feels inclined to doubt it. It rather seems that he knew *before* he left for Ch'angsha what kind of verdict to hand down after due enquiry. Still, why this sudden turnabout, at whatever juncture? A very simple explanation immediately suggests itself.

Moscow had recently decided that the time was ripe now to seize control of Wuhan's army — making T'ang a puppet. A plenum of the Comintern's Executive Committee — its eighth, held at the end of May — had openly proclaimed this. A resolution of the plenum made it clear to everyone, including T'ang and his like, how Moscow meant to deal with them. There was to be a thorough purge of any army "elements" still hostile to the revolution — or rather to the Comintern. New units under new commanders would replace these "elements" — elite units raised and trained directly by the Communists.[66]

These units would *not* go to form a separate Red army, since any separatist notion remained taboo in Moscow. Stalin expressly reminded a group of Chinese students that he had every intention of keeping Wuhan's friendship. This went for its army too: why should he try to split it as long as there was any chance of dominating all of it? [67]

The Comintern Executive had shown at its last plenum

* He reversed himself again in 1949 to rejoin the side of the Communists. His reward was the post of vice-chairman in the Hunan Provincial Government.

how to achieve this domination — but only in bare outline. Its emissaries down in Wuhan needed more instructions before they could even attempt to carry out its program. Stalin now sent them such instructions in a lengthy wire which they received on June 1, 1927. To form the army's new elite corps, 20,000 party men and 50,000 followers were to be recruited. A military tribunal under a puppet president was to indict — and to convict — "reactionary" officers. All "contact with Chiang Kai-shek" would be severely punished, as would be the use of soldiers to put down the "people." Stalin admitted that this purge might prove to be quite difficult; but what was the alternative? He saw none whatever.[68]

As usual, he put his trust in his apparatus: it would dispose of his opponents, in Wuhan as in Moscow. It would dispose of Chinese generals as of domestic Trotskyites: Wuhan and Moscow came to blend in his wishful thinking. But — *pace* Trotsky — Stalin's thinking as an *apparatchik* did not in any way preclude his thinking as a Marxist. He still continued to believe that most of Wuhan's generals would gladly let him steal their power if he spared their property. As long as no one touched their land or that of their families, they would allow the Communists to "reform" the army.

It therefore remained necessary to restrain the peasants — to stop all rural violence, though not official praise of it. According to the Comintern, the struggle of the peasants had now become the "inner content" of the revolution.[69] Those simple enough to believe that an inner content should also take some outer form learned soon to think more subtly. Such simpletons had been found high up in the Comintern, obstructing the smooth operation of its highest organ. The Comintern Executive had found at its last plenum that they controlled its subcommittee framing China policy. Two out of three committee members — Treint and Togliatti* — demanded a sustained offensive in the Chinese countryside. Bukharin, the remaining member, then in league with Stalin, attempted to convince these two that they were in error. But they refused to be persuaded till he called in Stalin to carry on the argument — and, of course, to finish it.[70]

Stalin was firmly resolved to stop the Chinese peasants from perpetrating more "excesses" that might wreck his program. There would be further incidents such as that at Ch'angsha unless the Chinese peasant leaders learned to curb their followers. The All-China Peasants' League would have to teach the peasants not to be so emotional about their revolution. The league instead of the army would have to stop excesses, said Stalin's latest telegram to his men at Wuhan.

Now the league's chairman, Mao Tse-tung, had the unusual duty of putting down an insurrection he himself had started. To stop excesses, he had written only four months earlier, was to engage in sabotage of the revolution.[71] Had he since then come to think (because Stalin thought so) that what had seemed like sabotage would *save* the revolution? He was quite capable, no doubt, of turning such a somersault; but had he done so in this case? It seems hardly probable.

Mao must have seen no less clearly than did those around him that Stalin's policy in China would presently defeat itself. The leading Communists in Wuhan, Chinese and Russian, had for some time been losing faith in the Kremlin's wisdom. Forebodings of catastrophe had prompted the proposal to pull the party out of Wuhan and escape northwestward. Now that such thoughts of escape had been ruled unorthodox, the only hope for survival lay in skilled procrastinating. But Stalin's

* Albert Treint, a French Communist, fell into disgrace shortly afterward. Palmiro Togliatti, then known as Ercoli, proved more adept in survival. To this day, he leads the Communist Party of Italy.

wire of June 1st demanded just the opposite: the forcing of a test of strength with the Wuhan Government.

When Borodin received the wire, he convoked a meeting between the Chinese party chiefs and the Soviet mission. The new instructions, he explained, were obviously ludicrous; but one could hardly tear them up: one could only shelve them. The party dignitaries present nodded their approval and went to tell their fellow leaders what had been decided. All of the Central Committee, hurriedly assembled, voted to give them its support: they *could* not follow orders.[72] A diplomatic reply was dispatched to Moscow: orders received; shall obey as soon as we can do so. . . .[73]

Actually this meant never, since the party leaders knew just as well as Borodin that they had reached an impasse. Not only with regard to Wuhan: even their own followers had, as we saw, found ways and means to ignore their orders. Would those of them who were peasants agree to stop their fellows? Would those of them who were workers agree to join the army? To form an army in an army was obviously nonsense; in uniform one must obey or be prepared for mutiny. Which general would be cowed by pressure from his soldiers? Which one of them would sit in judgment over fellow generals? The notion that the Wuhan army could be purged swimmingly of anyone resisting Moscow bordered on the fatuous. All of the army's high command was made up of traitors if "contact with Chiang Kai-shek" constituted treason. Such contact had just been resumed out of sheer necessity: Wuhan had found that without Chiang it could progress no further.

Its army advancing northward had (unbeknownst to Stalin when he sent off his telegram) suffered disastrous losses. The main body of its troops had been advancing slowly, at steadily increasing cost, along the P'ing-han railway. Near Chumatien it had met the main force of the enemy, Manchurians under the command of Manchuria's "crown prince." * A battle royal ensued; the Wuhanites won it; but victory cost them dear: they could move no farther. Between the exhausted victor and the retreating loser a vacuum opened up: an inviting vacuum. Into this vacuum moved a circumspect neutral: the canny warlord Feng Yü-hsiang, pro-Christian and pro-Soviet.

Feng had sat out the great battle waiting for its outcome; the victor would be his ally; he would share the victory. But now he saw that the victor was only a bare skeleton, a skeleton in need of props to avoid collapsing. No one had won at Chumatien except the nonparticipants: first, Feng himself; then, Chiang Kai-shek, also adept in waiting. The two came presently to terms and served Wuhan notice that if it broke with its allies, it might join their partnership. If only it cast out the Reds, there would again be unity among the heirs of Sun Yat-sen, the true-blue Chinese patriots. How could the Wuhanites say no? Pass up a chance of compromise with rivals who, if they used force, could easily defeat them?

In fact, even if the odds had been less against it, Wuhan would still have seized this chance to avoid more bloodshed. How could it have engaged in war against external rivals while being threatened from within by its so-called allies? The threat had now become immediate; Stalin wanted action; the Eighth Plenum's China theses mirrored his impatience. True, at this plenum he had ousted all of his opponents — Trotsky and those who followed him — from every party office. But Stalin was not content simply to prove them powerless; he also wished to prove them wrong — sinfully in error. The more they ventured any doubts about his

* This was Chang Hsüeh-liang, the son of the warlord Chang Tso-lin. The "young marshal" gained world-wide attention at the end of 1936, when he kidnapped Chiang Kai-shek at Hsian.

China policy, the more determined he became to succeed at Wuhan. Now was the time to subjugate their brethren in the Kuomintang, had been the Eighth Plenum's message to the Chinese Communists.

It had of course also told them how they were to do this: *reorganize the Kuomintang into a federation.* Replace its Bolshevik structure by a more elastic one in which whole groups and associations would be leagued together. Make workers and artisans, peasants and soldiers — each through their union, guild, or "club" — affiliate with the Kuomintang.[74] In short, remould the Kuomintang on a well-known model: that of the British Labour Party, Lenin's intended victim.[75]

Memories of 1920! Memories of Lenin, so hallowed as to sanctify even the master's blunders! Lenin had falsely believed that the Labour Party, thanks to its federate structure, would prove an easy victim. Now Stalin assumed just as falsely that the balky Kuomintang, if only given the same structure, would also prove more tractable. His error derived straight from Lenin's, only it was grosser: he thought that his intended victims would *help* him to dispose of them. Lenin had hoped that the leaders of the Labour Party would prove too weak or too smug to put up resistance. In fact, he must have thought them fools, for he boasted openly: we shall provide them the support a rope gives to a hanged man.[76] If this seems dubious realism, let us consider Stalin's: he counted on his good allies to order their own hanging.

He counted on his friends at Wuhan not merely to tolerate but to promote the preparations for their own destruction. Unless they helped actively, it would be impossible to give their party a new structure and to purge their army. The Soviet mission in Wuhan had to win their patronage for Stalin's program of reform — or else ignore the program. As we have seen, Borodin reached a quick decision: it would be futile to ask Wuhan kindly to commit suicide.

However, there was one member of the Soviet mission who disagreed with Borodin: orders remained orders. The Indian Roy had joined the mission only a few weeks earlier, but, having been sent out by Stalin, was an important newcomer. As such, he viewed the local scene, of which he was quite ignorant, with the superior eye of one who knows the needs of policy. Though Borodin and Ch'en Tu-hsiu also knew the policy, they could not bring themselves to share Roy's purist sense of discipline. In fact, they had drawn together, forgotten their old quarrels, because of their common dislike of Roy's overzealousness.[77]

Thus, when they found it necessary to shelve Stalin's orders, Roy sallied forth on his own to do his master's bidding. He took the wire of June 1, which listed Stalin's wishes, and showed it to Wang Ching-wei, the key figure at Wuhan. For this he has been called a fool, a blunderer, and whatnot;[78] but given Stalin's policy, could he have acted otherwise? Wang would have had to be informed sooner or later just how it was now proposed to push him further leftward. Even if he had never seen the text of Stalin's wire, he would have learned before long what Stalin meant to do to him. Roy forced the pace of events by his indiscretion; but he did not change their direction, he did not change history.

Nor did he even succeed in proving himself loyal and his superior, Borodin, guilty of obstructionism. Instead, the mighty machine in which they both functioned ground out the justice of machines: Roy had broken discipline. Since Borodin was still the chief of the Soviet mission, Roy, having tried to circumvent him, had been insubordinate.* Within a

* We have it on Roy's own authority that Borodin remained to the end in supreme command of the mission. *Revolution and Counterrevolution in China*, p. 552 (note).

month, ungrateful Moscow dismissed its faithful servant on the advice of Borodin, who had informed against him.[79]

Meanwhile, Wang Ching-wei, Stalin's prospective puppet, slowly prepared his reply to the puppet-master. Wang acted with the circumspection required by his weakness and with the boldness necessary to save his independence. Before he could break with supporters who aimed at undermining him, he had to make peace with rivals who offered to support him. After his interview with Roy, he went off to Chengchow (a railway junction north of Wuhan), where Feng Yü-hsiang awaited him. Repeating what he had learned of Stalin's intentions, he signified his readiness to expel the Communists. Feng was already doing so: in his own *Kuominchün* or "National People's Army," a Red hunt was in progress. Seeing that Wuhan was prepared to follow his example, the "Christian general" agreed to serve it as a mediator. He undertook to mediate between it and Nanking, to reconcile Wang with Chiang, to reunite the Kuomintang.* Before the month of June was over, Feng had kept his promise: the Kuomintang stood united—at least against the Communists.[80]

Or we should say: *almost* united; for in Wang's own circle, the rapprochement he proposed had met with opposition. Immediately after returning from his trip to Chengchow, he had convoked the presidium of the left-wing Kuomintang. It met at night at his house, met ten nights in succession, gradually dropping its objections, yielding to his eloquence. Finally a majority voted to support him, accepting the distasteful prospect of a move to Nanking. Only two presidium members—both well-known public figures—resisted his persuasive-

* Chiang had moved his capital to Nanking at the end of March. It is possible that Wang Ching-wei set out for Chengchow hoping that Feng Yü-hsiang might agree to make a common stand against Chiang (Fischer, *The Soviets in World Affairs*, II, 669; Isaacs, *The Tragedy of the Chinese Revolution*, pp. 255–56). If he did have such hopes, they must have collapsed as soon as he met his new friend.

ness and cast their votes against him. His flashy foreign minister, Eugene Ch'en from Trinidad, and Madame Sun, the founder's widow, proved to be intransigent. Both went to Moscow soon after; hence one may justly wonder whether they ceased to follow Wang to keep faith with Stalin. Especially Madame Sun arouses this suspicion, having since then cast in her lot with the Chinese Communists.* But as one probes the circumstances of her break with Wuhan, it does not seem that she — or Ch'en — acted as tools of Moscow.

Rather it seems that she and Ch'en went into opposition because they thought that Chiang Kai-shek could still be "eliminated." They thought that Wuhan could and should continue to oppose him instead of striking any bargain such as Wang thought necessary. Whether or not to oust the Communists was not the real issue; the question was *when* to do it — now or sometime later. Wang wanted to expel them now as part of his bargain; no, said the two, better wait: they are your lesser enemies. First finish Chiang; then, if you wish, get rid of the Communists: this, it appears, was the gist of their entire argument.[81]

They were outvoted, as we saw, by Wang Ching-wei's supporters — those who believed that the break should be made immediately. But even this majority did not want an *open* break; it issued no manifesto; why affront the Russians? Far better to throw out the Reds without any shouting; that way there was at least a chance of keeping Moscow's friendship. Any open violence attending the expulsion could easily be disavowed as the work of "rightists."

The ruse may seem quite transparent, but Stalin did not see through it; in fact, he took it to be proof of how very right

* She now holds an exalted, though hardly influential, position in Peking: that of a vice-chairman of the Standing Committee of the National People's Congress. There are thirteen such vice-chairmen.

he was. Now that the Kuomintang right wing had stepped up its terror, the need to support the left seemed all the more pressing. Until the Wuhan Government had coped with this menace, it needed *genuine* support — not that of the killing kind. The planned assault from within upon its independence would therefore have to be postponed until a little later. It sounds absurd, but it is true: once Wuhan had defied him, Stalin became the more determined to retain its friendship.

Even as late as July 7, the organ of the Comintern ran a report by Bukharin full of praise for Wuhan. It was a "well-known fact," it said, that under Wuhan's patronage the Chinese Communists were free to expand their influence.[82] The Chinese Communist leaders must have been surprised at this: as far as they themselves could see, their influence was waning. They had just recently dissolved their armed workers' pickets — their chief reliance in the cities — to conciliate Wuhan. This had been perfectly consistent with their latest orders not to antagonize Wuhan while it fought the "rightists" (as we have seen, the "rightist" menace was Wuhan's own invention; but since Stalin believed in it, his faithfuls could not say so). Moreover, the Communists had on their own initiative walked out of the government, in which they had been puppets. The party's two ministers had gone on "leave of absence"; and everybody knew, of course, that they would *remain* on leave. Their quick withdrawal, in disgust, from the Wuhan Government had not been authorized by Moscow nor by the Soviet mission.[83]

But even Moscow, given time, had to see eventually that it was Wuhan itself which posed the "rightist" menace. The "well-known fact" of Wuhan's friendship had to be retracted within a week after Bukharin had solemnly established it. The Comintern Executive resolved that its ally had suddenly, perfidiously gone over to its enemies.[84] The next day, on July 15, the Kuomintang Executive announced with due formality the ouster of the Communists. But Wang Ching-wei was just as eager as Chiang had been before him to draw a line between foreign and domestic Communists. Wuhan denied any intent to cut its ties with Moscow; in fact, it publicly announced that it wished to strengthen them. High-ranking Kuomintang leftists were to go to Moscow to lay a new and firmer basis for continued friendship.[85]

Stalin himself was very eager to keep friends with Wuhan, but not with "traitor" Wang Ching-wei: *he* had to be toppled. The Communists would have to show to Wang's misguided followers that they had also been betrayed by their unworthy leader. Given the proper agitation among the party "masses," the Kuomintang would purge itself of its present leadership. Next time it held a party congress, its rank and file would see to it that Wang Ching-wei and his fellows would be removed from office.[86]

Or such was now Stalin's hope — a strangely *naive* hope in one who erred rather seldom on the side of innocence. Such hope is usually born of hopeless situations; and Stalin's was no exception: he had reached an impasse. He was more handicapped than ever by the Opposition, which lunged at him frontally now that he had cornered it. For the first time in its campaign against his China policy, the Opposition had abandoned all equivocation. It had abandoned if's and but's and all the subtle formulae by which Zinoviev had intended to leave room for compromise. It had decided late in June that subtlety was useless and now spoke out in very plain and very telling language. It now demanded a clean break with Wuhan and the Kuomintang — or, since the break was a fact, its simple recognition.[87] How then could Stalin recognize the facts that confronted him? The logic of his high position forced him to ignore them. He felt compelled to pretend (to himself and others) that Wuhan minus Wang Ching-wei remained a faithful ally. He had to cling to the belief that the left-wing Kuomintang, helped by the masses behind it, would eject the "traitor." Therefore he would not countenance any suggestion to force the issue with Wang by recourse to violence. As soon as he received reports that the Chinese Communists were planning to stage a putsch, he interposed his veto. He sent them a telegram reminding them sharply that violence at this time would be futile heroism. Factually he was right: they had no chance of winning; but then what else were they to do? Simply await the firing squad? In any case, it was too late; when they received the wire (it was July 28), they all but stood committed. Some of the foremost party leaders had slipped out of Wuhan to organize an armed revolt at Nanch'ang, in Kiangsi. By now, these leaders — Chou En-lai, T'an P'ing-shan and others — had set a date, August 1, for the insurrection.

In three days they would stage a putsch that Stalin had forbidden unless their comrades in Wuhan could stop them in the meantime. The small group around Ch'en Tu-hsiu that had remained at headquarters hastily sent an emissary — Chang Kuo-t'ao — to Nanch'ang. Though Chang set out immediately, he did not reach Nanch'ang until July 31, the day before the rising. By then, it would have been hard to call off the venture, even if those about to launch it had agreed to do so. Actually they were far from willing to give up their project; the putsch, they said, would take place, whatever Stalin thought of it.[88]

Accordingly, on August 1, the troops around Nanch'ang — *all troops of the Kuomintang** — rose up in rebellion. Most of

* Hence there is irony in the fact that Communist China commemorates the foundation of its People's Liberation Army on the anniversary of the Nanch'ang revolt.

these troops scarcely suspected that they were rebelling; they simply carried out orders, unconcerned with politics.* They may have numbered anywhere from three to fifteen thousand: the lower estimate is Isaacs', the higher one is Moscow's.[89] Their generals were Yeh T'ing, the party's leading soldier, and an ex-bandit named Ho Lung, who had joined it recently† (Yeh had been a brigadier in Chiang Kai-shek's army: the only Red officer above battalion level).[90] It was no accident, of course, that Communist officers — Yeh, Ho, and many lesser names — had clustered at Nanch'ang. The reason was that there, in Kiangsi, stood the Fourth Army Corps — the one in which the Communists enjoyed the greatest latitude. The general in command of this congenial army was Chang Fa-k'uei, a Cantonese and a stalwart "leftist." [91]

However, "leftist" though he was, Chang did not help the rebels; in fact, he lost no time at all in moving in against them. This though they had considerately named him to high office, co-opting him, without his knowledge, into their shadow government. Their "revolutionary committee" included five such members elected behind their backs and serving *in absentia*. Thus Madame Sun and Eugene Ch'en had also been co-opted though both were on their way to Russia when the rebellion started. Perhaps they sided inwardly with the Nanch'ang rebels; any connexion beyond this was purely fictitious. But from the rebels' point of view, it was very sensible — in fact, almost necessary — to maintain this fiction. It helped them to preserve a semblance of unity with Wuhan — the shade, so dear to Stalin's heart, of the defunct alliance. This

* Their chief concern was to go home. Most of them were Cantonese; hence they hailed their leaders' decision, after the fall of Nanch'ang, to make a dash to the south. (Information obtained from Mr. Chang Kuo-t'ao.)

† Yeh died in an airplane crash in 1946. For Ho, Nanch'ang was the beginning of a brilliant career: he is now a vice-premier in the Peking government.

way they were less vulnerable to possible charges that they had separatist designs — as in fact they did have.

The party leaders in Wuhan also found it useful to pretend blandly that the rising was leftist, not Communist. One faction of the Kuomintang, they explained officially, had risen up against the other: they themselves were neutral.[92] By playing neutral, they could hope to escape Stalin's censure for having failed to prevent the unwanted rising. Since he had only just warned them not to resort to violence, some such excuse, however lame, seemed absolutely necessary. Actually it turned out that no excuse was needed; Stalin had meanwhile changed his mind; he gave the coup his blessings! Once the insurgents had struck, he found their prospects hopeful, exaggerating their strength as he had once belittled it. He had opposed violence, but now the sheer thrill of it, even as felt from a distance, overcame his caution. Thus Marx had warned the Paris workers against using violence and then, when they ignored his warning, hailed the Paris Commune.

However, quite unlike the Commune, the episode at Nanch'ang was only a *coup de main*, not a profound upheaval. Within a week, Chang Fa-k'uei had expelled the rebels, who fled (it was their first "long march") toward the Southern coast towns. When Stalin's press proudly announced the seizure of Nanch'ang, the rebels had already lost it to Chang Fa-k'uei's "Ironsides." [93]

The loss of Nanch'ang was to Stalin only a routine loss, a setback after other setbacks, all — he thought — temporary. He went on hailing the rebels as though their flight southward were yet another forward plunge of the Chinese working class. But even he could not maintain that the successive fiascos which had preceded that at Nanch'ang had been a chain of victories. It could no longer be denied that someone had blundered; yet it could never be admitted that Stalin was that someone. The Comintern solved the problem by rigging up a devil who could be blamed, in retrospect, for the godhead's errors.

The chosen culprit — the arch-sinner whose inveterate sinfulness had somehow escaped previous notice — was the Chinese party chief. It now emerged that Ch'en Tu-hsiu had been an opportunist, an advocate of least resistance, of convenient compromise. He had perverted his instructions to support the Kuomintang by not only supporting it but yielding to its tyranny. He and his minions had wound up by blocking Moscow's efforts, and those of their own followers, to resist the Kuomintang.[94]

Such were the charges against Ch'en — astonishing charges! The facts had not been distorted: they had been inverted. Ch'en had disliked Moscow's orders — that much was quite accurate; but on what grounds? As we saw, on grounds of Marxist principle. He had upheld principle against Moscow's lack of it — had erred by being *not enough* of an opportunist. If he had strayed from the doctrine, he had only done so under direct and constant pressure from the top in Moscow. Only under Russian pressure, and often under protest, had he consented to submit to Kuomintang supremacy. When torn between his own beliefs and loyalty to Moscow, he had invariably wound up by remaining loyal. And what was now his reward? He stood accused of treachery, of disobedience to orders, of systematic sabotage. To save the myth of Stalin's foresight and scientific judgment, the myth of his own villainy had had to be created. Only this myth could explain how an unerring policy, based on unshakable assumptions, had ended in disaster.

Among Ch'en's mentors, Borodin was the most deeply implicated; but he was not attacked till later and never quite so strongly.[95] Already early in July, he had wired Stalin that he was ready to give up: he had lost his usefulness. He had received friendly hints from the Wuhan Government that if he wished to go on leave, no one would detain him.* Under the circumstances, Stalin also saw no reason why he should not set out for home as soon as that was feasible.†

Now Borodin was free to go as soon as his successor, who had already been appointed, could take his place in Wuhan. He did not have to wait long: before the month was over, the new chief of the Soviet mission had assumed his duties. His name was V. Lominadze; like Stalin, he was Georgian; in fact, the rumor had sprung up that he was Stalin's nephew.[96] He had — this much at least was true — won his "uncle's" confidence by siding with the Stalinists in factional quarrels.

As a reward, he had received his present assignment to save the Chinese revolution — and Stalin's heavy stake in it. The Chinese Communist Party had to be beheaded and at the same time revived: a difficult enterprise. First, Lominadze had to probe the feelings of its leaders: who would be willing to assist in the operation? He could be sure that Ch'en Tu-hsiu had aroused some jealousies, that some of Ch'en's closest comrades would gladly help to oust him. Who were they and which one of them had enough authority to engineer Ch'en's dismissal from within the party? Moscow had given Lominadze very loose instructions; he was to get rid of Ch'en; *how* was his own business. He was completely new to China; yet no one had told him whom to install as Ch'en's successor, which one of all these strangers. Had there been many candidates competing for his favor, the choice would have been difficult and completely arbitrary. But it turned out that in fact there was no competition and therefore no necessity to

* By this time, Madame Sun was the only Kuomintang leader whom he still saw regularly. (Information obtained from Mr. Chang Kuo-t'ao.)

† The Russians had to take the difficult inland route home, since Shanghai was in the hands of Chiang Kai-shek, who might have put them in jail.

do any choosing. Only one candidate emerged; the other leaders canvassed refused to step to the helm while the ship was foundering.

Nor was this all: they even balked at taking the *first* step, at heaping blame on Ch'en Tu-hsiu to exculpate Moscow. Some of them went to the length of telling Lominadze that at least part of the blame should go to his employers. This, he replied, was not advice given by good comrades; it sounded more like an outburst of petty-bourgeois nationalism. They understood: the coming purge of the "opportunists" might well be widened to include some "nationalist" offenders. Cowed, they fell back without as yet giving in completely; they still believed it possible to achieve a compromise. On their behalf, Chang Kuo-t'ao suggested a solution: the party's Central Committee would take the blame collectively. No leader would be singled out for vicarious punishment; no one, not even Ch'en Tu-hsiu, would be made out a villain. It was a generous proposal; but how could Lominadze, with clear instructions to oust Ch'en, possibly agree to it? He turned it down out of hand; the Central Committee could, if it wished, share the blame; but Ch'en would still get most of it. There was no need for Lominadze to argue any further: he knew that he would have his way, since he had found a henchman.[97]

That henchman was Ch'ü Ch'iu-pai; he was the party leader who had, alone among his comrades, supported Lominadze. He was also the only party leader who spoke fluent Russian: out of his twenty-eight years, he had spent four in Moscow.[98] Hence it was only natural that some of Moscow's emissaries had sought him out like a guide-post in a foreign landscape.* He had

* There was only one Soviet emissary — Voitinsky — in whose eyes he had found no favor. His relations with Borodin were all the more cordial. In fact, a word of recommendation from Borodin may have helped him win the confidence of Lominadze. (Information obtained from Mr. Chang Kuo-t'ao.)

become their favorite, so much so that his comrades had nicknamed him sardonically the "communist comprador." However, his willingness to serve Lominadze did not derive entirely from loyalty to Moscow. He had his own private reason, different from Moscow's, for aiming, as Moscow did, at Ch'en Tu-hsiu's dismissal.

That reason was his rivalry with a party comrade who overshadowed him by virtue of being Ch'en's protégé. For *expertise* in matters Russian and in Marxist theory, Ch'en always turned to P'eng Shu-chih, his chief of propaganda. Ch'ü therefore felt himself slighted and unjustly thwarted: *he* was the party's leading expert on Russia and on Marxism. True, P'eng had been in Russia too; he too knew the language; but he was only competent where Ch'ü was pre-eminent.[99] Their ranks were technically the same: they were both department heads; but what a difference between them in actual influence! P'eng was the second in command of the entire party — not merely Ch'en's favorite but his *alter ego*. If Ch'en were ousted — that was clear — P'eng's special position would automatically collapse: he too would fall from power.[100]

This is exactly what happened and what Ch'ü was aiming at when he agreed to see to it that Ch'en would be ousted. His task was made much easier by the severe disruption, verging on outright dissolution, of the party hierarchy. Since mid-July, when Wang Ching-wei had formally expelled them, his former Communist comrades found life in Wuhan dangerous. Frequent descents by the police on their meeting-places, and even on their private homes, had forced them into hiding. Some had already fled the town either to make for Nanch'ang or else to sit out the crisis in the surrounding countryside. Ch'en Tu-hsiu had sought refuge in a village somewhere near Wuhan; there he was relatively safe but, of course, isolated.

To all intents and purposes, he had laid down his office before the Central Committee formally deposed him.

Instead of "Central Committee" one should say "rump committee"; for it was only a rump that voted to dismiss him. On August 7 there met, at Ch'ü Ch'iu-pai's instance, a small group of party leaders and minor party functionaries. Three or at most five of them Central Committeemen; the others — about ten in number — simply served as stand-in's.[101] Since this assembly clearly lacked the necessary quorum, all of its votes and resolutions were actually invalid.[102] The chroniclers of the party disregard this detail to represent the occasion as a moral turning-point. Groveling opportunism was at last abandoned, Marxist morality remembered and fully reasserted. However, to an eyewitness, the party's resurrection looked somewhat forced and somewhat staged: in fact, somewhat farcical. To its recording secretary, the August 7 Conference seemed very much like theatre: a Ch'ü Ch'iu-pai production. Ch'ü was the author and producer of this one-act comedy apart from being its director and its leading actor.[103]

The conference was held in Hankow; but those who took part in it pretended after disbanding that they had met in Kiukiang. This was to cover their tracks, to fool their pursuers; whether it fooled them or not, it did fool historians.* The delegates, true and bogus, met in a parlor — the living room of a house belonging to a sympathizer. The August heat made them dull; they struggled against drowsiness; all windows had to be kept shut to discourage eavesdropping. The heat was Ch'ü Ch'iu-pai's ally; no one in his audience felt in a

* So much so that many of them name Kiukiang as the site of the conference. Others name Lushan, a mountain resort nearby. What added to the confusion is that Borodin and retinue passed through Kiukiang at the end of July to spend several days in Lushan before leaving the country.

mood to object or even to raise questions. He read a lengthy resolution sketching out the future, then — to account for the past — a circular letter. Both documents had been written by him and Lominadze; both won immediate approval from everyone present. To read them off had taken Ch'ü exactly two hours; then there was just the show of hands, and everything was over.[104]

The resolution pointed out what was already obvious: all party work from this time forward had to be clandestine. Only by going underground could the party save itself, and only by violence could it stage a comeback. But violence had to be used with cool deliberation; spontaneous outbursts here and there would only be wasteful. Nothing was said in this connection about the coup at Nanch'ang, a guarded silence being wiser till one knew the outcome.[105]

The conference might well have kept a similar silence about the late *entente cordiale* with the left-wing Kuomintang. Instead, it had to lend support to Stalin's kind of realism and treat the ghost of the alliance as a living person. It simply had to ignore the ouster of the Communists and speak as though July 15 had somehow never happened. The Kuomintang, it announced, would yet be reorganized — reorganized and, by that means, reduced to submission.[106]

The open letter to the party which the conference rubberstamped exposed the "opportunist" errors of the party leadership.[107] Ch'en Tu-hsiu escaped outright denunciation (only once was he even mentioned): this may have been a concession to those who had defended him. (Vilification takes time, like sanctification: Ch'en's name had to be painted grey before it could be blackened). The only other party leader mentioned in the letter was T'an P'ing-shan, who had tried in vain to "correct" the peasants. T'an had stood so much in the limelight as minister of agriculture that he made an ideal target for retrospective slander.* Mao Tse-tung, who had also had a hand in curbing the peasants, did not have to be blamed for it: he had been less conspicuous. Moreover, up to recently, he had roused them to rebellion; and now the party was returning to the use of violence.

In fact, it now had so much use for men of his experience that he was given a seat in the new Politburo.[108] This was a caretaker body hastily appointed to guide the party for six months, till its next full congress.† Both Ch'en Tu-hsiu and T'an P'ing-shan had naturally been excluded; otherwise the new leadership looked much like the old one.[109] All of the "new" party leaders from Ch'ü Ch'iu-pai downward had held responsible posts before August 7. All of them had contributed in this or that capacity to making "opportunism" an effective policy.[110] Hence their indictment of the past was basically a confession: a strange case of Dr. Jekyll bringing Hyde to justice.

As yet untouched by this indictment was the massive Russian whose guilt (if failure was a crime) almost equalled Stalin's. While his tutees tried to outlive the lesson he had taught them, the luckless Michael Borodin was trekking back to Russia.‡ He was an embittered man, embittered by failure and by the knowledge — gained late — of having been hoodwinked. To an American writer who had joined his retinue,

* Though T'an's conduct in office had allegedly been "shameful," no one prevented him from taking a leading part in the Nanch'ang rebellion. His Cantonese origin fitted him well for this part, since most of the rebel troops were Cantonese. When they dashed south, he became, informally at least, their principal party commissar.

† Actually its next congress — the sixth — did not convene until almost a year later, in July 1928.

‡ There he was relegated to the obscurity of minor administrative and editorial posts. He died in 1953.

he gave a sad summary of what he had learned in China. "When the next Chinese general comes to Moscow and shouts 'Hail to the World Revolution,' " he warned, "better send at once for the G.P.U. All that any of them want is rifles." [111]

CHAPTER VI

AFTERMATH AND RETROSPECT

The defeat of the Chinese revolution, being a defeat for Stalin, compelled him to vindicate his China policy not only as a policy but also as a correct application of Marxist-Leninist tenets. Why had the "science" of revolution failed to produce the expected — and often predicted — results? Because Ch'en Tu-hsiu had "betrayed" it was the eventual answer; but until Ch'en could be dismissed, a different answer was needed. Until August 7, it was thus given out not that Ch'en had misled the party but that the party itself was at fault, being still too untrained to be orthodox.

Already in early June, the chairman of the Comintern, Bukharin, had sounded the theme that the Chinese Communists were not "100% Bolsheviki." He considered them immature because, unlike their Russian comrades, they had never "absorbed the whole Marxist experience of the West European Social Democratic movement." [1] We may doubt that Stalin saw the matter in the same light, but he did arrive at exactly the same conclusion. He found it "ridiculous to suppose that the Chinese Communist Party could be transformed into a real Bolshevik party overnight." [2]

Trotsky and the Opposition agreed with Stalin on this: the fiasco in China could only be due to deviations from the true doctrine. But in their view, it was Stalin himself who had perverted the doctrine and who had thus brought about the defeat of the Chinese revolution. The theoretical roots of this argument have already been analyzed in Chapter I, so that our only present concern is with its practical aspect. Let us see how Trotsky proposed to save China — or rather how, looking backward, he thought that China might have been saved if he had sat in the Kremlin.

To be sure, Trotsky never said point-blank that the Chinese revolution would have been certain to succeed if he himself had guided it. But he did ascribe the debacle in China almost wholly to Stalin's errors, thus implying that he, in Stalin's place, might well have avoided it. The Chinese Communists had, after all, come to grief by joining the Kuomintang, by forming a bloc which he, for his part, had opposed "from the very beginning." He had opposed it consistently from 1923 onward — or so he maintained in a private letter written seven years later.[3] But elsewhere he has frankly admitted that the bloc was at first quite useful; hence one may wonder how firm a stand he had really taken against it.

By 1926, in any event, Trotsky had reached the conclusion that at one time it had been "perfectly correct" to form the bloc with the Kuomintang.[4] It had been correct (he later explained) as long as the Chinese Communists lacked really wide and solid support among the urban workers. Only after they had gained such support through the May 30 Movement did their membership in the Kuomintang lose its original usefulness.[5] That was in mid-1925; and indeed, from what Trotsky tells us, it seems that he did at this point demand their immediate withdrawal.[6] However, in mid-1926, when this move might have seemed still more urgent, Trotsky not only failed to demand but perhaps even voted against it.

Here we must revert to our account of how, in March of that year, the Soviet leaders failed to react to Chiang Kai-shek's coup in Canton. It will be remembered that soon after the coup, the Politburo's Committee on China issued a report which simply ignored the whole unpleasant occurrence. No particulars need to be repeated here except for the very striking one that over this session of the committee presided none other than Trotsky.

It is quite possible that the committee missed the new trend in Canton because its intelligence from that city was tardy and insufficient. But when the entire Politburo met approximately two months later, it must have been fairly well informed about Chiang Kai-shek's intentions. He had clearly defined them on May 15, when the Kuomintang, at his instigation, laid formal restraints — not to say, fetters — on its Communist members. Yet the Politburo, undeterred, resolved with complete unanimity not to pull out of the two-party bloc because of the new "adjustment." Trotsky, still a Politburo member, presumably voted with it, unless — and this seems rather unlikely — he failed to attend this session.*

As a matter of fact, he himself has admitted that during the period in question he no longer took an open stand in favor of leaving the Kuomintang. He had retreated because, to keep the Opposition united, he was forced to compromise with allies who disagreed with his viewpoint. Half-hearted Oppositionists like Zinoviev and Radek shied away from provoking a showdown with Stalin by demanding a showdown in China. Hence the Opposition never demanded an outright break with the Kuomintang until the actual break was at hand, in June 1927.[7]

At least this is Trotsky's own explanation of why he had not been bolder; and it is one that we can accept as long as we supplement it. Undoubtedly, Trotsky did make concessions to his more cautious allies; but what he conceded was still, at the time, of minor importance to him.

The whole China question, we have reason to think, engaged little of Trotsky's attention until early in March 1927,

* Had he been absent, Zinoviev, to whom we owe a detailed account of the session, would most probably have mentioned that fact.

when his interest in it grew suddenly. That this interest could not have been great before is demonstrated by a letter which he wrote to Radek on March 4 to clarify his position. The ignorance which pervades this letter would be difficult to explain in anyone of his high intelligence who had given thought to the subject.

In what year should the Chinese Communists have withdrawn from the Kuomintang? Trotsky admits that he himself is still debating the question. "Already in 1923," is one of his tentative answers; or in '24 or '25, but certainly not any later.[8] The last years of the Chinese revolution, he explains, are not very clear in his memory; and this by itself is not at all strange in a statesman of his versatility. Still, if China had ever held his attention for more than a fleeting moment, would he have forgotten in what year the Communists entered the Kuomintang? How could they have *left* it in 1923, the very year when in reality all but a very few of them were only about to enter it? *

Also, had Trotsky paid much attention to the Chinese revolution, he would not have been quite so ignorant about the Chinese Communists. As it was, he wrote in his letter to Radek that even to call them Communists might no longer be legitimate: they seemed to have sold their birthright. Was it not likely that they had absorbed so much of the Kuomintang spirit that they would not even *want* to regain their original independence? If this was the case (and he feared that it was), then the revolution in China could only be saved by founding a new, a genuine Bolshevik party. This new party would establish itself "not only outside the Kuomintang but also outside the existing 'Communist' Party of China."[9]

Apparently Trotsky had forgotten, in so far as he previously

* Only four Communists — Ch'en Tu-hsiu, Li Ta-chao, Ts'ai Ho-shen, and Chang T'ai-lei — had joined the Kuomintang as early as 1922.

knew, how often the Chinese comrades had balked at being tied to the Kuomintang. But within a month (by the end of March) he saw their position more clearly; for in the interval he had begun to pay serious attention to China. So much so, in fact, that on March 22 he wrote in his private journal that the crisis in China worried him more than anything happening elsewhere.[10]

This crisis had not arrived overnight but had been building up slowly ever since the split between Chiang Kai-shek and the left Kuomintang at Wuhan. For over a month, Chiang had conducted open, though undeclared, warfare against the workers' and peasants' unions and their Communist leaders. However, not until March 31 did Trotsky sound his first warning (or at least the first one to be recorded) of a military coup in China. Even then, he made only the oblique remark that "fears of a Chinese Bonaparte" were "apparently rather strong" among Chinese revolutionaries.[11] This was not long (a mere twelve days) before Chiang staged his coup in Shanghai; hence Trotsky did not even have the time to vent his misgivings in public. An article by which he had meant to do so never saw publication, but stood him in good stead later on, supporting his claims to foresight.[12] By then, it was easy to forget that his foresight had only been short-range and that, for a prophet, he had been slow to point to imminent danger.

Once Chiang Kai-shek's victory was complete, Trotsky wrote that the time to prevent it had been in mid-1926, at the start of the Northern Expedition. Soviets should have been formed at that time both inside the Kuomintang army and among the people along its path who had risen up to help it. Trotsky believed that in this way the Communists could have seized power "if not in all of China at once, in a very sizable part of it."[13] How they could have wrested it from Chiang and his generals without halting the northern campaign or even causing its total defeat, he never stooped to elaborate. To him the soviet meant much the same as the party machine did to Stalin: a political instrument in which he had faith, because he had used it successfully.

But neither in Russia nor anywhere else had soviets ever succeeded in winning control of a body of troops while also keeping it fighting. Only in times of disastrous defeat, of mutinous disaffection, had soviets ever come to the fore as alternate centers of power. In China, the army of Chiang Kai-shek was far from defeated or mutinous: the upheavals which its progress set off did not affect its own discipline. Things would have been different, Trotsky thought, if only there had been soviets; then soldiers and workers, soldiers and peasants could have combined their forces. Army officers trying to stop this would have been shot by the soviets: it was as simple and easy as that — or could have been with the right leadership.[14]

That the officers might have struck the first blow, as they actually did a year later, Trotsky preferred to overlook in the interest of his argument. Yet even supposing that he was right, that soviets could have seized power, why had he neglected to call for them at the critical moment? If he had, the records would certainly show it, since no thrust at Stalin's policy failed to evoke the strongest response from Stalinist platforms and journals. He himself claims only that the Opposition called for soviets in China "at the beginning of 1926," which means: *before* Chiang's campaign had started.[15] It therefore appears that the Opposition called for soviets "at the beginning" and then, to preserve its own unity, adopted a more cautious platform. The Trotskyites probably yielded to pressure from their ally, Zinoviev, whose following made up roughly one half of the whole Opposition.[16] How unwilling they were to lose this support is shown by their long acquiescence in a common platform that stopped warily short of demanding a break with the Kuomintang.

Only the year after, on the eve of Chiang's coup, was Trotsky finally able to revive his demand for Chinese soviets with the full consent of Zinoviev.[17] The imminence of a crisis in China — and of a defeat for Stalin — had apparently stiffened Zinoviev's back and driven him closer to Trotsky. But not the whole way: he still insisted just as firmly as ever that the Chinese Communists could and should remain members of the Kuomintang.[18] Trotsky, ostensibly of the same mind, expressed his actual feelings — his mounting impatience with the two-party bloc — in his personal notes and letters. There he made it equally clear, however, that after leaving the Kuomintang, the Communists should remain its allies and cooperate closely with it.

Not with the old Kuomintang, to be sure, but with one that had been remoulded — "purged" and "hardened" were Trotsky's words — under pressure from the masses. To build up such pressure and to apply it would be the task of the soviets, in which the two parties would find a link replacing their present connection. It would thus become possible to "work hand in hand with a *revolutionary* Kuomintang" while also keeping a "vigilant eye" on this untrustworthy ally. It was "nonsense, nonsense, nonsense" to assert that the advent of soviets would cause an immediate and total break between the two allied parties.[19]

How little Trotsky was inclined to favor such a rupture becomes apparent as we read some of his memoranda.* Here is an excerpt:

"The Communists cannot, of course, relinquish their sup-

* In these, he clearly distinguished between his own position and Zinoviev's; hence there can be no doubt that the passages quoted above express his true opinion.

port of the National Government and of the National Army. Nor does it seem that they can give up their participation in the National Government." [20]

The government to which Trotsky refers is the left government at Wuhan; the date of his comment March 22, 1927. The inclusion of Communist ministers in that ill-fated government thus had his approval, or passive consent, when originally resolved upon. Not until later did he condemn this "experiment with ministerialism" as a perversion, at Stalin's hands, of basic Bolshevik principles.[21] By then, the failure of the "experiment" had opened his eyes to its unorthodox features, which had somehow escaped him as long as it seemed that its outcome might be successful. Thus the basic Bolshevik principle that failure is a deviation was no less natural to him than to his hated rival.

Also, though quick to pounce upon Stalin's defeats in China, Trotsky was slow, as Stalin was, to grasp their impact fully. Like Stalin, he clung to the hope that, for all their reverses, the Chinese Communists might yet emerge the final victors. When they lost Shanghai in mid-April, he maintained, like Stalin, that though their loss was grave indeed, it was by no means fatal. They could retrieve it, he believed, sometime "in the near future," if only Stalin changed his mind and let them set up soviets.[22] Even in summer and in autumn, when fiasco followed fiasco, Trotsky still thought that victory might lie around the corner. A "rising wave" of revolution, he noted in September, might be approaching and, with it, a chance to capture power.[23] Just at this time, Communist troops—the troops that had seized Nanch'ang and, after losing it, dashed south—fought for the port of Swatow. They lost it too: no wave arose to rush in to their rescue, although the signs of its approach had seemed so clear in Moscow. Hence Trotsky soon revised his judgment (and, in addition, history): the putsch at Nanch'ang — he said now — had always been opposed by him. He had predicted its collapse already very early: at the Eighth Plenum of the Comintern's Executive Committee.[24] That was in May — about six weeks before the mere idea of staging the unlucky putsch occurred to its participants! Uncanny foresight or, more likely, canny self-deception: Trotsky himself no doubt believed in his prophetic powers.

One can see why: even Stalin seemed to pay them tribute, adopting all of his proposals after first denouncing them. Stalin discovered before long that China needed soviets and slowly worked his way around to saying so in public. First he announced in late July: "The slogan of soviets is correct now," then waited for about two months before he called for action.[25] By then, the Chinese Communists had all but lost the cities; only in Canton had they kept a fairly solid foothold. The prospect of a Canton soviet now caught Stalin's fancy; here the unhappy trend in China might at last reverse itself. He needed good news from that quarter after all the bad ones; he wanted to report a triumph to his party comrades. They were to meet in mid-December for their Fifteenth Congress; if Canton could be seized by then, he would reap in the glory.[26]

The Canton Communists themselves, when learning of the honor for which they had been singled out, attempted to decline it. They wired Moscow that they saw no chance at all of winning; why risk the lives of many workers (and their own) for nothing? More wires were sent back and forth in a long-distance argument; at last the Cantonese gave in under relentless pressure.[27] Thus came about the reckless putsch known as the Canton Commune: three days of bloody soviet rule (December 11–13), then bloodier reprisals. The net achievement: Canton lost, its party branches shattered, with not even as many left as had been saved in Shanghai.[28]

Under the circumstances, Trotsky found it not too difficult to demonstrate the utter folly of the Canton Commune. Ever since Stalin had begun to call for Chinese soviets, Trotsky himself no longer did: he now thought Stalin reckless. Yet if Stalin had taken his advice on how to capture Shanghai, would the result have differed much from that obtained in Canton? Would soviets, hastily set up in March or even April, have stayed the hand of Chiang Kai-shek, as Trotsky thought they might have? Is it not far more probable that Trotsky, if in power, would have lost out to Chiang Kai-shek still sooner than did Stalin?

Some would say: no, how could he have; he would never, like Stalin, have forced the Chinese Communists to truckle to the General. They would scarcely have been so powerless at the decisive juncture if they had not been tied to Chiang as members of the Kuomintang. Trotsky would soon have cut this tie, restored their independence — the independence they had lost as a result of Hangchow. Lost? An objection comes to mind: they had not truly lost it, since even in the Kuomintang they functioned as a unit. Most of the Kuomintang with the exception of its leading organs had, as we saw, become in fact a Communist appendage. This proved to be embarrassing after the final rupture: how was this tightly knit alliance to be disentangled? Many local party units fell into confusion: which party was it that was theirs? from which should they take orders? Even in 1928, such units still existed: in name, part of the Kuomintang; in outlook, vaguely Communist.[29]

Among the reasons why the Kuomintang prevailed over the Communists, the pressure of its discipline seems therefore unimportant. Though technically as centralized as its Russian model, the Kuomintang had not achieved nearly as tight a discipline. Trotsky, believing that it had, therefore overrated the strength of its internal curbs as used against the Communists. His notions of the latent power that the caged-in Communists would manifest once released were equally inflated. In short, he made more of the fact of their dual status — regarding it *in vacuo* — than its importance warranted.[30]

But if this status by itself had not enchained the Communists, what of the crippling self-restraint that Stalin had imposed on them? He had compelled them, as we know, to obey the Kuomintang, to give it proper "coolie service" while it fought the warlords. However, it should be recalled that in May 1927, seeing the warlords in retreat, he had changed his tactics. He had presented his ally, the government at Wuhan, with what amounted in effect to an ultimatum. Surrender to the Communists, he had warned implicitly, or else risk being overthrown by a mass upheaval. Reconstitute the Kuomintang so that we can rule it or else face our greater numbers in an open battle. Wuhan, he fancied, would surrender rather than risk battle: even its army seemed no match for the surging masses.

A gross miscalculation this; but was Trotsky's formula for bringing Wuhan to its knees so radically different? Trotsky had also hoped to win simply by force of numbers, by facing Wuhan with the threat of popular upheavals. He, too, had thought that Wuhan, cowed, would permit the Communists to "purge" and "harden" it at will: to conquer it internally. He, too, had thought that, to win, the Chinese brother party would have to go on working closely with the Wuhan leaders.[31] True, he had thought that without soviets this would be unfeasible: soviets would have to arm the people to make Wuhan tractable. But then, Stalin had also tried to arm the Chinese masses, even before he came around to advocating soviets. His telegram of June 1st had ordered the formation of a "reliable" armed force of workers and of peasants. This, as we know, had been the threat which Wuhan promptly countered by breaking with the Communists and ruthlessly suppressing them. A very strong response indeed, considering that the forces which Stalin had proposed to raise were to form part of Wuhan's. Would the establishment of soviets, a still sharper challenge, have failed to cause as violent — as final — a reaction?

The contrary seems likelier, since Wuhan had the upper hand, with nearly its entire army ready to support it. Communist influence was weak among the men in uniform; surely it would have taken time to undermine their discipline. Meanwhile, the peasant soldiery carried out its orders, even when told to open fire on its so-called brethren.

The case was different, of course, where Communist commanders stood at the head of local troops, as in the Nanch'ang area. However, nearly all these troops perished in vain endeavors to seize and hold an urban base: first, Nanch'ang; later, Swatow. It had been planned to send a column out of Swatow southward to attack Canton at the time of the Canton Commune. Instead, the conquerors of Swatow were dislodged and scattered, the few among them who survived escaping to the mountains. The Canton Commune had to do without the promised succour — without support from *any* troops except one local regiment. This was a unit of cadets from near-by Whampoa: too loyal to the revolution, they also perished needlessly.

Concurrently with these events, another insurrection, of different origin and type, was taking place in Hunan. There Mao Tse-tung had gathered up a motley band of followers: uprooted peasants, stray deserters, miners from the Hanyang mines. With this band as a nucleus, Mao hopefully expected to raise an army strong enough to conquer all of Hunan.[32] In this he counted, as before, on the rebellious peasants to lend his cause the sweep, the drive, the fury that it needed.

Bent on achieving his own end, Mao blandly disregarded the niceties of the rules of conduct handed down from Moscow. Though Stalin still dwelt on the need for close ties with the Kuomintang, Mao set out in all openness to cut these ties completely. He also called for Chinese soviets, risking all the dangers of being termed a Trotskyite — or *thinking* that he risked them. He did not know that he was safe — that only a week earlier Stalin had done a turnabout and sanctioned Chinese soviets. The fact that without knowing this Mao did what he thought proper must be considered side by side with all his feats of compromise.[33]

The methods to which Mao resorted in this time of crisis would not have earned him any blame if they had been successful. But they were not: the Hunan peasants, though no less embittered than they had been six months before, were now less free to show it. When they had risen up before, the army of the Kuomintang, still their ally at least in name, had not moved in to stop them. But now it acted with dispatch and chased the troublemakers — Mao and his dwindling band of men — into the nearest mountains. On Chingkanshan, a mountain fastness popular with bandits, Mao, seeking refuge, found instead the doorway to his destiny.

We now know that this forced retreat to the barren hinterland was but the first one in a row — and that it led to victory. In areas well beyond the reach of government authority, the Communists could gather strength and wait their opportunity. Circuitous as was their route from Chingkanshan to Peking, it followed contours that run back far into Chinese history. Old dynasties had been destroyed, and new ones had been founded, by gangs of outlaws swooping down from strongholds in the mountains.[34]

But only very few such gangs had ended up in power; the vast majority remained obscure and happy bandits. Who then could possibly have known in 1927 that the "bandits" on top of Chingkanshan would some day rule the country? The prospect seemed remote indeed; and to faithful Marxists, their hopes pinned on the working class, it had to seem still more so. The Chinese Communist elite — the leaders blessed by Moscow — therefore withdrew their confidence from Mao and his strange followers.

They did so in a resolution that the Central Committee (not fully present, to be sure) passed on November 14.[35] The blame for the defeat in Hunan went to Mao exclusively; he was dismissed from three positions: *all* his higher party posts.* Thus punished for his ill success, he also received warning that by persisting in his course he would bog down in heresy. It was "erroneous to make light of the strength of the workers and to regard them as no more than helpmates of the peasants." [36] A workers' uprising remained, in the official doctrine, the prime condition of success in the entire struggle.

To drive this lesson home to Mao, his direct superiors in the Hunan provincial party branch sent him a cutting letter. Was it not true, they wished to know, that his "Workers' and Peasants' Army" consisted in reality of *lumpenproletarians?* Reports had reached them — true reports, as Mao has since admitted — that two "converted" bandit chiefs had joined him with their followers.[37] Mao answered bluntly: *lumpenproletarians* did serve in his army; and how could he dispense with them? They were splendid fighters. In fact,

* These were: alternate member of the Politburo, secretary of the Hunan Provincial Committee, and secretary of the Party Front Committee.

they were invaluable for the simple reason that, under present circumstances, they were irreplacable.[38] Workers and peasants *should* replace them: that was undeniable; but both of these were hard to find on the top of Chingkanshan. Such was the gist of Mao's defense: a plea for pure expediency; but he had learned sufficient caution not to flout the doctrine. In winding up his argument, he kowtowed with due piety in front of the official image of the revolution. Of course, he said, unless the party followed urban leadership, it would be certain to fall prey to some "erroneous tendencies." [39] Mao could not have pursued his chosen course, his own "erroneous tendency," if he had not been so adept in conforming — verbally.

He maintained later that the party had endorsed his own view, as against that of his superiors, at its next full congress. This congress, the party's sixth, had been held in Moscow in the summer of 1928; it could not have met in China. There the police would have made sure that delegates attending it would have been seized — and executed — soon after assembling. Instead, the delegates drank wisdom at its very fountainhead; any decision made in Moscow was naturally Moscow's. Hence we can say that if the congress sanctioned Mao's adventure, he must have found some high-placed sponsors in the Soviet hierarchy. But had the congress sanctioned it? Indeed, it would appear so; or else would Mao have thought it had? [40] He had read its program. Here was a section that commended his guerrilla warfare; here was a lengthy resolution on how to win the peasants.[41] The congress also saw to it that Mao was reinstated in one of the three party posts from which he had been ousted. Again, he became secretary of the Front Committee, or we should say: resumed the title that described his functions.[42] These functions he had actually never ceased to exercise, having continued all along to rule supreme on Chingkanshan.

The party, ruling nowhere else, had actually, as Mao noted, begun to place much greater stress on working in the countryside. But had it therefore, as Mao thought, accepted his idea that peasants, bandits, *anyone* could act as proletarians? Certainly not; that becomes clear as we read the program — the whole program, not parts of it — of the Moscow congress. Here it was pointed out again that any revolution, including an agrarian one, required urban leadership. This was not merely verbal tribute to a time-worn tenet but a profession of true faith, of faith prepared to prove itself. And prove itself by force of arms: the program of the congress prescribed a nationwide revolt to retake the cities. Such a revolt could not be staged from one day to the other; but all the needed preparations were to start immediately.[43]

To reunite the stranded party with the stranded working class, a *labor* leader was entrusted with the party leadership. The workers' hero Li Li-san, whom the May 30 Movement had catapulted into fame, again stepped to the forefront. Li, having pleased his Russian hosts at the Moscow congress, now returned home safely supreme in the party's councils. He led it for the next two years, until 1930, without assuming the position of secretary-general. This honor he left without risk to a faithful adjutant, the former boatman Hsiang Chung-fa, also a labor leader.[44]

Li came away from the Sixth Congress knowing what it wanted and threw himself into the task of carrying out its program. His comrade Mao — who, of course, had not been at the congress — meanwhile obeyed the party's will as he chose to interpret it. It soon became obvious that Mao's interpretation of what the Sixth Congress had meant imputed his own thoughts to it. The course of action he pursued and that which Li embarked upon could not be reconciled for long: a clash was unavoidable. What brought it on was the question of how the cornered party, having to husband its few troops, could use them most effectively. Mao favored sallies and retreats in contrast to pitched battles: why waste one's strength storming cities if one could not hold them? But Li, with orders to revive the shattered labor movement, could not adopt a strategy that left the workers stranded. To win them back for the cause, he had to take some cities, take them at almost any cost, or else fail in his mission. This was a simple corollary of current party doctrine; but militarily it was a reckless proposition. It left the military officers in the party's service with only one alternative: be loyal or be sensible. The loyalists followed Li and carried out his orders but were obstructed at each turn by Mao Tse-tung's adherents. At last, the conflict culminated in an open battle: loyalist troops engaged with Mao's — and were soon defeated. The "incident" (how much blood has been shed in "incidents"?) took place at Fut'ien, Kiangsi Province, late in 1930. It led to the first big purge in the party's history — a purge of loyal followers of the party leader! [45]

To strike at Li in this fashion would have been unthinkable if he had not been losing power for some time already. As it was, failure — the collapse of the first offensive aimed at retaking a big town — had already doomed him.[46] Early in 1931, the Comintern dismissed him and ordered him to come to Moscow to reform through "study." Moscow, it seemed, had thus wound up its own protracted "study" of whether Li's approach or Mao's held out the greater promise.

But if a choice had been made in favor of Mao's strategy, this choice was not as clear nor final as it seems in retrospect. Mao gained prestige and influence from his opponent's exit, but he did not step in his place, and those who did distrusted him.[47] The policy of Li Li-san, it turned out eventually, had only been put on a shelf, not thrown into the discard. This had been wise, considering that the other policy — the novel course pursued by Mao — was only an experiment. Indeed, by 1935, it looked very probable that Mao would fail more dismally than Li had failed before him.

In the autumn of 1934, the armies of the Kuomintang opened a well-prepared campaign to finish off the Communists. The Red enclave in Kiangsi Province was their immediate target; it was the biggest of its kind, with ten million inhabitants. A full-fledged soviet government functioned in this area ever since 1931; Mao held the highest post in it. But now this post, the government, the area that it governed had to be quickly given up: the enemy was coming.

The exodus that ensued — the party's flight from Kiangsi — revived some orthodox misgivings in the Soviet capital. Marxist objections to Mao's course seemed again more cogent as his retreat removed the party into virtual no-man's land. His plan to march 6000 miles to the northwestern borderland, against resistance all the way, seemed likely to miscarry.* The prophets of the Comintern hastened to insure themselves: this was the time to go on record deprecating Maoism. They planted a long article in their official journal restating the entire case for Li Li-san's old policy. In fact, unless the "Li" who signed it was another person, this article was Li's own work — his first step toward a comeback.

Glancing at it in the pages of *The Communist International* of March 5, 1935, one might think it dealt with history.[48] No word of Mao nor of the trek to the northwestern border: instead, much talk of Borodin and the Northwestern Theory.

* Whether Mao himself first proposed this plan, and exactly when it was firmly adopted, remain debatable questions (see Robert C. North, *Moscow and Chinese Communists*, pp. 164, 173–74). It seems fairly certain, however, that if Mao had not yet adopted it when beginning the Long March, he did adopt it after three months, when stopping at Ts'unyi in Kweichow Province.

But soon one grasps that "Li's" concern is not with bygone blunders: he writes about a *present* need — the need for urban bases. History enters his discussion only for one purpose: to show that his own leadership had been the correct one. Recounting all the classic virtues of his abandoned policy, he naturally neglects to mention why it was abandoned. He twists its terrible defeat into a great accomplishment and arrogates to himself even Mao's successes. "The success of the soviet movement," he writes, "was decided by the battles in Canton and Changsha, by the concentration of the work of the Communist Party in the industrial districts of Shanghai and Wuhan. . . ." Now the party would surely suffer defeat if by excessive reliance on peasant guerrillas and peasant support, it lost touch with the proletariat. "*The center of gravity in the work of the Communist Party* [would have to] remain with the proletariat, in the *large industrial centers*"[49] (emphasis in original).

This in the pages of a journal whose official status made any view expressed in it equally official. But Li's political revival was of short duration: within six months, Mao had proved his greater staying-power. His Russian patrons, in this case, had been *too* foreseeing; thus, when they saw him re-emerge, they revised their vision. In short, the Stalinists decided to accept his presence — quite unlike Trotsky, who refused to grant him recognition.

Trotsky agreed with Li Li-san (known as a "semi-Trotskyite") in taking not too kind a view of the Chinese "peasant war." Not that he was therefore guilty — as his opponents clamored — of "underrating" the importance of the Chinese peasants. He knew their value, knew quite well how greatly their allegiance would help the Chinese Communists to attain to power. But he assessed the peasants' value by his Marxist standards: they were to give an "impetus" to the workers' struggle.[50] Again it seems that he and Li were in complete agreement; but actually, on closer sight, there appears a difference.

Li seems to have been quite content (judging by the record) to leave the workers' liberation to a peasants' army. Trotsky, however, felt misgivings: even "Marxist" peasants were bound to clash with the workers: classes remained classes. Peasants did not shake off their class by joining the Red Army, nor did they therefore cease to harbor peasant aspirations. These remained incompatible with workers' aspirations — with what the workers had to do to carry out their mission. As soon as the Red peasant troops occupied the cities, this latent conflict would break out in one form or another. Unless the workers were forewarned, the Chinese revolution might end (as had the one in France) in a peasant triumph. But who was there to warn the workers of the peasant menace now that the Chinese Communists championed peasant interests? The Chinese Trotskyites, of course: the motley opposition group united around Ch'en Tu-hsiu and his closest followers. On them Trotsky placed his hope for saving China's working class from the insidious influence of the bogus Communists.

Trotsky had wondered for some years — since 1927 — whether the Chinese Communists deserved their party label. Now he felt sure that they did not: since 1927, even their proletarian label had become fictitious. They championed peasants, motley paupers, not the proletariat; the real party of the workers was the opposition group. The coming struggle of the workers against peasant dominance would therefore bring them face to face with a double enemy. Their struggle with the peasantry, a struggle between classes, was also one between factions: true and bogus communists.[51]

Thus Trotsky's sharp analysis ends in utter phantasy, the

Chinese workers helping him to strike back at Stalin! Doctrine supported his objections to the Chinese "peasant war"; but what inspired these objections looks much more like rancor. Would he have raised them at all, or raised them quite so strongly, if strict adherence to the doctrine had been his only interest? Trotsky had proven in the past that, very much like Stalin, he could be orthodox or not, depending on his purpose.

Yet orthodoxy had its hold even on the hierarchs — a hold quite difficult to break, even for a Stalin. As we have seen, even Stalin met the Chinese "peasant war" with the distrust — the condescension — of the faithful Marxist. True, in the end he let it be: a very wise decision but one (like many of its kind) basically passive. He stood committed to support the Chinese revolution; one day the "peasant war" was *it:* how could he *not* support it?

And yet and yet: as we come down to more recent history, we still find Stalin skeptical of the Chinese "peasant war." It had by then become a war for the defense of China against invasion by Japan; yet Stalin remained skeptical. He called the Chinese brother party "margarine Communists":[52] a view with which we are familiar, since it had been Trotsky's. Whatever aid some of his troops gave to the Chinese Communists after the Japanese defeat, he did not commit himself. He did his best not to be drawn into the Chinese civil war, observing what was on the whole a scrupulous neutrality. Why this aloofness? One might think, since Stalin spoke like Trotsky, that his distrust of Mao Tse-tung derived from Marxist prejudice. Perhaps it did to some extent, but one rather hesitates to ascribe too much Marxist faith to the Marxist pontiff. Does it not seem much likelier that Stalin's circumspection derived from bitter memories of 1927? Nowhere had he been outwitted as badly as in China; the Chinese ground was treacherous; he had cause to shun it.

The more so since his defeat of 1927 had actually marked the collapse of a whole idea. The hope of world revolution had been disappointed just where its prospects of fulfilment had appeared the brightest. World revolution *Stalin's* hope? One reads and hears the opposite: *Trotsky* still dreamed the global dream; Stalin had ceased to do so.

Ever since 1924, Stalin had preached the notion that Russia could transform herself even in isolation. Socialism would be built in a single country now that the workers of the West had failed to capture power.[53] The Comintern no longer dragged them into insurrections; henceforth it spread its influence by entering alliances. "United fronts" became the fashion in Europe and Asia: pure marriages of convenience, but with romantic overtones. These unions with "progressive" parties proved of short duration: they fell apart one by one — at great cost to the Communists.* But did they matter very much? Weren't they purely marginal to Stalin's central enterprise of building a new Russia? Some foreign parties might be wrecked, some foreign comrades perish, but "socialism in one country" remained unaffected.

However, have we in this study found a domestic Stalin calmly content to cultivate only his Russian garden? No, we have seen him eagerly attending to his neighbor's — determined to spread socialism to *another* country. In China, he found fertile ground: an elemental readiness (no longer to be found in Europe) to receive the gospel. In China, he formed an alliance tighter, more cohesive (and therefore in the end more costly) than its Western counterparts.† The road to Paris led through Peking, as Lenin had predicted; the

* The first alliance to collapse was with Poland's strong man Pilsudski. That was in 1926. The next year saw not only the debacle in China but also the dissolution of the Anglo-Russian trade-union council in Britain.

† There was no "bloc within" in the West nor, apart from the Kuomintang, any "bourgeois" member of the Comintern family.

liberation of the West would follow that of China. The prospect remained rather distant, but it did move closer according as the Chinese people got in step with history. World revolution seemed alive in its Chinese setting, alive and moving on apace — till 1927.

Thus "socialism in one country" — Stalin's isolationism — did not preclude a lunge abroad where such a lunge seemed promising. In fact, his doctrine of retreat and his Chinese venture were perfectly compatible in everything but logic. The doctrine had been a response to defeats in *Europe;* it marked a giving up of hope for expansion *westward*. But such frustration in the West rendered any prospect of a recoupment in the East all the more attractive. Some tsars had felt the eastward pull now felt by their successors — this pull now felt as noble zeal to free the Asian masses. Stalin was somewhat predisposed to feel it the more strongly because Asia had long been at the core of his strategic thinking.[54] Yet it was Trotsky, the most Western of the leading Bolsheviks, who had been boldest in his vision of Oriental conquest. Trotsky had once proposed a plan to send Soviet cavalry across the mountains into India, there to fight the British.[55] But this had been a fleeting vision; Trotsky's usual outlook remained profoundly European — and, in this sense, provincial.

Not that Trotsky advanced a "Western" view against Stalin's "Asian" one; if they felt such a difference, they never said so openly. Instead, they eagerly disputed subtle points of doctrine, each a defender of the faith against the other's heresy. Stalin had made a formal creed of isolated socialism expressly to refute a tenet Trotsky had adopted. This was the notion (germinally an older Marxist concept) of revolution moving on in unbroken "permanence."

"Permanent revolution," such as Trotsky preached it, meant first of all a revolution crossing Russia's borders. Crossing them westward to escape its backward Russian setting, in which it would be almost certain to bog down unfinished. Trotsky had also, to be sure, thought of the possibility that backward Asia might be first to learn from backward Russia. But glancing at diverse perspectives does not change one's outlook: Trotsky still wanted, hence expected, victory in Europe.[56]

"Permanent revolution" denoted, in the second place, one moving up from stage to stage without ever stopping. As long as there were communists to act as social catalysts, society could be transformed at a steady tempo. In the Russia of 1917, the bourgeois revolution had been succeeded very soon by the proletarian one. In retrospect, the two-in-one looked genuinely "permanent," ascending through the bourgeois stage to proletarian altitudes. The bourgeois task had been fulfilled — "feudalism" ended — without letting the bourgeoisie entrench itself in power. The bourgeois phase had been over no sooner than it started because the party of the workers had taken charge of history.

If this was so (and it was in the eyes of Trotsky), why had the *Chinese* revolution failed to become "permanent"? Why had the Chinese bourgeoisie succeeded in arresting it just at the point where the workers should have taken over? Because of Stalin's foolishness, was Trotsky's simple answer; because of all his fond illusions about the bourgeois Kuomintang. But as we look at these illusions in the present context, we find that one of the most foolish was at bottom Trotskyist. Stalin provoked the break with Wuhan, the ultimate catastrophe, by thinking that the time was ripe to make a bid for power. The warlords or "feudalists" had not yet been defeated when he prepared to terminate the bourgeois revolution. His telegram of June 1, 1927, called on the Chinese Communists to take the helm at Wuhan. They were to move to the forefront of the revolution and thus ensure that its advance would be duly "permanent."

The Chinese revolution was already "permanent" in that it was Leninism outward bound for conquest. Trotsky had dreamed of an advance into "progressive" Europe, but he had not ignored the prospects Asia had to offer. If he had been in Stalin's place, he would have seen, as Stalin did, that China offered the best chance of propagating communism. China, by 1924, was the only country through which the world revolution could possibly spread outward.

China was therefore the only country (apart from the Soviet Union) where Stalin practiced, in his own way, the principles taught by Trotsky. Yet China was also the very country whose revolution, miscarried, brought the dispute between the two men to its ultimate bitter climax. Is this a paradox? Undoubtedly so; and one that is all the more striking because the same logic, of the same creed, served both disputants in their argument. One cannot but marvel at the way in which logic supports the passions, the biases and the dishonesties of men who struggle for power.

Bibliography
Notes
Index

BIBLIOGRAPHY

The sources listed below have been divided into primary and secondary ones, although this division may be even more arbitrary here than it is usually. For instance, writings by Communist leaders have been classified as "primary" even though they are often less accurate than "secondary" accounts. On the other hand, some writings which have been classified as "secondary" contain translations or summaries of original texts.

I. Primary Sources

A. Books, Documents, and Articles in Oriental Languages.

Ch'en Tu-hsiu, *Kao ch'üan-tang t'ung-chih shu* (A Letter to All Party Comrades) (Shanghai, 1929).

——— (under pseudonym of Ch'en Shih-an), "Kuo-min-tang yü Kung-ch'an-tang-chu-i-che" (The Kuomintang and the Communists) in *Chung-kuo Kuo-min-tang chiang-yen-chi* (Collected Kuomintang Speeches), 3 vols., (Shanghai, 1924).

——— "Shih-yüeh ko-ming yü tung-fang" (The October Revolution and the Far East), *Hsiang-tao chou-pao* (Guide Weekly), November 15, 1926.

Chin shih-wu-nien-lai Shanghai chih pa-kung t'ing-yeh (Strikes and Lockouts in Shanghai in the Last Fifteen Years) (Shanghai, 1933).

Ch'ü Ch'iu-pai (Ku Shuhaku), *Chūgoku daikakumei* (The Great Chinese Revolution) (Tokyo, 1933). A translation from the Chinese.

——— *Chung-kuo ko-ming chih cheng-lun wen-t'i* (Debatable Problems of the Chinese Revolution) (Wuhan, 1927).

——— *Chung-kuo ta-ko-ming yü kung-ch'an tang* (The Great Chinese Revolution and the Communist Party) (1928).

Kung-ch'an kuo-chi tui Chung-kuo ko-ming ch'üeh-i-an (Resolutions of the Comintern on the Chinese Revolution) (Shanghai, 1930).

Li Li-san, "Chung-kuo ta-ko-ming ti chiao-hsün" (Lessons of the Great Chinese Revolution), introduction to *Kung-ch'an kuo-chi tui Chung-kuo ch'üeh-i-an.*

Mandalyan, T., *Wei-shen-ma Chung-kuo Kung-ch'an-tang ti ling-tao po-ch'an* (Why did the Leadership of the Chinese Communist Party Go Bankrupt?) (Moscow, 1927). A translation from the Russian.

Mao Tse-tung, *Mao Tse-tung Hsüan-chi* (Selected Works of Mao Tse-tung), first edition (Tung-pei shu-tien, 1948) and second edition, 4 vols. (Peking, 1951).

P'eng Shu-chih, *Kung-ch'an lien-shih-i t'an-hua* (Speeches to the Communist Joint Conference) (Shanghai, 1930).

——— "Wo-men pei-fa kuan" (Our Views on the Northern Expedition) *Hsiang-tao*, September 10, 1927.

Su-lien yin-mou wen-cheng hui-pien (A Compilation of Documents on the Soviet Conspiracy) (Peking, 1928).

Tai Chi-t'ao, *Chung-kuo ko-ming yü Kuo-min-tang* (The Chinese Revolution and the Kuomintang) (Shanghai, 1925).

T'an-ho Kung-ch'an-tang liang ta-yao-an (Two Important Cases for Impeaching the Communist Party) (Nanking, 1927).

Teng Chung-hsia, *Chung-kuo shih-kung yün-tung chien shih* (A Short History of the Chinese Labor Movement) (Chin-ch'a-chi, 1946).

Ts'ai Ho-shen, "Lun Ch'en Tu-hsiu chu-i" (On the Principles of Ch'en Tu-hsiu), *Ch'en Tu-hsiu p'ing-lun* (A Critical Discussion of Ch'en Tu-hsiu) (Peiping, 1933).

Wu-chuang pao-tung (Armed Uprisings) (Shanghai, 1929).

B. Books, Documents, and Articles in Western Languages.

Brandt, Conrad, Benjamin Schwartz, and John K. Fairbank, *A Documentary History of Chinese Communism* (Cambridge, 1952).

Chiang Kai-shek, *China's Destiny* (New York, 1947).

——— *Soviet Russia in China* (New York, 1957).

Die Chinesische Frage auf dem 8. Plenum der Exekutive der Kommunistischen Internationale (Hamburg, 1928).

Dridzo (Losovsky), S. A., *Revolution und Konterrevolution in China* (Moscow, 1928).

Eudin, Xenia, and Robert C. North, *Soviet Russia and the*

East 1920–1927 (A Documentary Survey). (Stanford 1957).

First Congress of the Toilers of the Far East (Petrograd, 1922).

Hilferding, Rudolf, *Finanzkapital* (Wien, 1910).

Hobson, J. A., *Imperialism* (London, 1902).

——— *Kommunisticheskii Internatsional v dokumentakh* (Moscow, 1933).

Lenin, V. I., *Oeuvres complètes* (Paris, 1935).

——— *Sochineniya* (3rd ed.) (Moscow, 1935).

Mao Tse-tung, *Selected Works*, 4 vols. (London, 1954).

Mif, Pavel, "Kitaiskaya Kommunisticheskaya partiya v kriticheskiye dni," *Bol'shevik* (No. 21, 23–24).

——— *Kitaiskaya revolyutsiya* (Moscow, 1932).

Neuberg A. (Heinz Neumann), *L'Insurrection armée* (Paris, 1931).

Pervyi s'ezd narodov vostoka (Petrograd, 1920).

Pervyi s'ezd revolyutsionnykh organizatsii dal'nego vostoka (Petrograd, 1922).

Protokoll des II. Weltkongresses der Kommunistischen Internationale (Hamburg, 1921).

Protokoll des Vierten Kongresses der Kommunistichen Internationale (Hamburg, 1923).

"Report of [sic] the Communistic Movement of the Youth in China." Translated document, in the Jay Calvin Huston Collection, Hoover Library.

Roy, M. N., *My Experience in China* (Calcutta, 1938).

——— *Revolution and Counterrevolution in China* (Calcutta, 1948).

Stalin, J. V., *Marxism and the National and Colonial Question* (New York, 1930).

——— *Sochineniya* (Moscow, 1947).

——— *Voprosy Kitaiskoi Revolyutsii* (Moscow, 1927).

T'an P'ing-shan, *Entwicklungswege der Chinesischen Revolution* (Hamburg, 1927).

The Second Congress of the Communist International as Reported and Interpreted by the Official Newspapers of Soviet Russia (Washington, 1920).

The Second Congress of the Communist International (Stenographic Report) (Moscow, 1920).

Trotsky, Leon, *Problems of the Chinese Revolution* (New York, 1932).

——— *The Third International After Lenin* (New York, 1936).

Ts'ai Ho-shen, "Istoriya opportunizma v Kommunisticheskoi partii Kitaya," *Problemy Kitaya*, No. 1 (Moscow 1929).

Voitinsky, "K voprosu ob oshibkakh Kitaiskoi Kompartii v revolyutsii 1925–27 gg.," *Problemy Kitaya*, No. 4–5 (1930).

Vsesoyuznaya Kommunisticheskaya partiya v rezolyutsiakh eë s'ezdov i konferentsii (Moscow, 1928).

Vtoroi Kongress Kominterna (Moscow, 1934).

Wilbur, C. Martin, and Julie L. How, *Documents on Communism, Nationalism, and Soviet Advisers in China 1918–1927* (New York, 1956).

Zinoviev, Grigorii, "Novyi etap Kitaiskoi revolyutsii." A document in the Trotsky Archives.

——— "Zayavlenie k stenogramme ob'edinennogo plenuma TsK i TsKK." A document in the Trotsky Archives.

II. Secondary Sources

A. Books and Articles in Oriental Languages.

Ch'en Tu-hsiu p'ing-lun (A Critical Discussion of Ch'en Tu-hsiu) (Peiping, 1933).

——— "Shu Onrai den" (A Biography of Chou En-lai), *Kaizo*, July 1937.

Chung-kung jen-wu (Chinese Communist Personalities) (Shanghai, 1949).

Chung-kuo hsien-tai ko-ming yün-tung shih (A History of Modern Chinese Revolutionary Movements) (Yenan, 1941).

Fang Lu, "Ch'ing-süan Ch'en Tu-hsiu" (Liquidating Ch'en Tu-hsiu), *Ch'en Tu-hsiu p'ing-lun*.

Hatano Kanichi, "Chugoku Kyosanto oyobi kogun" (The Chinese Communist Party and the Red Army), *Saikin Shina nenkan* (Modern China Yearbook) (Tokyo, 1935).

Hsü Shan-fu, "Kung-ch'an-tang feng-lieh shih" (A History of Splits in the Communist Party), *Hsien-tai shih-liao* (Current Historical Materials) (Shanghai, 1933).

Hu Hua (ed.), *Chung-kuo hsin-min-chu-chu-i ko-ming shih*

(A History of the New Democratic Revolution in China) (Shanghai, 1950).

Hua Kang, *Chung-kuo ta ko-ming shih* (A History of the Great Chinese Revolution) (Shanghai, 1932).

Hua Ying-shan, *Chung-kuo Kung-ch'an-tang lieh-shih chuan* (Biographies of Heroes of the Chinese Communist Party) (Hongkong, 1949).

Kung Ch'u, *Wo yü hung-chün* (I and the Red Army) (Hongkong, 1954).

Li Ang (pseudonym of Chu Hsin-fan), *Hung-se wu-t'ai* (Red Stage) (Chungking, 1941).

Liu A-sheng, *Chung-kuo min tsu min-chu ko-ming yün-tung shih chiao-ch'eng* (A Textbook on the History of Chinese National Democratic Revolutionary Movements) (Sui Teh, North Shensi, 1941).

Obikawa Tsunetada, *Shina seiji soshiki no kenkyu* (Researches in Chinese Political Organizations) (Tokyo, 1933).

Okubo Yasushi, *Chükyo sanjunen* (Thirty Years of Chinese Communism) (Tokyo, 1949).

Po Ch'i, "Chung-kung t'ou-k'ao ti-san kuo-chi i hou" (After the Chinese Communists Became Dependent on the Comintern), *Kung-ch'an-tang tsai Chung-kuo* (The Communist Party in China) (Hongkong, 1943).

Shina Kyosanto no gaikan (A Survey of the Chinese Communist Party) (Tokyo, 1930).

Shina Kyosanto undoshi (A History of the Chinese Communist Movement) (Tokyo, 1932).

Shina ni okeru Kyosan undo (The Communist Movement in China) (Tokyo, 1933).

Shindo Teiichiro, "Ku Shuhaku den" (A Biography of Ch'ü Ch'iu-pai), *Kaizo* (August 1936).

Ssu-ma Hsien-tao, *Pei-fa hou chih ko-pai ssu-ch'ao* (Ideological Tendencies among the Various Factions after the Northern Expedition) (Peiping, 1930).

Tanaka Tadao, *Kuo-min ko-ming yü nung-ts'un wen-t'i* (The National Revolution and the Agarian Question) (Peiping, 1932). A translation from the Japanese.

Wen Shu, "Ch'en Kung-po fan-cheng chi" (The Story of Ch'en Kung-po's Conversion) *Hsien-tai shih-liao*, Vol. I.

B. Books and Articles in Western Languages

Asiaticus (Hans Müller), *Von Kanton bis Schanghai* (Vienna-Berlin, 1928).

Cheng Tien-fong, *A History of Sino-Russian Relations* (Washington, 1957).

Ch'ien Tuan-sheng, *The Government and Politics of China* (Cambridge, 1950).

Dedijer, Vladimir, *Tito Speaks* (London, 1953).

Deutscher, Isaac, *Stalin* (London, 1949).

——— *The Prophet Armed* (London, 1954).

Eberhard, Wolfram, *Conquerors and Rulers* (Leiden, 1952).

Fischer, Louis, *Men and Politics* (New York, 1941).

——— *The Soviets in World Affairs*, 2 vols., (New York, 1930). A new unaltered edition of this work was published by the Princeton University Press in 1951.

Fitzgerald, C. P., *Revolution in China* (New York, 1952).

Fuse, Katsuji, *Soviet Policy in the Orient* (Peking, 1927).

Hsiung, S. I., *The Life of Chiang Kai-shek* (London, 1948).

Hurwicz, Elias, *Die Orientpolitik der Dritten Internationale* (Berlin, 1922).

Isaacs, Harold, *The Tragedy of the Chinese Revolution* (Stanford, 1951).

Kara-Murza, G., "K voprosu o klassovoi sushchnosti Sun'yat-senizma," *Problemy Kitaya* (Moscow, 1931), No. 6–7.

Liu, F. F., *A Military History of Modern China (1924–1949)* (Princeton, 1956).

Nelson, William E., "One Party Government in China," *Far Eastern Survey*, May 19, 1948.

Nikolaevsky, Boris, "Revolyutsiya v Kitae," *Novyi Zhurnal*, VI (New York, 1943).

North, Robert C., *Kuomintang and Chinese Communist Elites* (Stanford, 1952).

——— *Moscow and Chinese Communists* (Stanford, 1953).

Orwell, George, *Animal Farm* (London, 1945).

Payne, Robert, *Mao Tse-tung* (New York, 1950).

Pipes, Richard, *The Formation of the Soviet Union* (Cambridge, 1954).

Snow, Edgar, *Red Star Over China* (New York, 1938).

Schwartz, Benjamin, *Chinese Communism and the Rise of Mao* (Cambridge, 1951).

Sharman, Lyon, *Sun Yat-sen* (New York, 1934).

Strong, Anna Louise, *China's Millions* (New York, 1928).

T'ang Leang-li, *The Inner History of the Chinese Revolution* (London, 1920).

Vilenskii-Sibiryakov, V. D., *Sun Yat-sen* (Moscow, 1924).

Wales, Nym, *The Chinese Labor Movement* (New York, 1945).

Whiting, Allen S., *Soviet Policies in China* (New York, 1954).

Wieger, Léon, *Chine moderne.* Seven volumes, containing numerous excerpts from the Chinese press (Peking, 1922–27).

Wolfe, Bertram D., *Three Who Made a Revolution* (New York, 1948).

Woo, T. C., *The Kuomintang and the Future of the Chinese Revolution* (London, 1928).

C. Periodicals, Newspapers, Reference Books.

Bol'shevik (Moscow).

China Yearbook (Shanghai and Tientsin).

Die Kommunistische Internationale (Moscow).

Far Eastern Survey (New York).

Gendai Chugoku Chosenjin meikan (Who's Who in Modern China and Korea) (Tokyo, 1953).

Hsiang-tao chou-pao (Guide Weekly) (Shanghai).

International Press Correspondence (Moscow).

Izvestiya (Moscow).

Kaizo (Reconstruction) (Tokyo).

Kommunisticheskii International (Moscow).

Kuo-wen chou-pao (National News Weekly) (Shanghai).

North China Herald (Shanghai).

Novyi Vostok (Moscow).

Novyi Zhurnal (New York).

Oriente moderno (Rome).

People's Tribune (Hankow).

Pravda (Moscow).

Problemy Kitaya (Moscow).

Saikin Shina nenkan (Modern China Yearbook) (Tokyo, 1935).

The Communist International (Moscow).
The Daily Worker (New York).
The Militant and *The New Militant* (New York).
Tung-fang tsa-chih (Far Eastern Magazine) (Shanghai).

D. Unpublished Manuscripts and Archives.

William Ayres, "Shanghai Labor and the May 30th Movement." A manuscript mimeographed by the Committee on International and Regional Studies, Harvard University, 1950.
Jay Calvin Huston, collected papers and documents, at the Hoover Library, Stanford, California.
Leon Trotsky, collected papers and documents, at the Houghton Library, Harvard University.

NOTES

Chapter I

Lenin and Asian Nationalism: Sources of an Alliance

1. It was rather a by-product of his thinking about the World War. Before the war, he had preached national self-determination chiefly with Eastern Europe in mind. But having branded the war as "imperialist" and adopted a neutral stand, he could not support nationalist causes in Europe without contradicting himself. His party comrades attacked him for this, maintaining that nationalism as such had now become outdated. He alone insisted that it had not, pointing to its now patent usefulness as an ally in Asia. See Richard Pipes, *The Formation of the Soviet Union*, pp. 41–49.

2. *Vsesoyuznaya Kommunisticheskaya partiya v rezolyutsiakh eë s'ezdov i konferentsii*, p. 212.

3. V. I. Lenin, *Sochineniya* (3rd ed.), XXIV, 550–51.

4. For Lenin's doctrine of imperialism see his *Imperialism: the Highest Stage of Capitalism* (1916) and scattered writings of earlier date such as "Backward Europe, Advanced Asia" (1913) and "The Socialist Revolution and the National Right of Self-Determination" (1916), *Sochineniya*, XVI, 395–96 and XIX, 43–44. Lenin derived the bulk of his doctrine from J. A. Hobson's *Imperialism* and from R. Hilferding's *Finanzkapital*.

5. See Lenin as quoted by Stalin in *Voprosy Kitaiskoi revolyutsii*, p. 35.

6. This slogan was officially adopted by the First Congress of the Peoples of the East, held at Baku in September 1920. *Pervyi s'ezd narodov vostoka*, p. 18.

7. *Protokoll des II. Weltkongresses der Kommunistischen Internationale*, p. 142.

8. Soviets, or councils of toilers' deputies, made their first appearance as organs of popular self-rule in the Russian revolution of 1905. Trotsky (not a Bolshevik at the time) took a prominent lead in this development; but the Bolsheviks under Lenin distrusted the soviet until it proved its worth in 1917. Bertram D. Wolfe, *Three Who Made a Revolution*, chapters XVIII and XXI.

9. *Protokoll des Vierten Kongresses der Kommunistichen Internationale*, p. 634.

10. *Protokoll des II. Weltkongresses*, p. 231.

11. *Ibid.*, p. 140.

12. For Lenin's draft theses see his *Oeuvres complètes*, XXV, 340–44. For Roy's supplementary theses see *The Second Congress of the Communist International*, pp. 576–79. For details of the conflict between Lenin and Roy, see *The Second Congress of the Communist International as Reported and Interpreted by the Official Newspapers of Soviet Russia*, pp. 31, 43–44, and M. N. Roy, *My Experience in China*, p. 18.

13. This was the Italian socialist Serrati. He and two others abstained from the unanimous vote in favor of the Theses. These seemed all the more contradictory because of a strange omission in their Russian and German texts. Here Roy's supplementary theses appeared as originally drafted, without the revisions to which he had later agreed as a concession to Lenin. Allen S. Whiting, *Soviet Policies in China*, p. 56.

Lenin for his part had made a small concession to Roy and revised his own draft to describe national liberation movements as "national-revolutionary" instead of "bourgeois-democratic." Eudin and North, *Soviet Russia and the East*, p. 68.

14. It is true that at one point he did speak of their aid as essential to victory in Asia. This would be a puzzling self-contradiction, were it not for the fact that, at open meetings of the congress, he would say almost anything to appear as a faithful lieutenant of Lenin's. Thus he even put up a spirited public defense of the very united-front strategy that he was attacking *in camera*. See Whiting, *Soviet Policies*, pp. 49–53.

15. *The Second Congress*, pp. 577–79.

16. J. V. Stalin, *Voprosy Kitaiskoi revolyutsii*, pp. 177–78, 184–86.

17. Compare draft theses in *Oeuvres*, XXV, 343, with the text as finally adopted in *Protokoll des II. Weltkongresses*, p. 230.

18. *Protokoll des II. Weltkongresses*, pp. 140–41.

19. *Ibid.*, p. 216; *Protokoll des Vierten Kongresses*, p. 591.

20. *Protokoll des II. Weltkongresses*, p. 140.

21. See for example, declarations by Grigorii Zinoviev and Bela Kun before the First Congress of the Peoples of the East at Baku (September, 1920), *Pervyi S'ezd Narodov Vostoka*, pp. 40, 177–78;

also, Zinoviev's speech before the First Congress of the Toilers of the Far East, in January 1922, *First Congress of the Toilers of the Far East*, p. 153.

22. *Protokoll des II. Weltkongresses*, pp. 648–654.

23. Sylvia Pankhurst, "Lenin and the British Labour Party," *Workers' Dreadnought*, April 9, 1921, p. 6.

24. *Protokoll des II. Weltkongresses*, p. 107.

25. *Ibid.*, p. 647.

26. *Ibid.*, p. 648.

27. Pankhurst, in *Workers' Dreadnought*, April 9, 1921, p. 6.

28. Stalin, *Voprosy*, p. 161; *Die Chinesische Frage auf dem 8. Plenum der Exekutive der Kommunistischen Internationale*, pp. 23, 123, 149.

29. Stalin, "Prospects of the Revolution in China," *International Press Correspondence* (hereafter designated as IPC), December 23, 1926, p. 1582.

30. Stalin, *Voprosy*, pp. 127, 169, 232.

31. Lenin, *Sochineniya*, VII, 201.

32. *Protokoll des II. Weltkongresses*, pp. 140–42.

33. See for example the Zinoviev Theses in Leon Trotsky, *Problems of the Chinese Revolution*, pp. 316–17; also Stalin, *Voprosy*, pp. 173–75.

34. E. Hurwicz, *Die Orientpolitik der Dritten Internationale*, p. 33.

35. *Ibid.*, p. 79.

36. *Vtoroi Kongress Kominterna*, p. 495.

37. This summary is drawn from the following sources: Hurwicz, *Orientpolitik, passim; Oriente moderno*, II, p. 249; *Protokoll des III. Kongresses der Kommunistischen Internationale*, pp. 998–99; *Die Chinesische Frage*, pp. 89–93.

Chapter II

The Comintern and Sun Yat-sen: Preliminaries of an Alliance

1. V. I. Lenin, "Demokratiya i Narodnichestvo v Kitae" (1912), *Sochineniya*, XVI, 26–31.

2. For an excellent treatment of Sun's conversion to one-party dictatorship, see William E. Nelson, "One Party Government in China," *Far Eastern Survey*, May 19, 1948, pp. 118–121.

3. Lyon Sharman, *Sun Yat-sen*, p. 241; Jay Calvin Huston, "The

Chinese Labor Movement," a manuscript in the J. C. Huston Collection; *Izvestiya*, No. 53 (605), March 9, 1919, p. 1.

4. The best analysis of Li Ta-chao's and Ch'en Tu-hsiu's roles in the May 4 Movement and of their subsequent conversion to Marxism-Leninism appears in Benjamin I. Schwartz, *Chinese Communism and the Rise of Mao*, chapter I.

5. See, for instance, Hatano Kanichi, "Chugoku Kyosanto oyobi kogun," *Saikin Shina nenkan*, pp. 1598–99.

6. Liu A-sheng, *Chung-kuo min-tsu min-chu ko-ming yün-tung shih chiao-ch'eng*, p. 115.

7. Hatano, in *Saikin Shina nenkan*, pp. 1598–99; Fang Lu, "Ch'ing-süan Ch'en Tu-hsiu", *Ch'en Tu-hsiu p'ing-lun*, p. 66.

8. Hatano, in *Saikin Shina nenkan*, pp. 1597–98.

9. *Ibid*., p. 1599.

10. "Chung-kuo Kung-ch'an-tang chien-ming li-shih" (A Short History of the Chinese Communist Party) in *Su-lien yin-mou wen-cheng hui-pien*, II, 16. This is a voluminous collection of documents seized during a police raid on the Soviet embassy in Peking on April 6, 1927. Moscow consistently denied the authenticity of these documents; but in a private letter by Zinoviev (undated), we find them described as "documents and falsified documents" (letter in Trotsky Archives). Most of them show nothing to cast doubt on their authenticity. The "Short History," for one, seems perfectly genuine, its bias and distortions being those to be found in all party documents.

An English translation of these documents, with introductory essays, appeared shortly before the completion of this manuscript (*Documents on Communism, Nationalism, and Soviet Advisers in China 1918–1927*). The editors, Professor C. Martin Wilbur and Miss Julie L. How, discuss the question of authenticity at great length (pp. 8–37). Having examined the question much more thoroughly than I have, they reach the same conclusion: the documents, except for a few whose origin remains dubious, are almost certainly genuine.

11. *Chung-kuo hsien-tai ko-ming yün-tung shih*, p. 89.

12. *Shina Kyosanto no gaikan*, p. 12. A study prepared for the Japanese General Staff in 1930.

13. Hsü Shan-fu, "Kung-ch'an-tang fen-lieh shih," *Hsien-tai shih liao*, I, 224. This volume is of very uneven quality, being a collection of articles by many contributors. Chief among these was Chu Hsin-

fan (Li Ang), writing under various pseudonyms (see Chapter III, note 12).

14. *Su-lien yin-mou*, II, 27.

15. *Chung-kuo hsien-tai ko-ming yün-tung shih*, p. 89; Harold Isaacs, *The Tragedy of the Chinese Revolution*, p. 58. The original edition of Isaacs' work appeared in England in 1938. It remains to this day the best account of the early phase of the Chinese revolution.

16. *Su-lien yin-mou*, II, p. 6.

17. Ts'ai Ho-shen, "Istoriya opportunizma v Kommunisticheskoi partii Kitaya," *Problemy Kitaya*, No. 1 (1923), p. 14. *Protokoll des Vierten Kongresses der Kommunistischen Internationale*, p. 630.

18. Ts'ai, in *Problemy Kitaya*, No. 1, p. 4.

19. Hsü Shan-fu, in *Hsien-tai shih-liao*, I, 225.

20. Ts'ai Ho-shen, "Lun Ch'en Tu-hsiu chu-i," in *Ch'en Tu-hsiu p'ing-lun*, p. 15, also *Chung-kuo hsien-tai ko-ming yün-tung shih*, p. 98.

21. Ssu-ma Hsien-tao, *Pei-fa hou chih ko-pai ssu-ch'ao*, p. 45.

22. *First Congress of the Toilers of the Far East*, pp. 153, 182, 192, 194.

23. *Pervyi s'ezd revolyutsionnykh organizatsii dal'nego vostoka*, pp. 12, 19. This is the Russian version of the proceedings of the congress. It is less comprehensive than the English version cited in note 22, but probably more accurate in its wording.

24. *First Congress*, pp. 194–95; *Pervyi s'ezd*, p. 60.

25. *First Congress*, pp. 174, 183, 196. It is interesting to note that this statement does not appear in the Russian version.

26. The text of this manifesto appears in Russian translation in *Novyi Vostok*, No. 2 (1922), pp. 606–612. The Chinese original is not available.

27. The text of the manifesto of the Second Congress is only available in Japanese translation, *Shina ni okeru Kyosan undo*, pp. 95–97.

28. *Ibid.*, p. 97.

29. *Su-lien yin-mou*, II, 29.

30. See the proclamation of the Third Congress of the Chinese Communist Youth Corps (February 1925), as quoted in *Pei-fa hou chih ko-pai ssu-ch'ao*, p. 44, also Ch'en Tu-hsiu, *Kao ch'üan tang t'ung-chih shu*, p. 2.

31. Ch'en Tu-hsiu, p. 2.

32. Isaacs, *The Tragedy*, p. 59.

33. Information obtained from Mr. Chang Kuo-t'ao.

34. Isaacs, p. 59 (footnote).

35. Resolution of the Executive Committee of the Communist International, dated January 12, 1923. The Russian text is quoted in full by Boris Nikolaevsky in "Revolyutsia v Kitae," *Novyi Zhurnal*, VI (1943), p. 234.

36. Ch'en Tu-hsiu, p. 2.

37. *T'an-ho Kung-ch'an-tang liang ta yao-an.* See Sun's marginal comments on page 5, written in December 1923.

38. *Su-lien yin-mou*, II, 27.

39. Isaacs, p. 59; *Su-lien yin-mou*, II, 28.

40. Okubo Yasushi, *Chukyo sanjunen*, p. 25; also Wang Ching-wei's report to the Second Kuomintang Congress as rendered in *Novyi Vostok*, No. 18 (1927), p. 8.

41. Ch'en Tu-hsiu, p. 2.

42. Sharman, *Sun Yat-sen*, p. 250. *The Foreign Relations of the United States* (1923) contains no reference to Sun's overture.

43. The English, and probably original, version of the Sun-Joffe Manifesto appeared in the *North China Herald* of February 3, 1923, p. 289. The first Chinese version appeared in the *Tung-fang tsa-chih* of January 25, 1923, pp. 10–11.

44. *T'an-ho Kung-ch'an-tang liang ta yao-an*, p. 7 (marginal notes).

45. "Report of the Communistic Movement of the Youth in China," translation of a document allegedly seized during the raid on the Soviet embassy in Peking on April 6, 1927, in the Jay Calvin Huston Collection.

46. *Protokoll des Vierten Kongresses*, pp. 632–33.

47. *Chung-kuo hsien-tai ko-ming yün-tung shih*, p. 98.

48. Ts'ai Ho-shen, in *Ch'en Tu-hsiu p'ing-lun*, p. 14; also Teng Chung-hsia, *Chung-kuo shih-kung yün-tung chien shih*, p. 104.

49. The full text of the manifesto of the Third Congress appears in *Hsiang-tao chou-pao*, June 20, 1923, p. 228. *Hsiang-tao* was the official Communist Party organ between 1922 and 1927.

50. See, for example, Hua Kang, *Chung-kuo ta ko-ming shih*, pp. 446–47.

51. Ch'en Shih-an (pseudonym of Ch'en Tu-hsiu), "Kuo-min-tang

yü Kung-ch'an-tang-chu-i-che," *Chung-kuo Kuo-min-tang chiang-yen chi*, I, 40.

52. T. Mandalyan, *Wei-shen-ma Chung-kuo Kung-ch'an-tang ti ling-tao po-ch'an?* pp. 4, 9.

53. Information obtained from Mr. Chang Kuo-t'ao.

54. See Mao Tse-tung's own account as rendered by Edgar Snow in *Red Star over China*, p. 159. This version of Mao's early career is still considered authoritative in Communist China.

55. Snow, p. 159.

56. Information obtained from Mr. Chang-Kuo-t'ao; partly confirmed in Snow, p. 159.

57. Ts'ai Ho-shen, in *Problemy Kitaya*, No. 1, p. 5.

58. Information given by Voitinsky to Mr. Chang Kuo-t'ao and obtained from the latter.

59. Information obtained from Mr. Chang Kuo-t'ao.

60. *Protokoll des Vierten Kongresses*, p. 615.

61. *T'an-ho Kung-ch'an-tang liang ta-yao-an*, pp. 14–15.

62. *Ibid.*, p. 6 (marginal notes).

63. *Ibid.*, p. 4 (marginal notes).

64. "Theses on the Oriental Question," *Protokoll des Vierten Kongresses*, p. 1038.

65. Resolution of the Executive Committee of the Communist International on the Chinese Question, May 1923. Quoted by G. Kara-Murza in "K voprosu o klassovoi syshchnosti Sun Yat-senizma," *Problemy Kitaya*, No. 6–7 (1–2), (1931), p. 178.

66. A letter by Borodin seized in the raid on the Soviet embassy in Peking on April 6, 1927. Quoted by J. C. Huston in "Sun Yat-sen, the Kuomintang and the Chinese-Russian Political-Economic Alliance," a manuscript in the J. C. Huston Collection, p. 75.

67. *Su-lien yin-mou*, II, p. 7.

68. H. Maring, "Die revolutionär-nationalistische Bewegung in Südchina," *Die Kommunistische Internationale*, No. 22 (September 1922), pp. 54–55; V. D. Vilenskii (Sibiryakov), *Sun Yat-sen'*, p. 178; S. A. Dridzo (Lozovsky), *Revolution und Konterrevolution in China*, p. 54; *Protokoll des Vierten Kongresses*, p. 615.

69. *T'an-ho Kung-ch'an-tang liang ta-yao-an*, p. 5.

70. Borodin's real name was Grusenberg. He had become a Social Democrat in 1903, the year in which the Russian Social Democrats

split into Mensheviks and Bolsheviks. He had first been a Menshevik, like Trotsky and others who later distinguished themselves in the Bolsheviks' service. Forced to flee Russia after the revolution of 1905, he had gone to America and stayed there till 1917. Then he became well-nigh ubiquitous as a Comintern agent, turning up in Mexico and in Spain; in Scotland and — again — in America; and as Kemal's adviser in Turkey.

71. Conversation between Borodin and two members of the Kuomintang Supervisory Committee, as quoted *ibid.*, p. 26.

Chapter III

The Communists in the Kuomintang: An Alliance in Operation

1. *T'an-ho Kung-ch'an-tang liang ta-yao-an*, p. 19; *Shina Kyosanto no gaikan*, pp. 25–26.

2. Bulletin of the Chinese Socialist Youth Corps, No. 7 (April 1, 1924), as quoted in part in *T'an-ho Kung-ch'an-tang liang ta-yao-an*, pp. 16–17.

3. Nine tenths of the local Kuomintang units were, according to a later Comintern report, under the direction of "left-wingers and Communists." *Die Kommunistische Internationale*, No. 9, p. 406.

4. Hatano Kanichi, "Chugoku Kyosanto oyobi kogun," *Saikin Shina nenkan*, pp. 1694–95; Ssu-ma Hsien-tao, *Pei-chiao hou chih ko pai ssu-ch'ao*, p. 50.

5. *T'an-ho Kung-ch'an-tang*, p. 2 (marginal notes).

6. T'ang Leang-li, *The Inner History of the Chinese Revolution*, p. 166.

7. Early in 1924 he wrote two articles restating his belief that the bloc with the Communists, being temporary, would not lead to the sovietization of China. Léon Wieger, *Chine moderne*, V, 38, and VII, 91–92.

8. H. Maring, "Die revolutionär-nationalistische Bewegung in Südchina," *Die Kommunistische Internationale*, No. 22 (September 1922), p. 55.

9. See, for example, *T'an-ho Kung-ch'an-tang*, pp. 4–5 (marginal notes); also a letter from Sun to Chiang Kai-shek, as quoted in S. I. Hsiung, *The Life of Chiang Kai-shek*, p. 161.

10. *Su-lien yin-mou wen-cheng hui-pien* II, 11; *Documents on Com-*

munism, Nationalism, and Soviet Advisers in China 1918–1927, p. 49.

11. *Pravda*, October 31, 1922, p. 3.

12. Li Ang (pseudonym) *Hung-se wu-t'ai* (The Red Stage), pp. 127–28. Li Ang was one of several pen names used by Chu Hsin-fan, a dissident Communist executed by the Kuomintang in 1945. "The Red Stage" is a chatty, highly personal volume, in many places of dubious accuracy. But its major claims are inherently credible and can be confirmed with the help of other sources.

13. *Ibid.*, pp. 42, 85.

14. Hatano Kanichi, in *Saikin Shina nenkan*, p. 1599.

15. Maring, in *Die Kommunistische Internationale*, September 1922; also "Report of the Communistic Movement of the Youth in China," in J. C. Huston Collection, p. 15.

16. Teng Chung-hsia, *Chung-kuo shih-kung yün-tung chien-shih*, p. 19; Nym Wales, *The Chinese Labor Movement*, p. 30.

17. Tanaka Tadao, *Kuo-min ko-ming yü nung-ts'un wen-t'i*, Part II, p. 74; "Report of the Communistic Movement," in the J. C. Huston Collection, p. 15.

18. Tanaka, p. 77; A. L. Strong, "Writer Compares Peasant, Soldier Excesses in Hunan," *People's Tribune*, July 30, 1927, p. 1.

19. A. L. Strong, *China's Millions*, p. 155.

20. G. Schüller, in *IPC*, No. 42 (August 1, 1928), p. 744.

21. *The Daily Worker*, February 6, 1926, p. 2.

22. A well-documented Western account of the May 30 Movement may be found in George Sokolsky's "Labor Strikes and the Anti-Foreign Agitation," *China Yearbook* (1926), p. 855ff. A detailed Chinese Communist account of the movement is given by Teng Chung-hsia in *Chung-kuo shih-kung yün-tung chien-shih*, pp. 198–242. An excellent unpublished account, well-documented by Chinese sources, is William Ayers' "Shanghai Labor and the May 30 Movement" (Committee on International and Regional Studies, Harvard University, 1950).

23. Shindo Teiichiro, "Ku Shu-haku den," *Kaizo*, Vol. XVIII (1936), p. 35; Hu Hua (ed.), *Chung-kuo hsin-min-chu-chu-i ko-ming shih*, p. 57; Hua Ying-shan (ed.), *Chung-kuo Kung-ch'an-tang lieh-shih chuan*, pp. 34, 39, 57, 159.

24. *Lieh-shih chuan* p. 63.

25. *Ibid.*, p. 64; Teng Chung-hsia, p. 202.

26. Hu Hua, p. 57.

27. For a record of the Profintern's pessimistic estimates of Chinese revolutionary prospects, see Whiting, *Soviet Policies in China*, p. 122ff.

28. I. Heller, "The Labour Movement in China," *The Communist International*, No. 17 (November 1925), p. 11.

29. *Lieh-shih chuan*, p. 39; Wales, *The Chinese Labor Movement*, p. 213.

30. Political Report of the Central Committee of the Chinese Communist Party (July 1926), as quoted in *Su-lien yin-mou*, III, 66; *Documents*, p. 275.

31. Teng, pp. 207–208; *North China Herald*, November 14, 1925, p. 294.

32. When the movement began the party had about 1,000 members; the Youth Corps, about 2,000. *Bol'shevik*, No. 23–24 (1927), p. 110. In Shanghai alone party membership quadrupled during the movement, from about 200 to 800. Nym Wales, *The Chinese Labor Movement*, p. 46.

33. Isaacs, *The Tragedy of the Chinese Revolution*, p. 78; *China Yearbook* (1926), pp. 925–27; *North China Herald*, July 11, 1925, p. 4.

34. The reorientation of the strike movement may be derived from statistics published in the appendix of *Chin shih-wu-nien-lai Shanghai chih pa-kung t'ing-yeh*. Part of this appendix has been summarized by William Ayers in the study cited in note (22) above.

35. See, for example, the Resolution of the Sixth Enlarged Plenum of the Executive Committee of the Comintern (February-March 1926) as rendered in *Kommunisticheskii Internatsional v dokumentakh*, p. 619.

36. *North China Herald*, August 1, 1925, p. 80; August 15, 1925, p. 16.

37. Teng, p. 230.

38. Marshal Tuan belonged to the Anfu (Anhui-Fukien) Clique, which had dominated the Peking government until Wu P'ei-fu drove it out of the capital in July 1920. He had staged his comeback after Wu, in turn, had been driven out (in October 1924) by the forces of the "Christian general," Feng Yü-hsiang.

39. Ch'en Tu-hsiu's political report to the Fifth Congress of the Chinese Communist Party (April-May, 1927), as summarized in *Bol'shevik*, No. 23–24, December 31, 1927, p. 99.

40. An excerpt from this speech appears in Sharman, *Sun Yat-sen*, p. 304.

41. Ts'ai Ho-shen, "Istoriya opportunizma v Kommunisticheskoi partii Kitaya," *Problemy Kitaya*, No. 1 (1929), p. 6.

42. T'ang Leang-li, p. 219.

43. Kautsky was a veteran leader of the German Social Democrats, who had earned Lenin's hatred by refusing to take a stand for socialist neutrality at the outbreak of the First World War. The Comintern functionary who looked after Hu was Karl Radek; his comments appear in a personal letter to Mussim, dated July 12, 1928 (in the Trotsky Archives). Although written with the benefit of three years' hindsight, this letter contains no suggestion that Radek knew at the time why Hu had been sent to Moscow.

44. A Japanese author lists Tai as one of those who joined the party at the time of its foundation (Hatano, *Saikin Shina nenkan*, p. 1597). But according to a Chinese Communist eyewitness, he did not become an actual party member, either then or later. Teng Chung-hsia, *Chung-kuo shih-kung yün-tung chien shih*, p. 239.

45. For Tai Chi-t'ao's views on the Communist-Kuomintang alliance, see his *Chung-kuo ko-ming yü Kuo-min-tang*. Brief second-hand summaries appear in Teng, pp. 239–241, and in T'ang Leang-li, p. 213.

46. *Die Kommunistische Internationale*, No. 7 (July 1926), p. 621.

47. Though Chiang's allegiance to the world revolution ended when he broke with the Communists, his view of the imperialist impact on China retained its Leninist ground-tone. See *China's Destiny*, chapter III.

48. The Kuomintang did have auxiliary organizations such as the San Min Chu I Youth Corps (1938–1947) through which to widen its popular base; but these never attained nearly the size of their counterparts in Communist China. It is interesting to note that the Kuomintang and its Youth Corps eventually became rivals, very much like the Communist Party and *its* Youth Corps during the 1920's. See Ch'ien Tuan-sheng, *The Government and Politics of China*, p. 127.

49. Ch'en Tu-hsiu, *Kao ch'üan tang t'ung-chih shu*, p. 3.

50. See the resolution of the Second Enlarged Plenum of the Central Committee, July 1926. *Su-lien yin-mou*, III, 71; *Documents*, pp. 279–280.

51. Ch'en Tu-hsiu's political report to the Fifth Party Congress, *Bol'shevik*, No. 23–24 (1927), p. 101.

52. Resolution of the Enlarged Plenum of the Central Committee, October 1925, as quoted in the resolution of the Second Enlarged Plenum of July 1926. *Su-lien yin-mou*, III, 70; *Documents*, p. 279.

53. Theses of the Fourth Party Congress, as quoted in *Die Chinesische Frage auf dem 8. Plenum der Exekutive der Kommunistischen Internationale*, p. 48.

54. Resolution of the Enlarged Plenum of October 1925 as quoted in *Die Chinesische Frage*, p. 49.

55. Resolution of October 1925, as quoted in *Su-lien yin-mou*, III, 70; *Documents*, p. 279.

56. Of course, such deception could not be practiced indefinitely. But in the beginning, the Communists practiced it with some success. Thus, in December 1925, while using the Kuomintang left as a spearhead against the right, they carried on direct negotiations with prominent rightists in Shanghai (Ch'ü Ch'iu-pai, *Chugoku daikakumei*, p. 74; *Ch'en Tu-hsiu p'ing-lun*, p. 21). Three months later, a Soviet adviser in Canton expressed his hope that Chiang Kai-shek's sallies against the right would give the Communists an "opportunity to be allied with some of the extremists of both right and left." Report by General Stepanov, *Documents*, p. 252.

57. *Su-lien yin-mou*, III, 70; *Die Chinesische Frage*, pp. 49–50.

58. Snow, *Red Star Over China*, p. 160.

59. P'eng had returned to his native Haifeng county in 1921 after graduating from Waseda University in Tokyo. The Kwangtung Board of Education, then under Ch'en Tu-hsiu's direction, had made him chief of its Haifeng bureau; but he held this post only briefly. Soon he devoted himself fully to the work of the Socialist Youth Corps, of which he himself had founded the Haifeng branch (the Corps, it will be recalled, was the party's chief link with the peasants). In 1927 he set up the first rural soviet of the type since made famous by Mao. When Kuomintang troops closed in on his base, he fled to Shanghai, where, in 1929, he was arrested and shot. *Gendai Chugoku Chosenjin meikan*, p. 207.

60. Hua Kang, *Chung-kuo ta-ko-ming shih*, pp. 159–161; Isaacs, pp. 67–69.

61. Mao began to act as such while in Canton in the winter of

1925–26; but not until the following spring did he formally take charge of the party's peasant department (*Red Star Over China*, pp. 160–1). It is improbable that he would have risen this high if Ch'en Tu-hsiu had been as hostile to his radical land program as he makes him out to have been (*ibid.*, p. 161). The party's own land program, as adopted the previous October, was itself far from moderate: it provided for outright confiscation of all land belonging to big landlords and officials, militarists and monasteries. *The Communist International*, No. 17 (November 1925), p. 28.

62. Even a year later, peasants made up only 5 per cent of its total membership. T'an P'ing-shan, *Entwicklungswege der Chinesischen Revolution*, p. 31.

63. *Su-lien yin-mou*, III, 103; *Documents*, pp. 300–301.

64. Lenin, *Sochineniya*, VIII, 187–88.

65. Stalin, "The Political Tasks of the University of the Peoples of the East" (a speech delivered at the university on May 18, 1925), *Marxism and the National and Colonial Question*, p. 216.

66. The Peasants' International, or *Krestintern*, had been formed in 1923 following the total debacle of proletarian revolution in the West. Moscow wished to recoup itself for its loss of influence among the Western workers by winning new adherents in the peasant parties of Eastern and Southeastern Europe. But the *Krestintern* never became an effective political instrument.

67. See, for example, the speech of a Stalinist henchman at the Eighth Plenum of the Comintern Executive, as quoted in *Die Chinesische Frage*, p. 48.

68. Stalin, in *Marxism and the National and Colonial Question*, p. 216.

69. *Ibid.*, pp. 216–17.

70. How completely it contradicted the tenets of Marxism-Leninism has been demonstrated by Trotsky in his *Third International After Lenin*, pp. 212–223.

71. Stalin, "The National Question in Yugoslavia," *Marxism*, pp. 202–203; also "The National Question Once Again," *ibid.*, pp. 227–28.

72. Stalin, "Prospects of the Revolution in China," *IPC*, No. 90 (December 23, 1926), p. 1581 (Russian original in *Voprosy Kitaiskoi revolyutsii*, p. 42).

73. *Die Kommunistische Internationale*, No. 9 (March 1926), p. 406;

Okubo Yasushi, *Chukyo sanjunen,* pp. 61–63; *Hankow Herald,* February 5, 1926, p. 2.

74. *IPC,* No. 21 (March 18, 1926), p. 330.

Chapter IV

The Communists in the Kuomintang: To Whom the Hegemony

1. Li Ang, *Hung-se wu-t'ai,* pp. 3–4, 7

2. Louis Fischer, *The Soviets in World Affairs,* II, pp. 633, 640; F. F. Liu, *A Military History of Modern China,* Chapter 2; T'ang Leang-li, *The Inner History of the Chinese Revolution,* p. 158.

3. The Canton-Hongkong strike had been called in protest against the so-called "Shameen Massacre" of June 23, 1925, a repercussion of the May 30 affair, which it resembled in its immediate origin. While imposing an embargo on foreign trade, the strike committee became in effect a side-government. According to Voitinsky, then chief of the Far Eastern Division of the Comintern, the committee was led by the Kwangtung branch of the Chinese Communist Party. *Problemy Kitaya,* No. 4–5 (1930), p. 97.

4. The whole "rescue" had been staged with such consummate skill that details remain to this day obscure. Two reports by General Stepanov of the Soviet military mission shed little light, since the Soviet mission itself had been caught completely off guard. This though one of its members had been warned of what was to come. *Documents on Communism, Nationalism, and Soviet Advisers in China,* pp. 248–250, 263.

5. This summary of the March 20 coup has been derived from: Hua Kang, *Chung-kuo ta ko-ming shih,* p. 235ff.; J. C. Huston, "Sun Yat-sen, the Kuomintang, and the Chinese-Russian Political-Economic Alliance," a manuscript, p. 133ff., and notes dated March 12 to April 26, 1926, in the J. C. Huston Collection; Isaacs, *The Tragedy of the Chinese Revolution,* chapter 6; T'ang Leang-li, *The Inner History,* p. 243ff.

Tien-fong Cheng in *A History of Sino-Russian Relations* (pp. 133–34) relates an "inside story" of the coup which he heard from Ch'en Li-fu, a prominent Kuomintang rightist. Little as we know about the coup, we can safely dismiss this story, because it runs counter to all we know about the political constellation both in Canton and Moscow at the time.

6. Ch'en Tu-hsiu's political report to the Fifth Party Congress, as quoted in *Bol'shevik,* No. 23–24, December 31st, 1927, p. 101.

7. Fang Lu, "Ch'ing-süan Ch'en Tu-hsiu," *Ch'en Tu-hsiu p'ing-lun,* p. 72.

8. Li Li-san, "Chung-kuo ta ko-ming ti chiao-hsün," *Kung-ch'an-kuo-chi tui Chung-kuo ko-ming ch'üeh-i-an,* p. 21; Hua Kang, *Chung-kuo ta ko-ming shih,* p. 452.

9. Ch'en Tu-hsiu, in *Bol'shevik,* December 31, 1927, p. 101.

10. Ch'en Tu-hsiu, *Kao ch'üan-tang t'ung-chih shu,* p. 3.

11. Its report of that date, "Voprosy nashei politiki v otnoshenii Kitaya i Yaponii" (in the Trotsky Archives), lists the following members in attendance: Trotsky, Chicherin, Voroshilov, Dzerzhinsky (only Trotsky and Voroshilov were members of the Politburo). That the two-party bloc in China was discussed without allusion to the coup of March 20 may be explained by the poverty of communications between Moscow and Canton. The committee may have known too little about the situation in Canton to appreciate its gravity.

12. This fear was also voiced in the contemporary Soviet press, as for instance in the *Pravda* of March 24, April 1, and April 11, 1926.

13. "Voprosy nashei politiki v otnoshenii Kitaya i Yaponii," pp. 2–4.

14. Stalin shared this assumption to the full; even a year later, he still believed that Moscow had "sufficient authority over the Chinese masses to make them accept [its] decisions." See his remarks to the subcommittee on China at the Eighth Plenum of the Comintern Executive, *The New Militant,* February 8, 1936.

15. Sung Hsiao-ch'ing, "Chou En-lai hsiao-chuan," *Hsien-tai shih-liao,* I, p. 146.

16. M. N. Roy, *Revolution and Counterrevolution in China,* pp. 399–401; *Die Chinesische Frage auf dem 8. Plenum der EKKI,* p. 95; J. C. Huston, notes dated April 26, 1926.

17. T'ang Leang-li, p. 247; J. C. Huston, "Sun Yat-sen, the Kuomintang, and the Chinese-Russian Political-Economic Alliance," p. 136.

18. For a complete rendition in English of the Kuomintang resolution of May 15, 1926, see T. C. Woo, *The Kuomintang and the Chinese Revolution,* pp. 176–77.

19. G. Zinoviev, "Zayavleniye k stenogramme ob'edinnogo plenuma TsK i TsKK," p. 1, a document in the Trotsky Archives, dated July 19, 1926.

20. Letter by the Central Committee of the Chinese Communist Party to the Central Committee of the Kuomintang, June 9, 1926, published in *Hsiang-tao*, No. 157 (June 9, 1926), p. 1526.

21. Ch'en Tu-hsiu, *Kao ch'üan-tang t'ung-chih shu*, p. 3.

22. *Ibid.*, p. 3.

23. Soviet aid to Feng Yü-hsiang is amply documented in *Su-lien yin-mou wen-cheng hui-pien*, III, 1–82; *Documents on Communism, Nationalism, and Soviet Advisers in China 1918–1927*, pp. 336–366.

24. The American consul in Canton had heard of the presence of this mission from two prominent Kuomintang leftists (J. C. Huston, "Sun Yat-sen, the Kuomintang, and the Chinese-Russian Political Economic Alliance," pp. 131–33). The mission in question may have been the same as a Soviet trade mission known to have reached Peking around this time (*The Central China Post*, February 27, 1928). Of course, this trade mission may well have included Comintern agents.

25. Fischer, *The Soviets in World Affairs*, II, 652.

26. Who composed this group is unknown; but we may venture the guess that it formed part of the Comintern mission in Shanghai, from which voices of protest against Stalin's policy made themselves heard later on (see the "Letter from Shanghai" in Trotsky's *Problems of the Chinese Revolution*, p. 397ff.). Our conjecture is supported by the fact that the group's thinking paralleled that of the Chinese Communist leaders, who made Shanghai their headquarters.

27. Leon Trotsky, "Kitaiskaya Kompartiya i Gomindan," p. 6, a document in the Trotsky Archives, dated September 27, 1926.

28. Zinoviev, "Zayavleniye," p. 2.

29. In August 1926, the Politburo's Committee on China complained that information from Canton "has not improved . . . but has rather become much worse" (see document quoted in *China Yearbook*, 1928, p. 805). An equally frank complaint to this effect may be found in Bukharin's report to the 15th Congress of the Bolshevik Party. *IPC*, November 4, 1926, p. 1251.

30. Zinoviev, "Novyi etap Kitaiskoi revolyutsii," p. 17, a document in the Trotsky Archives, dated July 2, 1927; "Voprosy nashei politiki v otnoshenii Kitaya i Yaponii," p. 9; also Fischer, p. 648.

31. Isaac Deutscher, *Stalin*, pp. 297–309.

32. Trotsky, "Pochemu my ne trebovali do sikh por vykhoda iz Gomindan," a document in the Trotsky Archives, June 23, 1927.

33. Resolution of the Central Committee of the C.P.S.U., adopted at the Plenum of July 1926, as quoted by Trotsky in "Novye vozmozhnosti Kitaiskoi revolyutsii, novye zadachi, novye oshibki," a document in the Trotsky Archives, dated September 1927.

34. Zinoviev, "Zayavleniye," p. 1.

35. Those who doubt Chiang's capacity to see beyond China's borders may be surprised by the judgment of a Soviet general who served directly under him. Chiang's grasp of world problems — wrote this general — was "extremely good," *Documents*, p. 251.

36. Fischer, *Men and Politics*, p. 140; *Soviets in World Affairs*, p. 648.

37. F. F. Liu, *A Military History of Modern China*, p. 29; *Documents*, p. 215.

38. Borodin had left Canton in early February and returned in May. It has been maintained that he agreed *before* his departure to support the drive to the north (Fischer, *The Soviets in World Affairs*, II, p. 648). But if, as the same source relates, one of his motives was fear of seeing Kwangtung invaded by Wu P'ei-fu's troops, he could not have supported Chiang's plan for a counterthrust until April or May. Only then did Wu's troops begin to threaten the south.

39. J. C. Huston, notes dated July 8 and August 30, 1926; T'an P'ing-shan, *Entwicklungswege der Chinesischen Revolution*, p. 8.

40. Speech by Chiang Kai-shek to a meeting of the Canton Kuomintang, May 25, 1926. *The Peking Leader*, June 19, 1926.

41. *Su-lien yin-mou*, III, 72–73; *Documents*, p. 281.

42. *Die Chinesische Frage*, p. 18; Zinoviev, "Novyi etap Kitaiskoi revolyutsii," p. 25.

43. Exactly who annulled it, and exactly why, cannot be firmly established. The Opposition said later that Stalin and Bukharin had been responsible; but since "Stalin and Bukharin" was a common formula in oppositionist usage at the time, this should not be taken too literally (Zinoviev, "Novyi etap Kitaiskoi revolyutsii," p. 25). The reason for the veto, according to the Stalinists themselves, was that the resolution had called for an end of the "bloc within"; but in fact it had nowhere done so. *Die Chinesische Frage*, p. 18.

44. *Su-lien yin-mou*, III, 72. The phrase "authoritarian one-class party" (*i-ko i chieh-chi-shih ti chi-ch'üan ti cheng-tang*) does not appear in the Wilbur-How translation, having been rendered, not

quite accurately, as "[party] in which political power is concentrated in one class," *Documents*, p. 281.

45. See, for example, Trotsky, *Problems of the Chinese Revolution*, pp. 92–95.

46. *Su-lien yin-mou*, III, 69; *Documents*, p. 278.

47. *Su-lien yin-mou*, III, 66, 69, 73; *Documents*, pp. 275, 278, 281.

48. *Ibid.*, p. 70. Wilbur-How's rendering of this passage—"we failed to . . . oppose the offensives of the Right and the armed Center"—is to be understood in the sense: we were *unable* to oppose, etc., *Documents*, p. 273.

49. *Su-lien yin-mou*, III, 63; *Documents*, p. 272.

50. Zinoviev, "Novyi etap Kitaiskoi revolyutsii," p. 17.

51. At the 15th Bolshevik Party Congress in December 1927, Stalin's spokesman Pavel Mif put the matter thus: "The [northern] campaign was not begun on the initiative of the Communists but by the bourgeoisie led by Chiang Kai-shek. The Communists were placed before the alternatives: either to aid the campaign . . . or to leave the initiative to the bourgeoisie . . . and thereby relinquish all the results [to it]," *IPC*, No. 1 (January 5, 1928), p. 29.

52. "Voprosy nashei politiki v otnoshenii Kitaya i Yaponii," p. 9. A marginal note in Trotsky's hand attributes the amendment in question to Stalin's authorship.

53. In June-July 1925, Borodin warned hot-headed Kuomintang officers against a direct attack on British-held Shameen Island (J. C. Huston, "Sun Yat-sen, the Kuomintang, and the Chinese-Russian Political-Economic Alliance," p. 183). In September, he pressed the Kuomintang leaders to seek a settlement of the strike (*Su-lien yin-mou wen-cheng hui-pien*, Vol. I; facsimile of minutes in Russian). This was in full accordance with a decision of the Politburo, taken the month before (*China Yearbook*, 1928, p. 805). Under such pressure, the Chinese Communist leaders instructed the party branch in Kwangtung not to prolong the strike (*Problemy Kitaya*, No. 1, p. 10).

54. Peasant union membership in Kwangtung and Hunan alone increased about threefold to more than three million in the latter half of 1926 (T'an P'ing-shan, *Entwicklungswege der Chinesischen Revolution*, p. 8). Trade-union membership, in April 1927, stood at 2,800,000—an increase of more than two million since the beginning of the Northern Expedition (*Problemy Kitaya*, No. 2, p. 31).

55. Stalin's speech to the Moscow party workers on April 5, 1927, as quoted in Isaacs, p. 185.

56. A partial list of the officers who made up the "Red Clique" at the Whampoa Academy appears in K. Hatano's biographical sketch of Chou En-lai in the July 1937 issue of the magazine *Kaizo* (p. 87).

57. Li Chi-k'u, "Natsional'no-revolyutsionnaya armiya Kitaya i politrabota v nei," *Revolyutsionnyi Vostok*, No. 2 (1927), p. 127.

58. *Ibid.*, p. 127.

59. *Ibid.*, pp. 132–33.

60. *Wu-chuang pao-tung*, pp. 94–95; A. B. Neuberg (Heinz Neumann), *L'Insurrection armée*, p. 165.

61. A Chinese military historian, F. F. Liu, maintains the opposite thesis. He asserts that the Communists, through their political commissars, came close to winning control of the army (*A Military History of Modern China*, pp. 18–21, 38–40, 43–47). They did undeniably try to control it, and even succeeded here and there, before the coup of March 20, 1926 (*Documents*, pp. 250–51, 258–59). But after the coup they grew more cautious, and their influence weakened. The most telling proof of their weakness lies in the subsequent course of events. At the decisive hour, they found only very few troops ready to fight on their side. See Chapter V.

62. Circular of the Military Committee of the Kwangtung branch of the Chinese Communist Party, quoted in Neuberg, p. 164.

63. *Wu-chuang pao-tung*, p. 96.

64. Nassonov, Albrecht, Fokine, "Letter from Shanghai," in Trotsky, *Problems of the Chinese Revolution*, pp. 421–22; Ch'ü Ch'iu-pai, *Chugoku daikakumei*, p. 83.

65. Nassonov, etc., pp. 421–22.

66. Zinoviev, "Zayavleniye," p. 2.

67. *Ibid.*, p. 2; Ch'en Tu-hsiu, *Kao ch'üan-tang t'ung-chih shu*, p. 4; G. Voitinsky, "K voprosu ob oshibkakh Kitaiskoi Kompartii v revolyutsii 1925–27 gg.," *Problemy Kitaya*, No. 4–5 (1930), pp. 84–87, 103.

68. N. Lenzner, "Ideologicheskie istochniki oshibok Kitkompartii," *Kommunisticheskii Internatsional*, No. 32, (106), p. 10.

69. Ch'en Tu-hsiu, *Kao ch'üan-tang t'ung-chih shu, passim.*

70. Ch'en Tu-hsiu, "Shih-yüeh ko-ming yü tung-fang," *Hsiang-tao chou-pao*, November 15, 1926, pp. 1849–50.

71. How such a suspicion could arise even in orthodox breasts has been explained to us by the Politburo's committee on China. "Undoubtedly," says a report of the committee, "the representatives of various agencies dealing with China have given themselves inadmissible big-power airs, compromising the Soviet regime and creating the impression that it might be imperialist." "Voprosy nashei politiki v otnoshenii Kitaya i Yaponii," p. 4.

72. Ch'en, in *Hsiang-tao,* November 15, 1926, p. 1850.

73. Ch'ü Ch'iu-pai, *Chung-kuo ko-ming chih cheng-lun wen-t'i,* pp. 101, 118; T. Mandalyan, *Wei-shen-ma Chung-kuo Kung-ch'an-tang ti ling-tao po-ch'an?,* p. 8.

74. "V s'ezd Kompartii i Gomindan," *Kommunisticheskii Internatsional,* No. 11 (85), p. 7.

75. Mandalyan, p. 10; Nassonov, etc., p. 427.

76. "Theses on the Chinese Situation," *IPC,* No. 11 (February 3, 1927), p. 233.

77. Address by Shao Li-tzu to the Seventh Plenum of the E.C.C.I., *IPC,* No. 91 (December 30, 1926), pp. 1605–06.

78. Voitinsky, in *Problemy Kitaya,* No. 4–5, p. 103; Nassonov etc., pp. 431–32.

79. *People's Tribune,* May 21, 1927, p. 1, and June 1, 1927, p. 1.

80. T'an P'ing-shan's report to the Seventh Plenum of the E.C.C.I., *Entwicklungswege der Chinesischen Revolution,* pp. 20–21.

81. Stalin, "Prospects of the Revolution in China," *IPC,* No. 90 (December 23, 1926), p. 1581; *Voprosy Kitaiskoi revolyutsii,* p. 162.

82. "Theses on the Chinese Situation," *IPC,* February 3, 1927, p. 231.

83. Bertram D. Wolfe, *Three Who Made a Revolution,* pp. 620–21.

84. Stalin was not, of course, the sole author of the theses; but they closely resemble, even in wording, a speech that he made at the plenum (*IPC,* December 23, 1926, p. 1581ff.). If we can believe M. N. Roy (and believing him is always hazardous), he himself was solely responsible for the drafting of the theses (Roy, *Revolution and Counterrevolution in China,* p. 538). On the other hand, we have Stalin's own word that the theses were written "not without my participation"—proof that the art of understatement is practiced even by despots (Stalin, *Marxism and the National and Colonial Question,* p. 238).

85. T'an P'ing-shan, *Entwicklungswege,* p. 22.

86. "Theses on the Chinese Situation," *IPC,* February 3, 1927, p. 233.

87. T'an, *Entwicklungswege*, p. 23.

88. "Theses," *IPC*, February 3, 1927, p. 232.

89. T'an's report to the Seventh Plenum, *IPC*, No. 91 (December 30, 1926), p. 1591.

90. Stalin, "Prospects," *IPC*, December 23, 1926, p. 1583.

91. T'an, *Entwicklungswege*, p. 24.

92. Stalin, "Prospects," p. 1582.

93. *Ibid.*, p. 1582.

Chapter V

A Defeat Out of Victory and a Devil Out of the Machine

1. See, for example, Hu Shih, "China in Stalin's Grand Strategy," *Foreign Affairs*, October 1950, p. 11ff.

2. Stalin, "Prospects of the Revolution in China," *IPC*, No. 90 (December 23, 1926), p. 1581ff.

3. P'eng Shu-chih, "Wo-men ti pei-fa kuan," *Hsiang-tao*, No. 170 (September 10, 1926), pp. 1723–25.

4. Stalin, "Prospects," *IPC*, December 23, 1926, p. 1582.

5. *Ibid.*, pp. 1583–84; "Theses on Chinese Situation," *IPC*, No. 11 (February 3, 1927), p. 231.

6. Pavel Mif, "Kitaiskaya Kompartiya v kriticheskiye dni," *Bol'shevik*, No. 5 (March 15, 1928), pp. 64–65; Asiaticus, *Von Kanton bis Schanghai*, p. 52.

7. Report by Chang Kai-lin, tax commissioner of the Hunan Provincial Government, to the Central Committee of the Kuomintang, dated December 27, 1926, *World-wide Soviet Plots*, p. 139.

8. An English translation of Mao's report, with critical commentary, appears in Brandt, Schwartz, Fairbank, *A Documentary History of Chinese Communism*, pp. 77–89.

9. *Hsiang-tao*, no. 191 (March 12, 1927); *Revolyutsionnyi Vostok*, No. 2 (1927); *Chung-yang fu-k'an*, No. 7 (March 28, 1927); *Chinese Correspondence*, No. 8 (May 15, 1927).

10. *Documentary History*, p. 83.

11. Stalin, "Prospects," *IPC*, December 23, 1926, p. 1582.

12. See, for example, *Mao Tse-tung Hsüan-chi*, I, 17.

13. Letter from Borodin to Chiang, dated January 12, 1927, in J. C. Huston Collection; Nassonov, etc., "Letter from Shanghai," in Leon Trotsky, *Problems of the Chinese Revolution*, p. 406.

14. Louis Fischer, *The Soviets in World Affairs*, II, 661; A. L. Strong, *China's Millions*, p. 252.

15. Fischer, p. 661; Léon Wieger, *Chine moderne*, VII, 143; Nassonov, *etc.*, p. 406.

16. Speech delivered at Nanch'ang on March 7, 1927, as rendered in Wieger, VII, 133.

17. Isaacs, *The Tragedy of the Chinese Revolution*, pp. 163–64, 180–1.

18. Ch'ü Ch'iu-pai, *Chung-kuo ko-ming chih cheng-lun wen-t'i*, pp. 102–103.

19. K. A. Wittfogel, "Streikkämpfe in Schanghai," *Die Kommunistische Internationale*, No. 41 (October 12, 1927), p. 2017.

20. Ch'en Tu-hsiu, *Kao ch'üan-tang t'ung-chih shu*, p. 4.

21. Isaacs, chapter XI; André Malraux, *Man's Fate, passim.*

22. Speech by Chiang Kai-shek reported in the *Min-chih jih-pao* of May 4, 1927, as quoted in Wieger, VII, 141.

23. *People's Tribune*, July 6, 1927, p. 2.

24. *Pravda*, April 15, 1927, p. 1.

25. Isaacs, Chapter IX.

26. *IPC*, No. 21 (March 24, 1927), p. 425.

27. Letter by Trotsky to the Far Eastern Secretariat of the Comintern, dated April 18, 1927; in the Trotsky Archives.

28. Speech delivered before the Moscow party branch on April 5, 1927, as quoted in Isaacs, p. 162.

29. Issac Deutscher, *The Prophet Armed*, p. 412.

30. Report by Blücher, dated September 30, 1925, in J. C. Huston Collection.

31. Report by Blücher, dated May 1926, in J. C. Huston Collection.

32. Stalin, "Questions of the Chinese Revolution," *IPC*, No. 27 (April 28, 1927), p. 544; Trotsky, *Problems of the Chinese Revolution, passim; The Soviet Union and the Fourth International*, p. 7.

33. *Pravda*, April 15, 1927, p. 1.

34. *IPC*, No. 44 (July 28, 1927), p. 983.

35. Isaacs, pp. 172–73, 210.

36. *Ibid.*, p. 165.

37. M. N. Roy, *Revolution and Counterrevolution in China*, pp. 519–20.

38. Roy, "Polozhenie vnutri K.P.K. ko vremeni V s'ezda," *Kommunisticheskii Internatsional*, No. 41 (115), October 14, 1927, p. 46.

39. Pavel Mif, "Kitaiskaya Kommunisticheskaya partiya v kriticheskii dni," *Bol'shevik*, No. 23–24 (December 31, 1927), p. 23.

40. Roy, in *Kommunisticheskii Internatsional*, October 14, 1927, p. 46.

41. Li Li-san, "Chung-kuo ta ko-ming ti chiao-hsün," in *Kung-ch'an kuo-chi tui Chung-kuo ko-ming ch'üeh-i-an*, p. 38.

42. Roy, *Revolution and Counterrevolution*, pp. 466–67, 546; Ts'ai Ho-shen, "Istoriya opportunizma v Kommunisticheskoi partii Kitaya," *Problemy Kitaya*, No. 1 (1929), pp. 24–27.

43. Roy, *My Experience in China*, p. 44.

44. Ts'ai Ho-shen, in *Problemy Kitaya*, No. 1, p. 25.

45. Mif, in *Bol'shevik*, December 31, 1927, p. 117.

46. *Ibid.*, p. 106; also see short summary in Roy, *Revolution and Counterrevolution*, pp. 548–49 (footnote).

47. Mif, in *Bol'shevik*, December 31, 1927, p. 117.

48. *Ibid.*, p. 114; Snow, *Red Star*, pp. 161–62; "Resolutions of the Fifth National Congress of the CCP," *Documentary History*, p. 96.

49. "Circular Letter of the Central Committee to All Party Members," *Documentary History*, p. 111; Snow, p. 162.

50. Roy, *Revolution and Counterrevolution*, p. 615.

51. Tanaka Tadao, *Kuo-min ko-ming yü nung-ts'un wen-t'i*, Part II, pp. 78–79; Ts'ai, in *Problemy Kitaya*, No. 1, p. 62.

52. Tanaka, Part II, pp. 75–76.

53. Ch'en Tu-hsiu's political report to the Fifth Party Congress, *Bol'shevik*, December 31, 1927, p. 110.

54. G. Voitinsky, "K voprosu ob oshibkakh Kitaiskoi Kompartii v revolyutsii 1925–27 gg.," *Problemy Kitaya*, No. 4–5 (1930), p. 93.

55. Ch'ü Ch'iu-pai, *Chung-kuo ta-ko-ming yü Kung-ch'an-tang*, p. 54.

56. *People's Tribune*, June 30, 1927, p. 1.

57. Ts'ai Ho-shen, in *Problemy Kitaya*, No. 1, pp. 39, 42; Isaacs, pp. 234–36; Roy, *Revolution and Counterrevolution*, pp. 482, 550–53.

58. Ch'en Tu-hsiu, *Kao ch'üan-tang t'ung-chih shu*, p. 5.

59. *People's Tribune*, May 27th, 1927, p. 1; May 29, 1927, p. 4.

60. Ts'ai, in *Problemy Kitaya*, No. 1, pp. 39, 42; Isaacs, p. 236.

61. *People's Tribune*, May 28, 1927, p. 5.

62. Ts'ai, in *Problemy Kitaya*, No. 1, p. 39.

63. *People's Tribune*, May 29, 1927, p. 4; Ts'ai, in *Problemy Kitaya*, No. 1, p. 48.

64. Letter from the Chinese Communist Party to the Kuomintang, June 16, 1927. Full text in *IPC*, No. 37 (June 30, 1927), pp. 783–84.

65. *People's Tribune*, June 29, 1927, p. 1.

66. "Resolution on the Chinese Question," *IPC*, No. 35 (June 16, 1927), p. 737ff.

67. Stalin, "Beseda Tov. Stalina so studentam universiteta imeni Sun Yat-sena," *Voprosy Kitaiskoi revolyutsii*, p. 182.

68. The exact text of Stalin's wire is unobtainable. We have an English version in Stalin's *Marxism and the National and Colonial Question* (p. 249); a Russian one in his *Sochineniya* (Vol. X, pp. 32–33); and a second-hand one in Ch'en Tu-hsiu's *Kao ch'üan-tang t'ung-chih shu* (p. 6). Strange to say, Ch'en's version, though only a summary, is probably the most reliable of the three. The Russian version, being the shortest, seems the most heavily edited. Ch'en's version is much sharper in its strictures on peasant "excesses" than are the other two.

69. "Resolution on the Chinese Question," *IPC*, June 16, 1927, p. 738.

70. Minutes of the subcommittee as published in *The New Militant*, February 8, 1936, p. 3.

71. Mao, "Report on the Peasant Movement in Hunan," *Documentary History*, p. 85.

72. This vote of support was unanimous, if we can believe Ch'en Tu-hsiu, who has made no secret of being opposed or outvoted at other times. *Kao ch'üan-tang t'ung-chih shu*, p. 7.

73. J. C. Huston, "Sun Yat-sen, the Kuomintang, and the Chinese-Russian Political-Economic Alliance," a manuscript in the J. C. Huston Collection, pp. 187–88.

74. "Resolution on the Chinese Question," *IPC*, June 16, 1927, p. 739.

75. This was in effect a concession to the Chinese Communists (see Chapter IV). One of these — T'an P'ing-shan — had openly mentioned the Labour Party as the model to be copied (*Entwicklungswege der Chinesischen Revolution*, p. 21). Moscow itself was less direct, having failed miserably in its efforts to beguile the Labourites.

76. Lenin, "Detskaya bolezn' 'levizny' v kommunizme," *Sochineniya*, XXV, pp. 224–25.

77. Information obtained from Mr. Chang Kuo-t'ao. Partly confirmed by Ts'ai Ho-shen in *Problemy Kitaya*, No. 1, p. 28.

78. Mao Tse-tung has called him a fool (*Red Star Over China*, p. 165); and Communist historians treat him no more kindly. He has gone down in their tradition as one of those who caused the subsequent fiasco.

79. Roy claims that he "declined" to stay at his post when finding himself thwarted (*Revolution and Counterrevolution*, p. 554). But this would have been tantamount to a rupture with Moscow, and he did not leave Moscow's service until about a year later.

80. Ts'ai, in *Problemy Kitaya*, No. 1, p. 29.

81. We have reconstructed their argument from an account by Wang Ching-wei's spokesman, T'ang Leang-li, a gentleman fond of imputing communist leanings to anyone (including Chiang Kai-shek!) who ever quarreled with Wang. That he fails to ascribe such leanings to Madame Sun and Eugene Ch'en leads one to think that these two were not as friendly to the Communists as the Communists themselves believed, but played both sides of the game. T'ang Leang-li, *The Inner History of the Chinese Revolution*, p. 283.

82. *IPC*, No. 39 (July 7, 1927), p. 873.

83. Ch'ü Ch'iu-pai, *Chung-kuo ta-ko-ming yü Kung-ch'an-tang*, pp. 64–66.

84. "Resolution of the E.C.C.I. on the Present Situation of the Chinese Revolution," dated July 14, 1927. *IPC*, No. 44 (July 28, 1927), p. 984.

85. *People's Tribune*, July 26, 1927, p. 1.

86. *IPC*, No. 44, p. 984.

87. Letter to the Politburo, dated June 25, 1927, and signed by Zinoviev, Trotsky, Radek, and Evdokimov. Also see Trotsky, "Pochemu my ne trebovali do sikh por vykhoda iz Gomindan," a manuscript dated June 23, 1927. Both documents in the Trotsky Archives.

88. Information obtained from Mr. Chang Kuo-t'ao. Mr. Chang's version of his role in the Nanch'ang uprising is partly confirmed by the Chinese Communist Central Committee's resolution of November 14, 1927. See *Kuo-wen chou-pao*, No. 2 (January 8, 1928), p. 7.

89. *IPC*, No. 64 (September 19, 1928), p. 1148; Isaacs, p. 280.

90. *Wu-chuang pao-tung*, p. 94.

91. T'ang Leang-li, *The Inner History*, pp. 284–85.

92. Mandalyan, *Wei-shen-ma Chung-kuo Kung-ch'an-tang ti ling-tao po-ch'an*, p. 10.

93. *IPC*, No. 48 (August 18, 1927), p. 1069.

94. *IPC*, No. 41 (July 14, 1927), p. 898; "Circular Letter of the Central Committee to All Party Members" (August 7, 1927), *Documentary History*, pp. 102–118.

95. Either he did not come under immediate pressure to confess or else he resisted it successfully. As late as 1936, a journal edited by Pavel Mif complained ominously of his silence and admonished him to "remember the necessity of self-criticism." *Problemy Kitaya*, No. 4–5, p. 104.

96. Unfounded as it was, this rumor gained credence among the Chinese Communist leaders, because Lominadze had obviously no interest in scotching it. Though only about 30 at the time, Lominadze did in fact have the confidence of the "boss." Thus he had recently been appointed secretary of the Youth International, succeeding Vuyovich, a supporter of Zinoviev. (Information obtained from Mr. Chang Kuo-t'ao and from Mr. Boris Souvarine.)

97. Information obtained from Mr. Chang Kuo-t'ao. For a partial confirmation, see *Documentary History*, p. 98.

98. He had gone there in 1920 after graduating from the Russian Language School in Peking. He covered the Russian upheaval for the Peking Morning Post (*Ch'en-pao*), translated Russian literature into Chinese, and also attended the Communist University for Toilers of the East. He died in 1935 before a Kuomintang firing squad.

99. P'eng had gone to Moscow in 1921 to attend the University for Toilers of the East. After graduation, he had stayed at the university as a lecturer till his return to China in 1924. He was executed by the Kuomintang in 1932.

100. Li Ang, *Hung-se wu-t'ai*, p. 16; Po Ch'i, "Chung-kung t'ou-k'ao ti san kuo-chi i hou," *Kung-ch'an-tang tsai Chung-kuo*, p. 241. Supplemented and partially confirmed by information obtained from Mr. Chang Kuo-t'ao.

101. Chu Hsin-fan (Li Ang) maintains that apart from Ch'ü himself, Hsiang Chung-fa and Li Wei-han were the only members of the Central Committee who attended (*Hung-se wu-t'ai*, p. 21). Chang Kuo-t'ao puts the number of delegates at five; but he speaks only from hearsay, not having been present himself. Chu Hsin-fan, on the other hand, attended the meeting as recording secretary.

102. Ch'ü Ch'iu-pai himself has admitted this (*Chung-kuo ta-ko-*

ming yü Kung-ch'an-tang, p. 66). But he maintains that as many as twelve members of the Central Committee attended.

103. Li Ang, pp. 18–21. Supplemented and partially confirmed by information obtained from Mr. Chang Kuo-t'ao.

104. *Ibid.*, pp. 19–20.

105. "Resolutions of the August 7 Conference," *Documentary History*, pp. 212–222.

106. *Ibid.*, pp. 122–23.

107. "Circular Letter of the CC (CCP) to All Party Members," *ibid.*, pp. 102–118.

108. Edgar Snow quotes Mao as saying that he had been in the Politburo ever since 1924 (*Red Star Over China*, p. 166). But there was no Politburo in the Chinese party until its Fifth Congress set one up in the spring of 1927.

109. Ch'en and T'an remained on the Central Committee for the time being. Exactly who belonged to the successive politburos of this period is difficult to determine. The membership lists drawn up by Mr. Robert C. North are admittedly tentative. North, *Kuomintang and Chinese Communist Elites*, p. 111.

110. P'eng Shu-chih, *Kung-ch'an-lien shih-i t'an-hua*, pp. 6–9; Li Li-san, in *Kung-ch'an kuo-chi tui Chung-kuo ko-ming ch'üeh-i-an*, p. 39.

111. Anna Louise Strong, *China's Millions*, p. 242.

Chapter VI

Aftermath and Retrospect

1. Report by Bukharin to the Moscow Committee of the C.P.S.U., dated June 4, 1927. *IPC*, No. 39 (July 7, 1927), p. 880.

2. Stalin, "Zametki na sovremennye temy," *Pravda*, July 28, 1927, p. 4.

3. Letter to Max Shachtman, dated December 10, 1930, quoted in Trotsky, *Problems of the Chinese Revolution*, pp. 19–20.

4. Trotsky, "Kitaiskaya Kompartiya i Gomindan," p. 2, a manuscript in the Trotsky Archives, dated September 27, 1926.

5. Trotsky, "Klassovye otnosheniya Kitaiskoi revolyutsii," p. 13, a manuscript dated April 3, 1927.

6. Trotsky, *Problems*, p. 19.

7. *Ibid.*, pp. 19–20; "Pochemy my ne trebovali do sikh por vykhoda

iz Gomindan," a manuscript dated June 23, 1927; also a joint letter by the Opposition to the Politburo, dated June 25, 1927, in the Trotsky Archives.

8. Trotsky, letter to Radek, dated March 4, 1927.

9. *Ibid.*

10. Trotsky, "Zapiska" (notes), dated March 22, 1927.

11. Trotsky, speech to the Politburo. Original text under date of March 31, 1927, in the Trotsky Archives.

12. The manuscript of this article is dated April 3 and entitled "Klassovye otnosheniya Kitaiskoi revolyutsii." A marginal note in Trotsky's hand explains that it did not go to press because the coup of April 12 intervened. If it had been suppressed by the Stalinists, as Harold Isaacs claims (*The Tragedy of the Chinese Revolution*, p. 161), Trotsky would almost certainly have made a note of that fact.

13. Trotsky, letter to Preobajenskii, dated 1928.

14. Trotsky, *Problems*, pp. 50, 103.

15. *Ibid.*, p. 155.

16. *Ibid.*, p. 19.

17. He did so on March 31, 1927, in a speech before the Politburo. The text of this speech (contained in the Trotsky Archives) is the earliest record to be found of a formal demand for soviets being made by the Opposition. Zinoviev seconded this demand in his "Theses on the Chinese Revolution," which he submitted to the Politburo on April 15, 1927 (see Appendix to Trotsky, *Problems of the Chinese Revolution*, pp. 367–371).

18. Zinoviev, "Theses on the Chinese Revolution," *ibid.* p. 362.

19. Trotsky, "O lozunge sovetov v Kitae," p. 6, a manuscript dated April 16, 1927.

20. Trotsky, "Zapiska," dated March 22, 1927.

21. Trotsky, *Problems*, p. 286.

22. Trotsky, "Polozhenie v Kitae posle perevota Chen-Kai-shi i perspektivy," p. 2, a manuscript dated April 19, 1927.

23. Trotsky, "Novye vozmozhnosti Kitaiskoi revolyutsii, novye zadachi, novye oshibki," p. 5, a manuscript dated September 1927.

24. Trotsky, *Problems*, p. 219.

25. Isaacs, *The Tragedy of the Chinese Revolution*, pp. 279–281.

26. *Ibid.*, p. 282.

27. Li Ang, *Hung-se wu-t'ai*, pp. 38–40.

28. Liu Hsiao-ch'i as quoted by Nym Wales in *The Chinese Labor Movement*, p. 56.

29. Ch'ü Ch'iu-pai, *Chung-kuo ta-ko-ming yü Kung-ch'an-tang*, p. 132.

30. Trotsky, "Klassovye otnosheniya Kitaiskoi revolyutsii," pp. 13–14.

31. In stressing the need for continued bonds with the Kuomintang, Trotsky described it as the "peasants' own party," comparable to the Social Revolutionaries in Russia ("Kompartiya i Gomindan," p. 1). This feeble comparison struck Radek as "extremely comical"—and rightly so. See Radek's letter to Mussim, dated July 12, 1928 (in the Trotsky Archives).

32. He had boasted in early August that he would succeed in recruiting 100,000 men (Li Ang, *Hung-se wu-t'ai*, p. 28). As it turned out, he found a bare 3000. Only one third of these remained in his train by the end of 1927. Snow, *Red Star Over China*, pp. 167–69.

33. He still thought ten years later that on the question of soviets he had defied the Kremlin (*Red Star*, p. 167). Yet he had not called for them till the beginning of August—till after Stalin had sanctioned them at the end of July.

34. A schematic outline of this type of dynastic succession appears in Wolfram Eberhard's *Conquerors and Rulers*, pp. 62–63.

35. Resolution of the Central Committee as quoted in *Kuo-wen chou-pao*, Vol. V, No. 2–3 (January 8–15, 1928), p. 1ff.

36. *Ibid.*, p. 6.

37. Snow, *Red Star Over China*, p. 170.

38. Mao's praise of his bandit troops has been greatly toned down in the latest edition of his works. He had originally described them as "especially good": two words that have since disappeared (*Hsüan-chi*, 1951, I, p. 68; *Hsüan-chi*, 1948, p. 523). So have whole phrases and parts of phrases. Both the English and Russian editions of Mao's works are loose translations of this bowdlerized version and therefore quite unreliable.

39. Mao Tse-Tung, *Hsüan-chi* (1948 edition), pp. 532, 538.

40. Once he was in power, Mao no longer gave out that the program of the Sixth Congress had been the same as his own. His own—wrote a party spokesman in 1951—"easily surpassed the decisions of the Sixth Congress in penetration and practicability."

Chen Yi, "Learn from the Marxist-Leninist Creative Style of Work of Chairman Mao," *Current Background No. 110* (United States Consulate-General, Hongkong).

41. Resolution of the Sixth National Congress on the Peasant Movement (September 1928), *Documentary History*, p. 156ff.

42. Li Ang, p. 70.

43. *Documentary History*, pp. 143–164; especially p. 164, Section XI.

44. Though vice-chairman of the All-China Labor Federation, Hsiang remained a political cipher. Thus it is often forgotten that he ever occupied the highest post in the party. Even Chinese sources erroneously list Li Li-san as secretary-general after the Moscow congress. The relationship between Li and Hsiang is discussed at length in Li Ang, *Hung-se wu-t'ai*, pp. 71–80.

45. Snow, pp. 174, 177–182; Kung Ch'u, *Wo yü hung-chün*, p. 255ff.; Li Ang, pp. 152–54.

46. In the summer of 1930, Communist troops under General P'eng Teh-huai (now minister of defense in Peking) had launched an assault on Ch'angsha and actually taken the city, only to be driven out again in a matter of days. It had been planned to launch a similar attack on Nanch'ang; but by skillful procrastination, Mao Tse-tung saw to it that the attack was delayed and finally given up. Li Ang, *Hung-se wu-t'ai*, p. 126.

47. Control of the party had passed to a group of youthful stalwarts recently returned from Moscow, where they had been protégés of Pavel Mif at the Sun Yat-sen University. Mao was soon made to feel their superior knowledge of Marxism and their superior standing with its Russian exponents. But ultimately neither advantage availed them against his superior political skill. Li Ang, pp. 154–55; Schwartz, *Chinese Communism and the Rise of Mao*, pp. 148–163.

48. Li, "The Conditions for Establishing Soviet Districts in the Interior in Semi-Colonial Countries," *The Communist International*, No. 5 (March 5, 1935), p. 222ff.

49. *Ibid.*, pp. 236–38.

50. "Tasks and Perspectives of the Chinese Revolution," a manifesto of the International Left Opposition, as quoted in *The New Militant*, October 15, 1932.

51. Trotsky, "Peasant War in China," a letter to the Chinese Bolshevik-Leninists, *The New Militant*, October 15–16, 1932.

52. One may doubt the sincerity of this remark and of others like it, because they were made in the presence of foreigners (Herbert Feis, *The China Tangle*, pp. 140–41n., 180). Were they calculated to foster Western sympathy for Mao's cause by freeing it from the Communist stigma? Possibly so. One need not believe Stalin's words, however, to detect a great reserve in his attitude toward the "margarine Communists." One need only recall that Moscow negotiated with the Kuomintang government to the very end. V. Dedijer, *Tito Speaks*, p. 331; James F. Byrnes, *Speaking Frankly*, p. 228.

53. For an excellent outline of Stalin's theory of socialism in one country, see Isaac Deutscher, *Stalin*, pp. 282–293.

54. *Ibid.*, pp. 208–210; also Deutscher, *The Prophet Armed*, pp. 456–58.

55. That had been in 1919, when the pressures of civil war prevented serious consideration of the plan (Deutscher, *The Prophet Armed*, pp. 456–58). By comparison with Trotsky's proposed method of liberating Asia, Stalin's efforts in that direction seem nothing less than subtle.

56. *The Prophet Armed*, chapter VI (especially p. 159); also Deutscher, *Stalin*, pp. 282–84.

INDEX

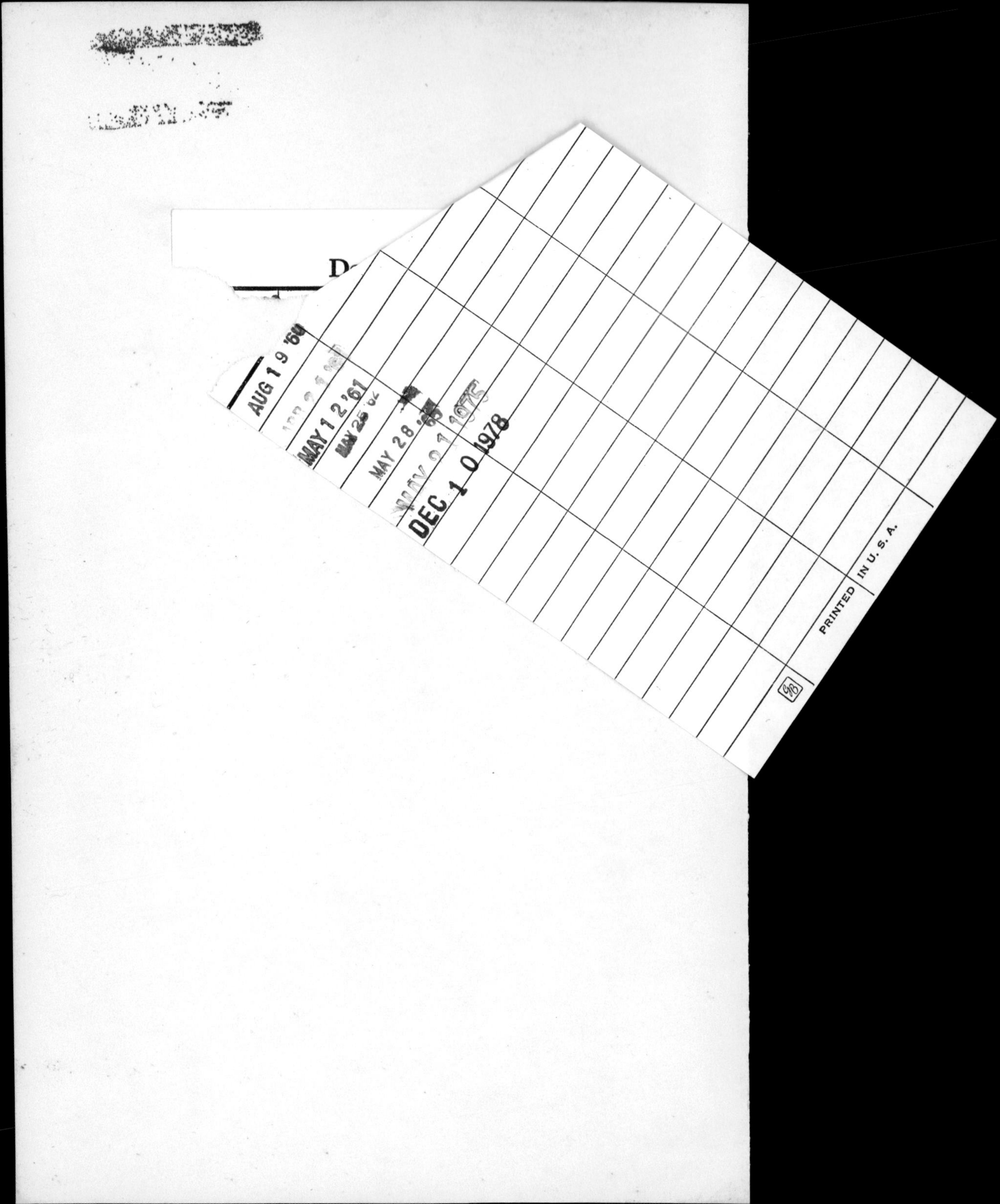
AUG 1 9 '60
MAY 1 2 '61
MAY 28
DEC 1 0 1978
PRINTED IN U. S. A.